THE ASSOCIATION of

TOP

TOP TRAINERS

1001 Practical Tips and Techniques
for Successful Dog Care and Training

TOP TIPS FROM TOP TRAINERS

Project Team
Editor: Heather Russell-Revesz
Copy Editor: Stephanie Fornino
Indexer: Joann Woy
Design: Mary Ann Kahn

T.F.H. Publications
President/CEO: Glen S. Axelrod
Executive Vice President: Mark E. Johnson
Publisher: Christopher T. Reggio
Production Manager: Kathy Bontz

T.F.H. Publications, Inc.
One TFH Plaza
Third and Union Avenues
Neptune City, NJ 07753

Printed and bound in China

10 11 12 13 14   1 3 5 7 9 8 6 4 2

Library of Congress Cataloging-in-Publication Data
The Association of Pet Dog Trainers' top tips from top trainers : 1001 practical tips and techniques for successful dog care and training.
    p. cm.
  Includes index.
  ISBN 978-0-7938-0640-9 (alk. paper)
  1. Dogs--Training. I. Association of Pet Dog Trainers. II. Title: Top tips from top trainers.
  SF431.A87 2010
  636.7'0887--dc22
                            2009032535

The Leader in Responsible Animal Care for Over 50 Years!®
www.tfh.com

CONTENTS

FOREWORD

Founded in 1993, the Association of Pet Dog Trainers (APDT) was the brainchild of noted veterinarian, animal behaviorist, and author Ian Dunbar, PhD, BVetMed, MRCVS, CPDT. In1980, Dr. Dunbar created the SIRIUS Puppy Training program, which was the very first home obedience program created specifically for puppies. Through his work with the SIRIUS program and working with other dog trainers and veterinarians, he saw a need for pet dog trainers to come together and provide support and education for each other.

Up until the time of the APDT's founding and first meeting in San Mateo, California, in 1993, most educational and networking opportunities for trainers were focused almost exclusively on competitive obedience training. There was little available for the trainer who worked in the home or who taught group classes for dog owners who simply wanted an obedience pet but were not interested in dog sports and competitions. Moreover, the information available on how to deal with behavior problems in the home was sparse, and the importance of puppy socialization for behavioral health was not widely promoted among trainers or veterinarians. Notes Barbara Long, CPDT,

president of the APDT Board of Directors, "Back then most of the clubs were for competitive trainers. When someone handed me the information on the first APDT conference in Orlando in 1993, I was so excited that someone thought working with pet dogs was important!"

What started as a small conference in 1993 has since expanded into the organization's flagship event, the APDT Annual Educational Conference and Trade Show. The event averages 1,000 attendees each year and draws speakers from around the world to present the latest innovative research in dog training and behavior, as well as provides educational opportunities for trainers new to the field in everything from class curriculum creation to business and marketing tips to dealing with behavioral issues. The accompanying trade show features many of the top manufacturers of dog training equipment, treats, and other pet-related products.

To ensure that APDT members received educational benefits throughout the year and not just from the annual conference, the *APDT Newsletter* was started in 1994. In September 2003, the name changed to the *APDT Chronicle of the Dog.* What began as a manually copied 8-page newsletter has morphed over the years into a bimonthly, full-color, glossy 60-page magazine that has been nominated for awards from the Dog Writers Association of America (DWAA) for several years in a row and in fact won for Best Special Interest Magazine in 2008. The *APDT Chronicle of the Dog* regularly features the industry's top trainers and behaviorists, such as Sophia Yin, DVM, Patricia McConnell, PhD, CAAB, Sue Sternberg, Pia Silvani, and many more.

The APDT's website, www.apdt.com, is a source of information for dog owners, veterinarians, shelter workers, and of course, dog trainers and animal behaviorists. Our "Trainer Search" feature allows the public to search for members in their area, research their services, and contact them directly. In 2009, we expanded our section on pet owner information with tips on dog safety, basic training and behavior, and choosing the right dog for you and your family. The site will continue to expand with more resources for pet owners and others in 2010 and beyond. The APDT has also expanded into the social media venue with a presence on sites such as Facebook, LinkedIn, and Twitter.

Today, the APDT has almost 6,000 members and a permanent office with staff in Greenville, South Carolina. The organization's goals for the future include a foundation to promote research into dog training and behavior and the creation of a standard curriculum for dog trainers that can be implemented in vocational schools, colleges, universities, and through online venues. The APDT is proud to be the largest organization in the world for professional dog trainers, and our mission is simple: to promote caring relationships between dogs and people by educating trainers in canine behavior and emphasizing professionalism and reward-based training. Through our mission, we achieve the APDT's vision of a world where everyone involved in dogs believes that all dogs are effectively trained through dog-friendly techniques and therefore are lifelong companions in a relationship based on mutual trust and respect.

Over the last several years, we asked our members to share successful hints and tips drawn on their dog training experiences. This collective knowledge has been assembled into *Top Tips From Top Trainers*, which features APDT members' expertise on all things dog. We knew our trainers would have a lot to say but were surprised by the breadth and depth of the tips we received. This wealth of information is sure to help anyone train, manage, and have a great relationship with her dog.

To learn about the APDT's latest endeavors, find information on membership, or locate a trainer in your community, we encourage you to visit our website at www.apdt.com.

A to Z Tips

ADOLESCENTS

The best advice for anyone with an adolescent dog (anywhere from 5 to 24 months old) is to hang in there! This can be a difficult time, and even dogs who have behaved well and were well trained as puppies can start losing all semblance of civility. Your adolescent dog is likely to forget previously reliable commands and turn to destructive chewing that can result in entire living room furniture disintegration. Plus, many owners give their adolescent dogs more freedom in the house once they are housetrained, which can result in serious damage. During this time many owners despair or feel like giving up on their dog—but please don't! Adhere to these simple rules: supervise, supervise, supervise; exercise, exercise, exercise; and train, train, and train some more!

> &SUE STERNBERG, Animals for Adoption
> and Great Dog Productions,
> Accord, NY, and Moab, UT

One of the hardest parts of dealing with canine adolescence seems to be the mere act of accepting that your dog *is* an adolescent. Despite residual cuteness and continued playfulness, your 4- to 5-month-old dog is now a teenager! And just as it isn't a good idea to treat a 15-year-old child like a 5-year-old, it doesn't serve you or your dog to excuse or ignore canine adolescent behavior as adorable puppy antics. You're quickly running out of time!

> &CYNTHIA BRUCKART, The Puppy
> Playhouse, Sherwood, OR

Adolescent dogs need strict rules and consistency more so than during any other developmental period in their lives.

> &SUE STERNBERG, Animals for Adoption
> and Great Dog Productions,
> Accord, NY, and Moab, UT

Adolescent dogs will "forget" their manners, name, and just about anything else you've taught them. Being consistent is the name of the game. Stepping back and trying to make things easier for dogs going through this period will help. They will try to see what they can get away with (maybe even every hour!), but be patient—this will pass.

> &LYNETTE TATAY, Nashville, MI

There are three important components to taming the energy of the canine adolescent: enrichment, enrichment, enrichment! Enrichment can include stuffing your dog's food into hollow toys, hand-feeding his dinner in exchange for basic behaviors, appropriate exercise, scent games, socialization with other dogs, and field trips about town.

> &CYNTHIA BRUCKART, The Puppy
> Playhouse, Sherwood, OR

Adolescent dogs need to be challenged with their training, and rewards need to be increased, not decreased, as we sometimes do as the dog gets more proficient.

> ⚬SUE STERNBERG, Animals for Adoption
> and Great Dog Productions,
> Accord, NY, and Moab, UT

The best way to deal with adolescent dogs is to exercise them every day until they are too tired to get themselves into mischief! Go out for a game of fetch, swim, jog, play with other dogs until they lie down and quit, and then repeat in a few hours. Agility training is also a great way to tire them out. A tired dog is a good dog!

> ⚬REENA S. WALTON, Pups-R-Us Dog
> Training, Redwood City, CA

Adolescent dogs need more control work interspersed in their bouts of aerobic exercise and outdoor activity. For example, interrupt your dog's exercise and play with control commands, such as *down-stay* or *sit*, and have him make sustained eye contact with you. Long *down-stays*, for a minimum of ten minutes at a time, are useful during evening indoor activities in the home.

> ⚬SUE STERNBERG, Animals for Adoption
> and Great Dog Productions,
> Accord, NY, and Moab, UT

More off-territory or new-territory walks are important for the adolescent dog. As dogs mature, they may root in to their home and surrounding area and become overly territorial. It is useful to take them off their territory once daily or to range farther during familiar walks so that they can't get too used to one region.

> ⚬SUE STERNBERG, Animals for Adoption
> and Great Dog Productions,
> Accord, NY, and Moab, UT

TOP TIDBIT

Spaying and neutering is the best way to prevent unwanted puppies from coming into the world and to prevent the pet overpopulation problem.

ADOPTION

When looking for a new puppy or dog, please search your local animal shelter first. You'll be amazed at how many different types of dogs are there and how great they can be. Many dogs living in shelters are already obedience trained. Of course, other sources (like breeders) can have great dogs, but to be able to give a home to a shelter or rescue animal is very special. All they want is a little companionship and a lot of love and care. The next time you are thinking about getting a new pet, give your local shelter or rescue agency a try—there's a dog waiting for you.

> ⚬ALICE
> PISZCZEK,
> CPDT-KA, BIG
> PAWS/little jaws,
> Naperville, IL

AGGRESSION

Dogs who display aggressive behavior are a major challenge. Aggression severely limits a dog's access in public and exposes the family to injury or major liability. If you have a dog in your family who has shown aggressive behavior, you need to seek professional help and exercise rigorous management in order to protect humans and other animals.

✑JIM BARRY, CDBC, CPDT-KA, Reston Dog Training, Reston, VA

As a professional behavior consultant for 17 years, I have literally seen thousands of "aggressive" dogs. When asked to assess an aggressive dog, three big questions need to stay in the forefront: 1. Has this dog actually bitten a person or animal? 2. Can I help them manage, extinguish, or curtail this act? 3. Is it best to look the owner in the eye and say no, you can't help them? The third point is the hardest to learn, but if you work with aggressive dogs, you have to know enough to say no—there is no learning curve with people's safety. How do you learn? Mentorship; seminars and reading; working with shelter dogs; repetition and time; and trusting your instincts.

✑ELAINE ALLISON, CPDT-KA, Shelter Director of the Humane Society of Wickenburg, Wickenburg, AZ

When on an aggressive dog consult, do not come with treats in your pocket. Certain dogs will start working you for treats as soon as they realize you have a resource, and they may get pushy and aggressive if the treats do not start flowing.

Fear-aggressive dogs should have treats tossed to them only. Hand-feeding can lead to aggressive snatching and even fear biting while taking the resource.

✑RACHEL B. LACHOW, CPDT-KA, Positively Obedient, Reisterstown, MD

AGILITY

When you're getting started in agility, it's all about attention—use treats, toys, or any other motivator you can think of to practice being the most interesting thing in the world to your dog, and test it out in new and increasingly distracting locations. In an agility environment, you will have to compete with other distractions like high-energy dogs and toys and people. Will you lose your dog in the middle of a run if someone is eating a cheeseburger at ringside?

✑ERICA PYTLOVANY, Woofs Dog Training, Arlington, VA

I love to introduce my beginner dogs and puppies to the agility tunnel during week 4 of classes. I've discovered that shy dogs blossom when they conquer the scary tunnel. I have a practice tunnel that is only 10 feet (3 m) long and has a greater diameter.

ROBIN BAIZEL, Reno, NV

When an agility-trained dog begins to fail in performance, look for a medical reason, beginning with the eyes. If a dog has nuclear sclerosis, he will not be able to see when he exits a tunnel, faces equipment in the sun, or goes from dark to light. Look for spinning, slowing down, and signs of stress, then check his eyes.

ANDREA CARLSON-CARTER, Courteous Canine, Inc., Lutz, FL

Socialization is key in preparing your dog for agility. It's heartbreaking when a dog and handler team put in hundreds of hours of training and then can't compete or go to "fun runs" because the dog can't handle being out in public. Make sure that you take your dog out to visit lots of new environments, and where permitted, bring him out to be a spectator at trials, matches, and training sessions. If your dog gets anxious as an observer, it will only be harder when you later add handler stress to the equation. Socialization may seem like a mundane detail, but a failure in this area stops more would-be agility teams than any other training challenge you can think of.

ERICA PYTLOVANY, Woofs Dog Training, Arlington, VA

ATTENTION, GETTING YOUR DOG'S

Getting your dog's attention is the first thing you should do during each training session. When you don't have his attention on you, you're wasting your breath and your cues. Start each training session with ten seconds of rewards just for giving you attention. Once you have your dog's attention, then you can get down to business.

JACQUELYN ENGLAND, A Dog's Life, Sunnyvale, CA

If you are trying to train a dog who won't settle and can't seem to focus, it could be that he is anxious or just fidgety. Get the dog up and moving around for a couple of minutes. Ask him to follow you, make a couple of right and left turns, and then go back to where you started and re-engage him in the training activity. While your dog is following you, it gets him focused on you and doesn't allow him to be thinking about jumping, fidgeting, etc. The movement helps connect the body to the brain through the nervous system. Gentle stroking also helps calm down dogs.

PAT HENNESSY, CAP2, CPDT-KA, N2paws, Leawood, KS

Is your dog ignoring you? Try talking less.

&JOANN KOVACICH, Grateful Dog Pet Care, Inc., Penfield, NY

Do you want a dog who watches you, comes when he is called, and heels? If so, remember this number: 10,000. That is the number of reinforcements that should be your goal in the first year of your dog's life for the simple acts of looking at you, walking toward you, and following you—basically, for "attention." Attention toward you is not a genetic trait—it is learned behavior. Your diligence in establishing a high rate of reinforcement for watching you, following you, and walking near you will lay the foundation for all training throughout the dog's life.

&PAM SHEEHAN, 4 Paws Training, LLC, Broken Arrow, OK

If a dog is looking at you on his own (sometimes called an "automatic check-in"), he's probably looking just as much for attention as for a treat. You can easily reinforce this outside of formal training sessions simply by returning the attention.

&ANN DUPUIS, CPDT-KA, Your Dream Dog, Randolph, MA

Do you want your dog to pay more attention to you? Train yourself to notice when he is looking at you—and return the gaze!

Smile and nod and say "Good dog!" Acknowledge his presence, give him a moment of social interaction with you, and then go on with what you were doing.

&ANN DUPUIS, CPDT-KA, Your Dream Dog, Randolph, MA

Attention is everything, and if you can't get and keep your dog's attention, you might as well be on another planet. To get his attention, make yourself more interesting to your dog.

&KATHERINE ROLLINS, CPDT-KA, Kat's K9 Cadets, Greeneville, TN

Attention is one of the most valuable things you can teach your dog, but it is often overlooked in obedience classes. Click and treat your dog for simply looking at you when you say his name. If he won't pay attention, you can't teach him anything else. If your dog looks at you anytime you ask, you can keep him out of all kinds of trouble.

&JULIE HUMISTON, CPDT-KA, Puppy Love Dog Training, Minneapolis, MN

I have my clients make curious sounds to gain their dog's attention. Using a fast high-pitched sound like "doodley doo doo" or using a "squirrel call" works very well. If you are having trouble keeping your dog's attention on you, these types of sounds will get him to look at you.

&DAINA BECKMAN, Behavior Specialist, Happy Tails Dog Behavior & Training, Hornell, NY

Getting and keeping your dog's attention around distractions sometimes feels like an impossible feat. However, a little change in your focus can lead to a big change in your dog's focus. Instead of trying to get your dog to pay attention to you, teach him to offer you his attention. With your dog on leash, stand quietly at a distance from something he is interested in, such as a person or a doggy pal. The instant your dog glances toward you, say "Yes!," give him a treat, and then give him permission to go visit. Your dog will learn that offering you attention is the fastest way to get access to what he wants. Plus, it will earn him bonus prizes from you! Soon, your dog won't be able to take his eyes off of you!

⁌LAUREL SCARIONI, CPDT-KA, Pawsitive Results Critter Academy, Santa Rosa, CA

ATTENTION-SEEKING BEHAVIORS

Attention-seeking behaviors, such as pawing, whining, and nudging, can make an evening at home less relaxing. I have found that with a little time and patience, plus charting the behaviors to help you ignore them, can help put a stop to them.

1. Write down all the ways your dog seeks your attention.
2. Choose the most annoying behavior to begin working on.
3. Note the time of day this behavior happens the most, and set aside a half hour of time to focus on this exercise.
4. Make a chart listing the days of the week and a space to put tally marks under them.
5. Place the chart across the room from where you will be during the training session.
6. During your planned half-hour time slot, instead of looking at or reacting to your dog when he performs the unwanted behavior, look at the chart, walk over to it, and put a tally mark down. Then return to what you were doing. Repeat this every time the dog performs the attention-seeking behavior.

Follow this program for a week and you'll see the tally marks decrease! Be consistent and persistent, and you will soon be ignoring the behaviors at other times during the day too. Repeat these steps for the other behaviors on your list.

⁌JENNIFER SHRYOCK, BA, CDBC, Family Paws, Cary, NC

Simply put, if your dog wants your attention, he should be required to work for it. If he approaches you for attention, request that he sit in the short period before he has a chance to jump on you. Reward your dog with a treat or simply give him the attention he desires.

⁌JENNIFER SCHNEIDER, CPDT-KA, Pick of the Litter Dog Training, Seattle/Tacoma Area, WA

B

BABY

Some tips in preparing your dog for your new baby's arrival are:

- Start your preparations well before your baby's arrival, at least three months prior.
- Make sure that your dog is well trained in obedience.
- If you plan to restrict your dog's access to the baby's room (or any other areas of your house), begin the restriction well in advance of the baby's arrival.

Use these tips in conjunction with, not as a substitute for, a training program.

CHRISTINA SHUSTERICH, BA, CBC, NY
Clever K9, Inc., Queens, NY

I had a client who was getting ready to have a baby, so we bought her two dolls: one that cried and held a bottle and one that crawled. She and her husband followed a routine using the dolls that would mimic a baby's routine. They used baby powder, lotion, etc., to get the dog used to new smells in the house. They took one of the dolls for a walk in the stroller with the dog. They fed, changed, and held the dolls just like they would with a baby so that they could learn how to incorporate their dog into the new household routine. This way, when the new baby came home, their dog was familiar with the baby and the new routine.

BONNIE KRUPA, CPDT-KA, Happy, Clean and Smart, Muncie, IN

When bringing a new baby home to a house with a dog, prepare the dog for the new family member. Get the nursery ready beforehand and let the dog explore the "new room." Have a family member bring home a blanket that smells like the baby. Before the birth, make sure that the dog knows a *sit-stay* and *leave-it*, then use those commands as needed when the baby comes home.

SHANNON COYNER, RVT, CPDT-KA, Ventura, CA

Desensitize your dog to the new member of the family in a positive way. Prior to the arrival of the baby, purchase a CD of a baby crying, cooing, and suckling. There are several available on the Internet, or get a prerecorded version from a friend. Allow the dog to begin listening to the CD on a low volume level. Gradually increase the volume over a couple of days. It is only necessary to play the sounds for five to ten minutes, once or twice a day.

HEATHER SCHAMERLOH, SmartDog Training, Dallas, TX

BACKYARD

Have you fenced in your backyard for your canine companions to enjoy some free time outside? Please provide them with shade, fresh water, and something to do.

Dogs left alone in the yard with nothing to do will learn to bark at your neighbors and at people passing by, chase cars along the fence, and engage in destructive behaviors. Provide them with interactive toys to engage them in activity. Better yet, step outside with them and play fetch or hide-and-seek, or have a five-minute training session. Your dogs will be happier and healthier, and your neighbors will thank you for having well-behaved members of the neighborhood.

ᴄ⃝JANET WEYERS, Stamford, CT

To keep a dog from being bored in the backyard, scatter his kibble around the yard. By the time he has finished finding it and eating it, he will be exhausted. A tired dog is a happy dog!

ᴄ⃝LYNETTE TATAY, Nashville, MI

Go out with your dog when he goes to the bathroom. Accompanying him into the backyard will create a well-supervised pet who will develop fewer backyard bad habits, like barking, digging, and ignoring his owner.

ᴄ⃝SUE STERNBERG, Animals for Adoption and Great Dog Productions, Accord, NY, and Moab, UT

B

BARKING

If your dog is barking excessively, determine why he is barking. Is he barking because he is undersocialized, so strange dogs overstimulate or scare him? If that is the case, invest in some training classes or day care, which will help him become more relaxed in the presence of new dogs. Is he barking because he is bored? Make sure that he has plenty of chew treats and toys, and give him ample exercise. Is he barking to get your attention? Start training him so that this behavior does not get him attention, but quiet, calm behavior does. If you need help with excessive barking, consult a trainer. Especially if barking is a fear response, it is very important that a qualified behavior counselor work with you to ensure that the fear does not grow.

ᴄ⃝DEVENE GODAU, CPDT-KA, Trainers Academy, LLC, Royal Oak, MI

TOP TIDBIT

In 1997, the United States Department of Agriculture (USDA) announced that keeping a dog outside on a tether was a cruel practice.

The best way to stop a dog from barking is to *ignore* the barking, thus not reinforcing this behavior. Even a simple "Fido, stop it," is attention that can reward the bad behavior, causing it to continue.

    ✒DAWN NARGI-FERREN, CPDT-KA, Metropolitan Pets, New York City, NY

Most dogs have no clue as to whether barking is something good or something bad. Sometimes when a dog barks, he is ignored (owner is in a jolly mood). Other times, the dog is encouraged (owner sees suspicious stranger outside the house). And yet other times, the dog is yelled at (owner has a headache). To help your dog know your rules, teach him what they are. Here is a good rule to start with: Barking is okay until the dog is told to hush.

    ✒CRYSTAL COLL, All Ways Pawsitive Pet Behavior and Training, Queen Creek, AZ

To reduce barking, teach your dog to "speak." Barking only gets rewarded if he follows the "*speak*" cue. Heavily reinforce him when he's quiet, especially when you haven't asked for it.

    ✒ANN DUPUIS, CPDT-KA, Your Dream Dog, Randolph, MA

Be careful not to reward excessive barking with *any* attention—even negative attention! Instead, completely ignore the barking. Reward the dog with attention when the barking stops. Plus, you can modify the dog's environment to remove stimuli that trigger the barking (e.g., closing the blinds on a window facing a busy street).

    ✒PHIL GUIDA, Director of Training, Canine Dimensions In-Home Dog Training, Marlton, NJ

Be sure to reward your dog during periods when he is quiet and not performing any unacceptable behaviors. For example, if he is sitting quietly and not barking, this is a perfect opportunity to reward him with his favorite treat or a belly rub.

    ✒DAWN NARGI-FERREN, CPDT-KA, Metropolitan Pets, New York City, NY

Many dogs who bark and lunge at other dogs on a walk are the same dogs who are home alone all day, looking out the window barking at dogs outside. I recommend covering the windows in the house so that the dog cannot practice barking at outside dogs. This, combined with additional training for walking outside, helps modify the behavior. For some dogs, just keeping them from barking at the window is enough to stop them from barking at other dogs when they are walked outside.

CAROL SIEGRIST, CPDT-KA, SIEGRIST LLC, Dog Training & Behavior Consultation, Philadelphia, PA

Barking is intrinsically reinforcing, so be creative in reducing a dog's opportunities to bark when you don't want him to and reducing any external reinforcements that unwanted barking may produce.

ANN DUPUIS, CPDT-KA, Your Dream Dog, Randolph, MA

Increase the amount of play, exercise, and distraction that your dog receives during the day. Inappropriate barking that occurs in the late afternoon and evening can be a sign that the dog is not getting enough physical and mental stimulation.

PHIL GUIDA, Director of Training, Canine Dimensions In-Home Dog Training, Marlton, NJ

Do not yell at a barking dog—to him, it's like you're joining the excitement. Instead, call him and engage him in an incompatible behavior like a *down*. After he is quiet, say "Shhh" and reward him. If he is too absorbed in barking to pay attention to you, try using a food lure or a body block to interrupt him. (This means placing yourself between the dog and what he is barking at.) Then step toward him, which will cause him to move away from the source of his barking. Make sure to ask for another behavior after he is quiet and before rewarding him so as not to reinforce the barking.

PAT BLOCKER, CPDT-KA, Peaceful Paws Dog Training, Aurora, CO

The first step in obtaining peace and quiet is to realize that lots of barking is caused by the dog being lonely, bored, frustrated, or frightened. These are all situations that you can help alleviate. A well-exercised, happy dog is more likely to sleep all day while you are not home. Spend time playing with, training, and exercising your dog.

CRYSTAL COLL, All Ways Pawsitive Pet Behavior and Training, Queen Creek, AZ

As a matter of ethics, do not have your dog surgically debarked. It is better to rehome the dog than to subject him to an inhumane procedure.

PHIL GUIDA, Director of Training, Canine Dimensions In-Home Dog Training, Marlton, NJ

For problem backyard barking, try taking your dog on a walk instead of letting him out into the backyard for exercise. The mental stimulation he'll get from the different smells while out on a 20-minute walk will tire him out (and help prevent nuisance barking) much faster than hours with the same nonstimulating smells in the same nonstimulating yard. If you feel that you don't have enough time to walk your dog, consider hiring a pet sitter/dog walker who can go over to your home while you are away and give Rover a much-needed break.

DANA COOPER, CPDT-KA, Woofers Canine Companion Training, Round Rock, TX

Use obedience commands to break the barking habit, which will give your dog an acceptable alternative behavior to perform.

PHIL GUIDA, Director of Training, Canine Dimensions In-Home Dog Training, Marlton, NJ

If your dog's excessive barking has already become a habit, don't expect to get it under control overnight. It takes weeks of repetition to replace an old habit with a new, more desirable one. If you keep up with behavior modification procedures (such as teaching the *quiet* command), you will see a new pattern of barking develop. Instead of barking relentlessly at the insignificant, your dog will be barking appropriately and for a reasonable length of time. It is important that you maintain the new good habit through practice and praise, or your dog may revive his old annoying barking habits again.

CRYSTAL COLL, All Ways Pawsitive Pet Behavior and Training, Queen Creek, AZ

Never use a muzzle for excessive barking. A muzzle does not allow a dog to pant, which is how he regulates his body temperature. Improper use of a muzzle can cause serious harm and even death. Instead, seek a trainer's advice for excessive barking because dogs bark for various reasons.

DARLENE KOZA, Scooter's School of Sit & Stay, Rochester, NY

BATHS

If your pup is not fond of the bathtub, try some of these steps. Feed him his dinner or yummy treats in or near the dry tub. Next, feed him in a tub that just had the water drained out and is still damp. Then feed him in 1 inch (3 cm) of tepid water, then 2 inches (5 cm), etc. Stop on any step where your dog slows down eating, working on desensitizing again when he is ready. Also, put down extra-long bath mats so that he doesn't slip.

P.J. LACETTE, the original Best Paw Forward, Osteen, FL

When teaching a puppy (or new adult dog) to enjoy baths, smear peanut butter or cream cheese on the inside of the bathtub. It will give him something to work on while getting bathed and teach him that the bathtub is a cool place!

VICKI RONCHETTE, CPDT-KA, CAP2, Braveheart Dog Training, San Leandro, CA

If your dog doesn't like the bathtub, try skipping it and just giving him a bath outdoors using a tiny wading pool or just a wooden platform. Use warm soapy water dipped from a bucket onto a sponge or bath netting.

P.J. LACETTE, the original Best Paw Forward, Osteen, FL

BEDS

I find that most dogs like a cozy bed with raised sides to snuggle next to, something I discovered while observing each successive foster dog try to squeeze into my cat's bed! Also, if your dog or puppy has a tendency to chew on his bed, provide soft, washable blankets as bedding. A supply of several blankets can be obtained from secondhand shops at reasonable prices and then donated to the local animal shelter when the dog or puppy graduates to a real bed.

ANN ALLUMS, CPDT-KA, Best Friends Animal Society, Kanab, UT

B BEGGING

To prevent begging, it is best to never feed your dog any table scraps, particularly while still sitting at the kitchen table. Occasionally feeding your dog from the table can make begging worse—this is called random reinforcement, which is similar to gambling at a slot machine. (Not knowing for certain if you are going to get rewarded can make the behavior persist more strongly than when reinforcement is certain.) So even occasionally feeding your dog from the table should be avoided.

CHRISTINA SHUSTERICH, BA, CBC, NY Clever K9 Inc., Queens, NY

My clients are sometime embarrassed that their dogs beg, but I always tell them that a behavior is only bad if it is dangerous to the dog, family, and visitors; bothersome to people or the dog; or causing the dog stress. If you enjoy those forlorn starving eyes watching while you eat, that's okay. You can even teach your dog that it is only okay to beg from certain people (but don't feed your dog any table food, as many of the foods we eat can make your dog sick). If you live with someone who enjoys those begging eyes but you don't, simply ignore the dog whenever you have food. Don't look at him, don't talk to him, and don't touch him. He will get the message that you are not going to share.

DAINA BECKMAN, Dog Behavior Specialist, Happy Tails Dog Behavior & Training, Hornell, NY

Does your dog beg at the table? Ignore him! Do *not* give him a tidbit! When he gets bored because you are not giving him anything and moves away from the table, throw a tidbit to where he is sitting. Do *not* call him over to you. Rewarding him when he's away from the table will encourage him to stay away from it and wait for good things to come to him.

ELAINE COUPÉ, For Pet's Sake & Memphis Agility, Oakland, TN

BODY LANGUAGE

Dogs are fluent readers of body language. It is their primary method of communication. If you exhibit an unintentional flail of an arm or a glance in an unintended direction, this can cause your dog to respond in a very different way than you intended.

DELTA SMITH, Dawgz Gone Good Inc., Leesburg, VA

Dogs are very aware of your body language. When interacting with your dog, pay close attention to the physical signals you are giving them. For example, when you call him to come, crouch down or move away from him. This body language will make him more comfortable coming to you.

KRISTINA N. GAGE, CPDT-KA, SmartDog Dog Training, Saratoga Springs, NY

In my culture (Cherokee), we are quiet. We observe and listen. If you take the time to sit and watch a dog, you may find out much about his personality. Is he restless? Barking? Licking his lips? In what position are his ears? Is he making eye contact? If a trainer can quietly observe the dog, she can read him very well and make a rational decision about the training approach that will be the most effective. Be quiet. Be still. Say nothing. Do not interfere at first. Allow the dog to be natural, and you will discover that he is speaking to you in his language. Then you can begin to speak to him in your language.

✎DAWN WATSON, Brother of the Wolf, LLC, AKC CGC Evaluator, Gloucester City, NJ

Using body language is like dancing, and you lead. Walking backward, direct the dog to come and follow you; stop abruptly, scuff your foot for sound emphasis, and open your arms with elbows bent as if you are welcoming your dog. Take one step forward and the dog will most often sit automatically. I often demonstrate this on my first meeting with a client to emphasize how much dogs respond to body language.

✎CYNTHIA KURTZ, The Pet Geek, West Linn/Sandy, OR

Good communication is the best way to get good behavior. Learn to read your dog's postures, expressions, movements, and vocalizations. Observe ear and tail positions, general body posture (especially "fluid" and "curved" versus "stiff" and "angular"), and facial expressions. Be precise. (Write down "mouth open, panting slightly, tongue hanging out, eyes bright, facial muscles relaxed" rather than "looks happy.") Study videos, books, photographs, and other people's dogs. Notice your own body language and how it affects your dog. Your body says a lot and your dog notices!

✎ANN DUPUIS, CPDT-KA, Your Dream Dog, Randolph, MA

Body language gives a more realistic signal from your dog's point of view. If you are disappointed in his behavior, decide on a body signal to let him know that. An example would be hands on hips with a turn of your head as you say "No cookies for you!" or a shrug of the shoulders as you say "Excuse me!" The words are not as important as the body language, but both used together will help get across your disappointment.

✎GLORIA J. WHITE, CPDT-KA, Pawsitive Waggers Training, Cincinnati, OH

B

Make sure that your body language matches what you are verbally telling your dog. They could be saying different things, and chances are the dog will respond to the body language first. After all, dogs don't talk to each other with words—they use body language and subtle expressions. Be aware of what your body is telling your dog.

DEBBY MCMULLEN, CDBC, Pawsitive Reactions, LLC, Pittsburgh, PA

Body language is a dog's primary means of communication. Your body movement/ position may relay a different message than your voice command. If a double message is conveyed, body language takes priority.

KAREN CAMPBELL, Karen Campbell's Pet Behavior Help Now!, Portland, ME

BREEDS

Gather as much information as possible about your dog's breed. If he is a mix, look up all the breeds with which he is mixed. This will give you a clue as to why your dog may be doing certain behaviors.

LYNETTE TATAY, Nashville, MI

Although we rarely see a Border Collie couch potato or a Basset Hound agility

star, our pets all have idiosyncrasies that especially endear them to us. As with any sentient being, each dog reveals distinctive interests, fears, emotions, and personalities. In other words, like us, every dog is a unique individual and should be respected as such. Some dogs learn commands immediately, others require a few hits and misses, while still others do best through observation. Some never quite outgrow their goofy adolescence, and some always need a very gentle hand to gain confidence. Always love your dog for that special "furry person" he really is.

AUDREY SCHWARTZ RIVERS, MS, PetShare: Pets and People for Positive Change, Houston, TX

BRUSHING

Some dogs do not want to hold still for brushing, especially young dogs. One trick is to put squeeze cheese or peanut butter at the height of the dog's head on the side of the refrigerator or washing machine. Then call him over and have him start licking the spot while you start to brush him. You may need to add more or just have several short brushing sessions until your dog is more relaxed with brushing.

You can also stuff a hollow toy with treats and cheese, and while the dog is lying down with the toy, do some brushing as well.

🐾HEATHER MOHAN-GIBBONS, MS, RVT, CPDT-KA, ACAAB, Collected Wisdom Animal Behavior, LLC, Milwaukee, WI

BUSINESS CARDS

You can encourage people to keep your business cards by printing helpful information on the back. All of my cards have a place for people to put emergency contact information for their pets, including their names; the name, phone number, and address of friends; and information about their veterinarian.

🐾WAYNE SHAFFER, ABCDT, Pawsitive Methods, Kelseyville, CA

CALMING SIGNALS 15

Calming signals are signals that dogs give off to avoid conflict; to avoid threats from people, dogs, and other animals; to calm down nervousness, fear, noise, stress, and other unpleasant things; and to make friends with other dogs and people. If you notice your dog doing any of the following, it may be a calming signal:

- turning his head to the side
- diverting his eyes to either side
- turning his back to you or turning to his side
- licking his nose
- freezing in position
- walking slowly using slow movements
- moving toward you in a curve
- yawning
- sitting or lying down
- sniffing with nose to the ground
- splitting up (physically going between dogs or people)
- wagging his tail in different ways
- making himself small
- lifting his paws up and down
- licking faces

🐾LISA HOLLANDER, ABC Certified, DogGone Proud Dog Obedience/Behavior Modification, Lexington, KY

CAMPING

Before you go camping with your dog, brush up on his obedience skills. Even if he responds to all of your cues at home, how sure are you that he will respond in an area with tons of distractions (the great outdoors, other campers in close proximity, the smells wafting off the grill, just to name a few)? Take him to a class where he can learn to work in the presence of other dogs and people. Take him to different parks and work on the following cues that I use all of the time at the campground: *down-stay*, *leave it*, and controlled walking. If your dog can master these commands, your trip will be safe and pleasant for all.

—DEVENE GODAU, CPDT-KA, Trainers
Academy, LLC, Royal Oak, MI

Whatever you are planning on camping in—a tent, a pop-up, a trailer, or a motor home—make sure that your dog gets used to it before you hit the campground. Think of all the new sights, smells, and sounds that he will be expected to tolerate at the campground. The more things you can get him used to beforehand, the more relaxed he will be. We put up our pop-up a few weeks before our trip and just hang out in there. We'll eat dinner in there and leave the door open so that our dogs can go in and out. Whenever they choose to relax in the camper, we reward them with treats so that they start to pair relaxing in the camper with great stuff!

—DEVENE GODAU, CPDT-KA, Trainers
Academy, LLC, Royal Oak, MI

CANINE FREESTYLE

Canine freestyle is a great way to have fun with your dog. It's like ballroom dancing for dogs. The object is to create an original dance, using music and movement, to showcase the teamwork between the two of you. Once you've selected your music, the next step is choreography. This means that you design steps and movements for your and your dog that relate to the music. Canine freestylers use a variety of moves to add interest to their performance. Obedience moves like *heel* and *stay* can be incorporated. Tricks can work well too. A beginner routine has about 20 different moves timed to precise points in the music. An advanced-level routine can have as many as 70 different moves.

—MARY LEATHERBERRY, CPDT-KA,
Good Dog! Santa Fe, Santa Fe, NM

Canine freestyle, also known as doggy dancing, is a sport that any dog can do. I teach freestyle for fun, not for competition, and I find that it is a great bonding experience as well as a fun activity–dogs love moving and people love music! One of the great things about freestyle is that each routine is customized to the individual dog. That means that while my Bearded Collie, who has hip dysplasia, can't do crawls or walk on her hind legs, she excels at heeling and weaving. My Bulldog mix is not as coordinated, but he really comes alive when I ask him to do rollovers, spins, and crawls to the beat. So rather than force certain behaviors on your dog, let him show you what behaviors he likes to do.

ᦾ ANN ALLUMS, CPDT-KA, Best Friends Animal Society, Kanab, UT

CANINE GOOD CITIZEN®

The American Kennel Club's (AKC) Canine Good Citizen (CGC) test is all about having a good relationship with your dog. Be proud of your dog's accomplishments, and don't get overly stressed about obtaining the certificate. The most important thing is the time you spend working with your dog and building your mutual bond.

ᦾ JACQUELYN ENGLAND, A Dog's Life, Sunnyvale, CA

The AKC's CGC is a real asset to pet owners and the general public. This test is really a demonstration of how well a dog can behave in public situations. It has proven itself useful in a number of different ways: In some cities, apartment rental companies request that a dog have his CGC before they will rent to a person. And there are therapy dog programs that use this test as the first stepping stone to becoming a certified therapy team. No matter what type of dog you have, the CGC is a great way to prove to the world that you can communicate well with your pet.

ᦾ DEENA MCIVER, K-9 Kind, Portland, OR

TOP TIDBIT

Canine Good Citizen (CGC) is an American Kennel Club (AKC) program designed to recognized dogs who display good behavior at home and in public and to emphasize responsible pet ownership to the community.

On a day warmer than 60°F (15°C), do not leave your dog in the car without air conditioning. The temperature rises quickly in a car—even with the windows open a crack. Many dogs have died from heatstroke this way. Imagine sitting in an enclosed car with a fur coat on when it's hot outside!

ᗡDARLENE KOZA, Scooter's School of
Sit & Stay, Rochester, NY

We are all aware that air bags are too powerful for our children (anyone who has had a child can attest to the fact that information about air bags is drilled into your head before you are even allowed to bring her home from the hospital), but do we ever think about the consequences of air bags for our dogs? Even a minor impact can set off the air bags with such power that it can crush a dog. Stop allowing your dog to ride in the front seat. To keep everyone safe, commit yourself to using a doggy seat belt or a crate. Not only will this keep your dog safe from air bags and reduce the ways he can distract you, but it

After training for the CGC test, you can easily proof each behavior (i.e., work on each behavior in many different situations) in the following way: Choose one behavior at a time, and have your dog do that behavior every time he wants something for a week. For instance, if you choose to work on the down, your dog must down before going outside, getting in the car, getting his food bowl, being petted, getting treats, etc. This is an easy way to work training into your schedule and gives your dog many opportunities to rehearse a behavior.

ᗡANN ALLUMS, CPDT-KA, Best Friends
Animal Society, Kanab, UT

CAR SAFETY

Always use a crate or canine seat belt for safety reasons! Put on your dog's seat belt, give him a treat. Repeat. Or crate train your dog to enjoy being in his den so that he will be comfortable in it during car rides.

ᗡTEOTI ANDERSON, CPDT-KA, Pawsitive
Results, LLC, Lexington, SC

will keep him confined upon impact—even a small impact can project a dog across the car, possibly even through a window.

ꭞDEVENE GODAU, CPDT-KA, Trainers Academy, LLC, Royal Oak, MI

Whether your dog rides in a crate or in the back seat with a seat belt, teach him to never get out of the car until you have fastened his leash to his collar. Practice getting into and out of the car at home, in a safe area where your dog cannot escape and run into traffic if he slips by you. Getting out of a car is serious business, as the surrounding area will most likely be dangerous for your dog. A dog who waits until you fasten his leash will be more likely to live to ride another day.

ꭞPAM SHEEHAN, 4 Paws Training, LLC, Broken Arrow, OK

Even though dogs really like it, it's not safe to let them stick their head out the window. A small rock or piece of debris could cut a dog's nose, eye, or head and cause serious injury. To be safe, secure your dog in your vehicle.

ꭞBONNIE KRUPA, CPDT-KA, Happy, Clean and Smart, Muncie, IN

Always lock the main power lock for automatic windows. If your dog accidentally steps on the window button, he could fall out of the car or get crushed in the window.

ꭞDEVENE GODAU, CPDT-KA, Trainers Academy, LLC, Royal Oak, MI

Teach your dog a solid *wait* before travel in the car so that he won't escape when opening the car or crate door on the road or at rest stops. Choose a special word that is not used in general conversation so that your dog won't jump out by mistake. Once he is properly leashed and you have control of him, you can use his release word to allow him to exit the car.

ꭞLAURA DORFMAN, CPDT-KA, kona's touch, inc., Glencoe, IL

CARSICKNESS

If your puppy or dog gets carsick, experiment with various changes to see if anything helps. Try positioning his crate or restraining device in different places in the car (front seat, back seat, cargo area). Turn on the air conditioner or roll down the windows so that air blows on his face. Cover his crate with a blanket. Drive him on an empty stomach. Feed him a few gingersnaps or dog treats with ginger added 30 minutes before leaving. You can also talk with your vet about options for medically minimizing the effects of carsickness.

ꭞDAWN ANTONIAK-MITCHELL, Esq., CPDT-KA, BonaFide Dog Academy LLC, Omaha, NE

Give your dog some diphenhydramine an hour before leaving. Of course, always consult your veterinarian before giving this or any other drugs to your dog.

&LAURIE ROBINSON, Valparaiso, IN

For dogs who have carsickness and drool while in the car, try the holistic remedy called Rescue Remedy. It comes in a bottle with a spray top, and all you have to do is spray it on the pads of the feet and put a bit in the mouth, and it can help reduce the anxiety and drooling in some dogs.

&CARMEN PETZ, Vancouver, Canada

Plan one long, fun car ride—at least four hours long. A weekend camping/hiking trip works wonders. Hours of endless driving on the highway help a dog get used to riding in the car, and the length will help him get over his carsickness. The extra bonus of stopping to hike and camp makes the car a fun place, and camping changes the car from a vehicle to a home. And just in case, remember to pack plenty of paper towels, odor-neutralizing cleaners, and towels to use as bedding.

&SUE STERNBERG, Animals for Adoption and Great Dog Productions, Accord, NY, and Moab, UT

CATS

Living with dogs and cats can be made easier by allowing the cats their own getaway places. The use of baby gates is a wonderful way to do this, but make sure that the gates are raised up about 6 inches (15 cm) off the ground so that the cats can slip under them instead of trying to jump over them. Jumping will slow a cat down, making her easier to catch and the chase behavior harder to extinguish. Also, jumping cats are more exciting to a dog than a cat who simply disappears!

&JESSICA JANOWSKI, Puppy Please! Dog Training, LLC, Goffstown, NH

CHEWING

Puppies need to chew. However, it obviously isn't pleasant when they use humans or furniture as chew toys! To prevent excessive mouthing, always have a toy on hand to redirect their chewing behavior (which may mean carrying one around), and have as many toys scattered all over the house as possible. Some good choices are washcloths frozen in the freezer; stuffed animals they can sink

their teeth into; rubber squeaky toys; and hard rubber chew toys. Be sure to have at least 20 toys of different varieties, and rotate them in groups of 10.

ᥱ⁄CHRISTINA SHUSTERICH, BA, CBC, NY Clever K9, Inc., Queens, NY

Be aware that chewing is a natural dog behavior. It is rewarding to the dog or he wouldn't be doing it. The dog has no ulterior motive for chewing, such as anger or spite—the behavior simply works for him! To truly change the behavior, which is what training is meant to accomplish, you need to either change the motivation for the behavior or redirect the behavior.

ᥱ⁄ANN ALLUMS, CPDT-KA, Best Friends Animal Society, Kanab, UT

If chewing is a problem with your dog, take preventive measures like putting your possessions out of his reach. Leave three to five very interesting toys on the floor for him, which should vary in type—some should have squeakers, some should be fuzzy, and some should be able to be filled with food. Praise your dog for chewing his toys.

ᥱ⁄LAURIE LUCK, CPDT-KA, KPACTP, Smart Dog University, LLC, Mount Airy, MD

Puppies and some adult dogs explore with their mouths. Creating a safe environment could mean the difference between life and death for your dog. Keep everything he should not have out of his environment.

Dog toys should be size appropriate—never give your dog a toy that is so small that it can get stuck in his mouth or throat or swallowed.

ᥱ⁄DAINA BECKMAN, Happy Tails Dog Behavior & Training, Hornell, NY

Some dogs chew on leashes as a way to pacify themselves. For example, in the shelter environment, dogs who become anxious when they see other dogs may chew on their leashes in lieu of barking, lunging, or showing some other kind of displeasure. A chain leash helps save leashes, but it does nothing to help the anxious dog. A hollow rubber toy, slid over the chain leash, will give the anxious dog a pacifier to chew on to help him stay calm in stressful situations.

ᥱ⁄PAMELA SEMANIK, CPDT-KA, Walton Hills, OH

It's important to know your dog's habits to spot if he has chewed on and swallowed anything dangerous. A change in defecating or urinating habits, vomiting, acting lethargic, or not eating or drinking are all signs of a blocked bowel or stomach or other serious problems. Most people wait longer than they should to call their veterinarian when their dog is sick. Call your veterinarian at the first sign of illness.

ᥱ⁄DAINA BECKMAN, Happy Tails Dog Behavior & Training, Hornell, NY

NYLABONE

Does your dog chew on his leash? Letting him chew on his leash makes walking with him rather difficult. Taking a walk soon becomes a game of tug-of-war! If you let your dog continue, it could also become a safety issue in addition to a behavioral one. The sturdy leash you bought yesterday could get frayed in minutes, and if your dog gets loose, he could be injured.

To stop this habit, apply some chew deterrent spray to the leash. If your dog loves the taste of chew deterrent spray, try using lemon juice or hot sauce. Also try exercising your dog at home before going for a walk; dogs who like to chew on their leashes often have a lot of pent-up energy. Burning some calories before

getting out in the neighborhood can sometimes help take the edge off. You may also want to teach your dog a *leave it* cue. This will teach him to leave the leash alone, as well as other items you want him to avoid.

ℰ TEOTI ANDERSON, CPDT-KA, Pawsitive Results, LLC, Lexington, SC

CHILDREN

Don't leave your kids and puppy or dog alone together unsupervised. If you can't supervise, use a crate, tether the dog to you, or tether him in a dog-proofed area or an x-pen.

ℰ DENISE DAWSON, CPDT-KA, All Breed Rescue and Training, Colorado Springs, CO

Direct eye contact can be confrontational to dogs, and children frequently stand at eye level to large-breed dogs. Children should be taught to ask before approaching a dog so that an adult can judge the dog's posture to determine if it is appropriate. If a child wants to pet the dog, she should learn to stroke him gently with the back of her hand, which keeps fingers from grabbing. Children don't know their own strength and are used to squeezing stuffed animals. Teaching them to be gentle and quiet helps them learn to be respectful.

ℰ PAT HENNESSY, CAP2, CPDT-KA, N2paws, Leawood, KS

A valuable lesson for children is to simply "be a tree." This applies whether it is their own exuberant puppy or the strange dog who is running toward them in a menacing way. Tell the story about the tree that has a very strong trunk and that they can be like that tree trunk if they fold their arms and tuck their fists into the armpits. "Be a tree" could save a child from serious injury. Explain to your kids that running away from a dog is likely to cause him to chase and attack.

ᴇᴢGLORIA J. WHITE, CPDT-KA, Pawsitive Waggers Training, Cincinnati, OH

Children are very excited when a new puppy comes into the home, but the puppy can easily become overwhelmed. Also, children can unintentionally be too rough with a puppy. Therefore, implement a "one hand rule." This means that only one person can be touching the puppy at a time, and that person can only have one hand on the dog. This will help prevent a child from trying to pick up or carry the pet and is less stressful on the puppy.

ᴇᴢLAURIE ROBINSON, Valparaiso, IN

What is appropriate behavior for children around dogs? An easy gauge is what I would allow the youngster to do with a human infant. Is the child old enough and strong enough to walk around carrying a wriggling baby? If not, she is too young to carry a puppy. I might permit that same youngster to sit on the floor and cradle an infant in his lap with my assistance, which is how he should cuddle a puppy. Would I allow a young child to drum her heels repeatedly into a baby or use the baby for a pillow? I stop a child who does those things to a dog just as quickly. This simple guideline makes it easier to allow for different age levels and decision-making skills. While a four-year-old would find it challenging to rest her head on her beloved

dog without a lot of wiggling, an older child or teen might be able to safely do that with the right well-trained dog in good health.

ᴇᴢP.J. LACETTE, the original Best Paw Forward, Osteen, FL

If you want your young children to act appropriately with your dog, let them help you take care of the daily chores involved with having a dog. Measure out the food together, wash his bowls together, and create a toy basket and help pick out toys for him together. Let your children take care of hanging up the leash and potty bags. Caring for an animal's daily well-being adds to a more balanced household!

ᴇᴢNANCY TANNER, CPDT-KA, Paws & People, LLC, Bozeman, MT

If your young child really wants to walk the dog but you feel that the family dog is too large for your child to handle, simply put two leashes on his collar. The child can hold one and you can hold the second for security.

ᴇᴢMICHELLE SEVIGNY, BA, DOGSAFE Canine First Aid, North Vancouver, BC, Canada

> **"Children should be brought up learning to treat dogs with respect."**

Parents should teach their children the responsibilities as well as the fun aspects of having a puppy. They need to teach them to play calmly and nicely with their dog because this teaches them to respect adult dogs later in life.

ॐDONNA S. RINDSKOPF,
Guide Dog Raiser, Doglovers
Obedience of Ramona, Ramona, CA

I often have little kids in my classes, so I teach them the following script when asking to pet a dog: Hello. My name is _____. May I pet your dog? Thank you!

ॐBONNIE KRUPA, CPDT-KA, Happy,
Clean and Smart, Muncie, IN

It is important that you teach children not to bother a dog while he's sleeping. Teach them to arouse him verbally and wait until he is fully awake before attempting to touch him. Accidents can and do happen, but in the case of a sleeping dog, any youngsters should be kept away, or the dog should be put away safely to nap in another room or his crate to prevent any mishaps.

ॐLISA PATRONA, Dip. DTBC, CPDT-KA,
PDT, CBC, Trainers Academy, LLC,
President, Troy, MI

CHILDREN, TRAINING WITH

Finding ways to include your children in the training of the family dog is a fantastic way to foster a positive relationship between them by practicing ways in which they can interact safely and appropriately. As always, very small children should be attended at all times when interacting with your dog, and full care should be taken that your dog can safely take food from children as appropriate to their age. A very young child can help if she sits with an adult who feeds treats to the dog while the child simply pets the dog as a reward. Training games should be suspended immediately if your dog shows any sign of possessiveness around food treats or appears stressed in any way.

ॐERICA PYTLOVANY,
CPDT-KA, WOOFS!
Dog Training Center,
Arlington, VA

Consultations with children can be chaotic, but planning ahead can help set everyone up for success. Discuss expectations with the parents prior to the consult. It is not reasonable to expect children to attend a two-hour session. Bring "novel" items with you, such as doggy coloring pages, small dog figures, or even a dog-related board game. Often the kids will enjoy these activities, and they will entertain them during times when they do not need to participate. Having items handy for consults with children can make everyone's experience much more pleasant and successful!

ꝏJENNIFER SHRYOCK, BA, CDBC, Family Paws (Dogs & Storks programs), Cary, NC

Sometimes it is useful for families of young kids (five to ten years old) to construct incentive charts for handling the new puppy or dog. They can list what commands or tricks they worked on and the day they did it. The parents can offer some kind of prize/reward for a certain number of days. This helps with kids who are a little jealous of the new puppy/dog or who might be a little too rough. It empowers them to get involved with the dog while teaching them the correct way to relate to him.

ꝏAMY W. DE BENEDICTIS, The Puppy Lady, Menlo Park, CA

When working with families with small children, use the game "Simon Says" to get the kids to help with training. For instance, the dog can practice how to down and stay while the kids run where you tell then to run, play with toys, jump up and down, shout, scream, etc. The kids have fun and offer controlled distractions while the dog works.

ꝏRACHEL B. LACHOW, CPDT-KA, Positively Obedient, Reisterstown, MD

When children are involved in my private in-home training lessons, I always try to keep them interested by periodically coming up with games for them to do with their dog throughout the lesson. I find that this keeps their attention throughout the lesson because they want to pay attention to all instructions so that they can win the next game. I carry a doggy bag with treats not only for the dog but for the kids as well.

ꝏJANICE DEMADONA, Dog Training With Janice, Orlando, FL

CHOOSING A DOG

Choosing the right dog is one of the most important decisions you'll face in the lifetime of your pet, so don't make a hasty or uninformed decision. Choosing wisely means years of happiness; choosing poorly means years of frustration. The best questions to ask are "What is my current lifestyle?" and "How would a dog fit into it?" Think about the person you are right now. Be honest with yourself; this is a potential 15-year or more commitment, so facing reality is important. Sharing similar energy levels and interests is the best way to choose a pet and create a lasting bond.

ᐱWENDY SCHMITZ, BA, CPDT-KA, CDBC,
Life with Fido, Fredericksburg, VA

Every dog is an individual, with certain predispositions or traits more or less apparent, depending on the dog's breed or breed mix. All dogs bark, bite, chase, jump, and do other "dog things." It's best to select a dog based on your lifestyle and his breed characteristics rather than appearance. Retrievers are playful,

sturdy dogs who have a lot of energy. Hounds howl. Terriers dig. Huskies run. Bulldogs walk to their food bowls. Regardless of breed, it is important to realize that all dogs have desirable and not so desirable attributes for living with us as companions. All dogs require proper training and socialization. There is no ideal dog. Whatever dog you choose, educate yourself and work to bring out the qualities that make him special and minimize the characteristics that are problematic, such as howling or chasing.

ᐱLUCINDA LUDWIG, Canine
Connection LLC, Dubuque, IA

The decision to bring home a new pet should be made with as much, if not more, foresight as buying a house or car. Having a dog is a long-term relational and financial commitment, up to 10 to 20 years. Furthermore, a dog is more than just an object to exist in a backyard; he is a living, emotional being who depends on a human family for his needs, which include a sense of belonging.

ঙ ANN ALLUMS, CPDT-KA, Best Friends
Animal Society, Kanab, UT

CLASSES

Before signing up for a group class, it is highly recommended that you attend one in advance. There are a large variety of training methods, styles, and personalities available. Most classes are nonrefundable, so you want to ensure that the class is a good fit for you and your dog. Some things to consider: You and your dog should be treated respectfully, there should be adequate space for the number of dogs, the building should be free of other distractions, and the parking and traffic should not a problem for you. Avoid signing up for classes if the trainer prohibits you from observing before paying.

ঙ HEATHER MOHAN-GIBBONS, MS, RVT,
CPDT-KA, ACAAB, Collected Wisdom Animal
Behavior, LLC, Milwaukee, WI

You may find that you have real problems getting your dog to walk nicely into the building the first few times you attend a class, which can be very frustrating. I have my clients wrap the leash under their dog's belly and bring the end back up, crating a makeshift harness. The dog doesn't pull because it tightens against his chest. This is just "first aid" for a couple of weeks. It's a good way to keep from getting frustrated at the start of class.

ঙ BETH HALEY, CPDT-KA, 4RK9S,
Cedar Rapids, IA

If you are a trainer running a group training class and you have two dogs in a class who constantly "talk" to each other, place a crate covered with a towel or a large piece of cardboard between the dogs. This will block their view of each other and help stop the barking. Of course, have the handlers work on redirecting the dogs' attention to them.

ঙ ROBERT JORDAN, CPDT-KA, Pavlov's
Dogs
Pet Dog Training, Mechanicsville, VA

For highly aroused (read: noisy!) dogs in your beginning class, try stationing the client and dog behind a solid high jump. Sometimes if he can't see the other dogs it cuts down on the noise level produced, and the client can focus on you, the instructor, instead of trying to keep the dog quiet.

ঙ CATHY BONES, CPDT-KA, Pacifica, CA

When I run my adult dog group class, at the very first meeting I want the dogs to come (instead of just the clients alone). It can be louder and more chaotic, but with good prescreening and a trained assistant, it goes remarkably well. I use a clicker and want to be there when people use the clicker with their dog the first time. Otherwise, I find that people practice the clicker for a week on their own before I see them again. I have found it is more effective and easier on people, the dogs, and me to get them off on the right foot with the right timing before sending them home to practice.

ꙅHEATHER MOHAN-GIBBONS, MS, RVT, CPDT-KA, ACAAB, Collected Wisdom Animal Behavior, LLC, Milwaukee, WI

CLICKER TRAINING

Using a clicker to train your dog is a valuable tool. The clicker makes the same sound no matter who uses it, and it sends a clear message to your dog that you are pleased with his behavior. The click is given when the appropriate behavior is performed. Think of the clicker as a camera: You take a picture (click) when you see the pose (behavior) that you like. After the click, reinforce the dog with something he likes (in most cases, food).

ꙅGLORIA J. WHITE, CPDT-KA, Pawsitive Waggers Training, Cincinnati, OH

The clicker bridges the gap between two species trying to communicate at the same time. If I am training a dolphin, a bird, or a dog, each has his own form of body language and sounds to communicate with me, but none of them is fluent in English.

So using words to train a new behavior to an animal that does not speak the language is not helpful. The clicker is simply a clean, efficient way to say exactly what it is you want regardless of species or language. Your training success will increase dramatically for new behaviors when you stop talking and start clicking!

ꙅHEATHER MOHAN-GIBBONS, MS, RVT, CPDT-KA, ACAAB, Collected Wisdom Animal Behavior, LLC, Milwaukee, WI

Clicker training can be great fun for you and your dog. Perfect your timing because what you click is what you teach. Make sure that the behavior you mark with the clicker is the behavior that you want repeated!

ꙅDEBBY MCMULLEN, CDBC, Pawsitive Reactions, LLC, Pittsburgh, PA

Clicker training requires good timing and focus on the part of the trainer to mark the precise behaviors you want to develop. To improve your timing and focus, have a helper bounce a tennis ball. Click each time the ball hits the floor. Encourage your helper to sometimes "fake it" by pretending to toss the ball. This will help you develop patience and focus so that you are only clicking an actual behavior, rather than one you anticipate will occur.

ᑭDAWN ANTONIAK-MITCHELL, Esq., CPDT-KA, BonaFide Dog Academy LLC, Omaha, NE

To help people work on timing when training with a clicker, I encourage them to watch favorite movies or reruns of television shows, especially horror movies or campy TV shows. The rules are that every time Jan Brady whines, someone says "like," or the killer stabs someone, you click. You can learn to anticipate the action so that the click happens almost simultaneously with the action on the screen.

ᑭJILL MILLER, CPDT-KA, Mad City Dog Training, Madison, WI

When clicker training, it is best to work with a hungry dog!

ᑭJENNIFER TUCK, Rip it Up! Dog Training, Skowhegan, ME

If you feel too clumsy to use a clicker as a reward mark, the next best choice may be clicking with your tongue. It's a more neutral sound than using your voice and a word.

ᑭJULIE HUMISTON, CPDT-KA, Puppy Love Dog Training, Minneapolis, MN

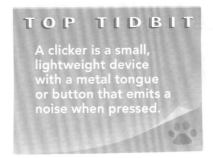

TOP TIDBIT

A clicker is a small, lightweight device with a metal tongue or button that emits a noise when pressed.

Clickers are not remote controls. Try to keep your hand still while clicking—don't let your hand become part of the signal. You may need to keep your hand behind your back or in a pocket, whatever you need to avoid the "point and shoot"!

ᑭPAM SHEEHAN, 4 Paws Training, LLC, Broken Arrow, OK

Clicker training is preferable to just using food as a reward because the reinforcement is immediate. Reinforcement for behavior must happen within one-and-a-half to two seconds of its occurrence for the dog to make a clear association between the two. When just using food rewards, actual delivery of the food will oftentimes not come for several seconds after the target behavior has occurred. Sometimes the food will not come until the dog is already disengaged from the target behavior, at which time you're not at all reinforcing the behavior you wanted! The clicker provides an effective way to "bridge the gap," which enables you to effectively capture the moment in time when the behavior is happening. The actual delivery of the food can be seconds later.

ᑭLISA PATRONA, Dip. DTBC, CPDT-KA, PDT, CBC, Trainers Academy, LLC, President, Troy, MI

Why is a clicker preferable to just using your voice? Because the distinct and consistent sound of the clicker provides clear and well-timed reinforcement. When using your voice as a reinforcer (instead of a clicker), even subtle changes in intonation can confuse the dog.

DEVENE GODAU, CPDT-KA, Trainers Academy, LLC, Royal Oak, MI

CLOTHES

If your dog needs a coat in cold weather and enjoys romping with other dogs, the best play clothes are those that fasten along his neck and spine, giving him full range of motion. Coats that fasten with Velcro on the chest have a tendency to pop open and are easily pulled off by other dogs during play. Coats that come down in front to the dog's knees restrict movement and interfere with play.

JOANN KOVACICH, Grateful Dog Pet Care, Inc., Penfield, NY

If you dress up your pet, make sure that the costume isn't annoying or unsafe. It should not constrict movement or hearing or impede his ability to breathe or bark. Keep a lookout for small, dangling, or easily chewed-off pieces on the costume that could cause your pet to choke.

JAMIE DAMATO, CPDT-KA, Animalsense Canine Training and Behavior, Inc., Chicago, IL

COLLARS

Try a collar with your name and phone number embroidered directly on it with no tags. The embroidered collar is great in case your dog gets out. Tags can be difficult to read, and your dog has to get close enough for the person to read it. With embroidered collars, the information can be read at a distance, making notification quick.

LAURA DORFMAN, CPDT-KA, kona's touch, inc., Glencoe, IL

Never use a choke collar on your dog—no training happens when a dog is under stress.

ANDREA CARLSON-CARTER, Courteous Canine, Inc., Lutz, FL

Using aversive collars, such as choke chains, can actually contribute to aggression issues while walking. As the dog lunges towards a person or dog, he gets a collar correction from the choke chain choking him. Over time, people and dogs

can become associated with an unpleasant correction. Dogs with a history of aggression toward people and dogs should never be walked with an aversive collar. A head halter is a much better collar choice.

    CHRISTINA SHUSTERICH, BA, CBC, NY Clever K9, Inc., Queens, NY

A flat buckle or breakaway collar is the safest choice if your dog needs to have a collar on while he is alone because there is no risk of him catching it on something and choking or strangling.

    JAMIE LURTZ, Solutions! Pet Services, Anaheim, CA

I *never* suggest the use of a choke collar or prong collar. Inexperienced owners can cause more damage than good.

    DARLENE KOZA, Scooter's School of Sit & Stay, Rochester, NY

COME (RECALL)

Playing games like hide-and-seek can make training the *come* (or *recall*) fun for both you and your young puppy. Just call his name, run in the other direction, and hide around the nearest corner. Act excited when the puppy finds you. When that gets too easy, start making it a little harder for him to find you. Soon you will have your puppy coming at the sound of his name, and you will have fun doing the training.

    TIMOTHY REISINGER, Tomah, WI

Dogs, just like humans, tend to forget things they don't practice a lot. Set aside at least five minutes every day to practice *recalls*. Practice them in the house, at the park, randomly during off-leash walks, in your front yard, and wherever else you go with your dog. Keep in mind that if there's somewhere you haven't practiced your *recall*, there's somewhere your dog might not remember what it means. Practice in many different locations—even by simply calling your dog to you several times during daily walks.

    JACQUELYN ENGLAND, A Dog's Life, Sunnyvale, CA

If everyone in the household puts ten small treats in their pocket each morning and sets a goal to, throughout the day, call the dog to give him a treat and then let him go about his business, you'll have the foundations for a good *recall*.

    SUSAN SMITH, CPDT-KA, CDBC, CTC, Raising Canine, LLC

Dog who come reliably in class or at home may not be entirely reliable in a new location. Dogs don't generalize well, and a different environment that's chock-full of distractions that you haven't trained him for creates the need to go back a few steps in your training. Work on basic *recall* exercises to help him understand that "Come!" means come to me no matter where you happen to be or whatever else is going on in the environment. Train for random and distracted *recalls*, and practice, practice, practice (always on lead). Use the most rewarding and yummy treats (leftover chicken, cheese, lunch meat) that he will only get when you are working the *recalls* with him. Be sure to work in different locations, not just in one place.

ꬲLISA PATRONA, Dip. DTBC, CPDT-KA, PDT, CBC, Trainers Academy, LLC, President, Troy, MI

When calling your dog in from outside or to you to go home from a dog park, use a different word other than your *recall* ("come!") cue, such as "here," "inside," or "time to go." Periodically call your dog with this cue, put the leash on (if at the park), or go inside and close the door. Then give him praise, treats, and pats, and allow him to go back to having fun outside or at the park. This will make it so that these cues do not mean "playtime is over."

ꬲCOLLEEN B. HURLEY, Orlando, FL and Gainesville, FL

I recommend teaching your dog to come to you on a whistle. Why? Because if he's ever lost, you want the *recall* cue to carry far, your voice not to give out, and if your dog is shy and will only come to your voice, no one else can help you look usefully. Every whistle sounds a bit different, so buy a few of the same kind and practice with them. If your dog ever becomes lost, there will be more than one whistle for searchers to use.

ꬲCERENA ZUTIS, CZ Dog Training, CA

You can reinforce a reliable *recall* when walking your dog on a loose leash. Every time you find him interested in anything along the way, say "Look! Look!" Then when you want the dog to recall, yell "Look! Look!" and he will be expecting something cool and come running.

ꬲDONNA SAVOIE, CPDT-KA, Pack of Paws Dog Training, Charlton, MA

Never call your dog to you and then reprimand him. If you do this, you will never get a good *recall* from him. Only good things should happen when your dog comes to you—no matter what.

ꬲLISA HOLLANDER, ABC Certified, DogGone Proud Dog Obedience/Behavior Modification, Lexington, KY

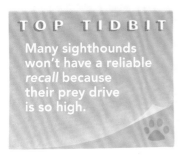
Find ' em is one of my favorite easy games for owners to play with their dogs, and it's a great reinforcer for *recall* training. All you have to do is start inside the house tossing one or two treats for the dog to find. Then move the game outside and toss one or two treats. Let the dog find them and then toss lots more.

JILL HALSTEAD, BA, CTC, Follow the Leader Dog Training Services, Richmond, VT

COMMANDS

It is best to integrate commands into your dog's daily life. You will find that using simple commands (*sit*, *down*, *stay*, *come*, and *heel*) will reinforce appropriate behaviors and discourage inappropriate behaviors.

JAMIE DAMATO, CPDT-KA, Animalsense Canine Training and Behavior, Inc., Chicago, IL

Be sure to say commands only once. Repeating commands several times trains your dog to not immediately obey.

CHRISTINA SHUSTERICH, BA, CBC, NY Clever K9, Inc., Queens, NY

Many dogs learn that when they hear "Come!" it means that fun is over—that it's time to come indoors or leave the dog park. Instead of only calling your dog to come when it's time to come inside, try calling him at various times during his outside time; when he comes, give him several treats and allow him to go back to the fun thing he was doing. Soon, your dog will learn that the word "come" means that he gets treats *and* gets to continue to have fun!

MEL BUSSEY-SILVERMAN, CPDT-KA, CDBC, Training Tracks Canine Learning Station, Oxford/Cincinnati, OH

For a reliable *recall*, always call your dog to do something more exciting than what he's doing at the time. Let's say you are sitting outside with a refreshment in your hand when you are called to come inside the house. You come running only to find out that the dishwasher needs to be emptied. Blah, next time you'd stay outside. But if you ran into the house and got $100, you'd be glad to run into the house every time!

DONNA SAVOIE, Pack of Paws Dog Training, Charlton, MA

When I have a client who constantly repeats commands, I will (teasingly) do the same. If the client is sitting down during my explanation, when I am ready for her to work with the dog, I will say to the client "Stand, stand, stand" until she does so, then ask how that felt. I will then (in a very friendly manner) point out her own behavior. This usually does the trick!

   HEPZIBAH E. HOFFMAN-ROGERS, CPDT-KA, Thunderpaws Canine Solutions, LLC, Seguin, TX

When giving commands, it is important to give the correct command with the desired action. If you want your dog to lie down, give only one command, such as "Down"– not "Sit down." Or if you want your dog off the couch say "Off," not "Down." Otherwise, you'll just be giving him mixed messages.

   DONNA S. RINDSKOPF, Guide Dog Raiser, Doglover's Obedience of Ramona, CA

When first teaching basic commands (such as *down*, *sit*, etc.) always make sure that you are in control of the dog before you give a command. Do not give a command to a dog when he is across the room. If he does not fully understand what you are asking of him, he may not comply, which means that you may have to go get him. The dog will quickly learn that if you're not near him, he can choose to obey or not, and you will have lost control. It can take a long time for you to regain control once it's lost.

   JENNIFER TUCK, Rip it Up! Dog Training, Skowhegan, ME

COMMUNICATION

How does one communicate with a different species? By learning its language since it cannot learn ours. Because dogs do not speak our language, they display their questions through their behavior.

   PENNY LOCKE, Dog Listener, All About Canines, Novato, CA

When communicating with your dog, the more versatility you give to body language, tone, and inflection, the more he will respond. You can do this by altering tone, pitch, and emphasis (i.e., showing a range of emotion in your voice), as well as being just as dramatic with body language. These techniques will all captivate the animal.

   CYNTHIA KURTZ, The Pet Geek, West Linn/Sandy, OR

Part of our responsibility in communicating with our canines is to try to learn their language. If a dog fails to give us what we think we are asking for, go back and reteach. Think about whether you may not have been clear or may not have set him up to succeed, or maybe it's just a matter of needing more training.

   RUTH BRUNETTE-MEANS, CPDT-KA, All Breed Rescue & Training, Colorado Springs, CO

Consider taking a class or reading some information to best educate yourself about canine language and communication. And realize that not everyone may agree with your ideas about dog training and behavior. Be prepared to agree to disagree!

   JAMIE DAMATO, CPDT-KA, Animalsense Canine Training and Behavior, Inc., Chicago, IL

> **"The average dog understands more than 150 words."**

training. It has been my experience that people talk too much, causing the dog confusion. When the word "no" or the dog's name is overused, it becomes nagging, and the dog will ignore you. He must be paying attention to you to learn the commands and work out exactly what you want.

ᐳDAINA BECKMAN, Dog Behavior Specialist, Happy Tails Dog Behavior & Training, Hornell, NY

Understanding that your dog is a different species that has difficulty learning and applying human forms of communication will make you a better trainer.

ᐳCYNTHIA EDGERLY, Bingo! Dog Training, Watsonville, CA

Contrary to popular belief, puppies do not emerge from the womb understanding English (or any other spoken language).

ᐳJOAN B. GUERTIN, Common Sense Dog Training & Behavior Solutions, Mabank, TX

Training your dog should be an enjoyable experience for you both. The more you understand about how your dog thinks and learns, the more effectively you can communicate. Clear communication means successful training and good behavior with no need for force or coercion

ᐳJAMIE DAMATO, CPDT-KA, Animalsense Canine Training and Behavior, Inc., Chicago, IL

Clarifying communication between a dog and people is essential for successful

Talk to your dog about everything that's going on. If you are taking him to run errands and then stopping at your sister's for a short visit, say "Honey, let's go in the car on errands and then we'll go see Auntie Laura." If you're going on a walk with his buddies, you might say "Okay, time for an adventure with your buddies!" The more words your dog knows, the better. "Walk," "Have din-din," and "Let's go see Rover" are all good, but don't forget to add other terms like "Let's see the vet," or "Time to get groomed."

ᐳJILL HALSTEAD, BA, CTC, Follow the Leader Dog Training Services, Richmond, VT

COPROPHAGIA

When your dog exhibits coprophagia, try adding crushed, fresh pineapple or grated zucchini to his diet. This will activate the enzymes in his gut and may reduce the desire to seek out and consume feces.

ᐳDANA COOPER, CPDT-KA, Woofers Canine Companion Training, Round Rock, TX

C Coprophagia (poop eating) is a hideous, disgusting, but completely normal doggy habit. I have found that scattering half a dog's normal ration of dry dog food in the yard will occupy the coprophage's nose and taste buds better than grass and poop. My advice is to stop stalling, buy a few good pooper-scoopers, and accompany your dog each and every time he goes out so that you can clean up after him immediately. Get into the habit. This works to stop coprophagia, and it benefits the relationship between you and your dog by ensuring that you're an integral part of his life and activities. While you're scooping, your dog will be sniffing out and eating kibble.

≈SUE STERNBERG, Animals for Adoption and Great Dog Productions, Accord, NY, and Moab, UT

Carry a pocketful of extra treats, and when you see your dog sniffing poop in that telltale way (like he's about to scarf it up), ask him to lie down and run over to him and reward him with a treat. Then scoop that poop! You'll be teaching your dog to help you locate the feces, like a bomb-detector dog who sniffs out and then passively indicates the location of a bomb.

≈SUE STERNBERG, Animals for Adoption and Great Dog Productions, Accord, NY, and Moab, UT

COUNTER SURFING

Prevention is the first step when dealing with counter surfing. This includes not leaving food on the counters or table unsupervised. When you are not in the kitchen, keep the counters and tables cleared so that your dog can't find any "rewards" on them, or prevent access to the kitchen. Prevention does not solve the problem long term, but it certainly helps interrupt the behavior from being practiced any longer so that it doesn't become a more ingrained habit.

≈ANN ALLUMS, CPDT-KA, Best Friends Animal Society, Kanab, UT

The best way I have found to extinguish counter surfing is to reward the dog for staying on the floor. I recommend spreading kibble under the toe kick of the floor every meal for two to three weeks. The dog must be out of sight when you do this, but soon he will start to look for food on the floor more often than on the counter. It is helpful to remove everything off the counter during this process. Once the dog learns to consistently look on the floor, start spreading less kibble on the floor every meal. Then begin doing it every other meal, then every other day, and so on. The dog will think the kitchen floor is giving him food and will continue to look on the floor instead of on the counter.

KARI BASTYR, MS, CDBC, Wag & Train, Denver, CO

Does your dog steal from the counter when you're not looking? Make a "monster." Get a piece of cardboard about the length of the counter. Rub a scent on the edge that is uncommon in your home (like coconut or almond). Place the cardboard on the edge of the counter so that it hangs over the edge about 1 inch (2.5 cm). Put several clean, empty cans on the cardboard. When your dog puts his paws on the cardboard, it will tip and the cans will fall, making a scary sound. Repeat this several times. Your dog will associate the scent on the cardboard with the monster. Now you can put the scent on the edge of the counter and your dog will stay away. Make sure that you are home when you set this up—you don't want your dog to chew on cans. When you hear the monster crash, you can immediately come back to pick it up.

DAINA BECKMAN, Happy Tails Dog Behavior & Training, Hornell, NY

Place double-stick tape on the edge of the counter. When your dog puts his paws up on the counter, they'll stick to it, which most dogs don't like.

CAROLYN KERNER, Dog Gone Right, Amite, LA

Counter surfing could be the result of boredom or lack of exercise. Making sure your dog is engaged throughout the day is a good way to help prevent this behavior.

MYCHELLE BLAKE, MSW, CDBC, Las Vegas, NV

Take a stale piece of bread or bun and cover it with hot sauce, then place it on the counter and leave. Let your dog get the bread without paying him any attention. Repeat. Generally, most dogs will stop eating the bread after about three pieces. Letting him learn on his own that he doesn't like what is available is the best way to teach this lesson.

CAROLYN KERNER, Dog Gone Right, Amite, LA

CRATES

Teach your puppy that crate time is nap time by draping a towel over the top of the enclosure. Watch to be sure that he doesn't chew the towel!

BECKY SCHULTZ, BA, CPDT-KA, Becky Schultz Dog Training and Behavior, Golden Valley, MN

A crate is an indispensable tool for new puppy owners. From day one, a crate helps in the potty training process, can be useful when traveling, prevents destructive behavior when the puppy cannot be supervised, and becomes a safe haven for him to use throughout his life.

ANN ALLUMS, CPDT-KA, Best Friends Animal Society, Kanab, UT

There are fabric crates, wire crates, plastic crates, and even "designer" wicker crates. Fabric crates are lightweight and collapsible, ideal for travel but not so great for a puppy or dog who'll try to chew his way out. Plastic or wire crates are a better choice when you're introducing your dog or puppy to the enclosure. To make a wire

crate more den-like, you can cover the sides and back with a sheet. Crate pads or a folded blanket or towel make the crate more comfy for your dog—but padding isn't recommended for pups or dogs who are likely to chew.

MARY LEATHERBERRY, CPDT-KA, Good Dog! Santa Fe, Santa Fe, NM

Owners can purchase a crate large enough for the anticipated full size of the puppy and barricade the excess space inside the crate where he might be tempted to potty.

ANN ALLUMS, CPDT-KA, Best Friends Animal Society, Kanab, UT

Many people feel bad about restraining their pets in crates. If you fit this description, once your dog is housetrained, buy the biggest crate your home can accommodate and you can afford. If you get a wire crate, give the crate a "den" feel for the dog by covering three sides with an old sheet attached with clothespins.

ELAINE COUPÉ, For Pet's Sake & Memphis Agility, Oakland, TN

When you bring your new puppy home, set up his crate in your bedroom. He is lonely and may be scared, and the bedroom will start reminding him that you are his family now. You'll also get eight free hours of bonding time just by having him sleep in your room! My husband just removed his bedside table and set up the crate in its place, covered the back half with a small blanket, placed a piece of wood on top, and voilà!—a bedside table/crate. Our new dogs settle in quite nicely!

PAULA KELMAN, CPDT-KA, Eagle Ridge Kennels, Buffalo, NY

Teach your puppy that crate time is nap time by draping a towel over the top of the enclosure. Watch to be sure that he doesn't chew the towel!

&BECKY SCHULTZ, BA, CPDT-KA,
Becky Schultz Dog Training and
Behavior, Golden Valley, MN

Teach your dog to be comfortable in a crate even if you don't think it will ever be needed. You never know when he will need to be crated at the groomer, the vet, or for a trip. It will be much less stressful for him to be confined if he is already accustomed to the idea.

&CYNTHIA FORD, Yuma, AZ

Select a crate that's large enough for your dog to stand up, turn around, and lie down in comfortably.

&MARY LEATHERBERRY, CPDT-KA,
Good Dog! Santa Fe, Santa Fe, NM

For a dog to truly feel at home in a crate, he needs to eat in it and sleep in it. I like to put the crate right beside my bed at first so that the dog or puppy doesn't feel too alone. When it was time for my crate-hating Doberman to learn to sleep in a crate, I gave her the choice between the cold, cold floor or a super-comfy, well-bedded dog crate. She paced and whined but eventually chose the crate. After a couple of nights, I started shutting the door, leaving her with a good chew toy of course.

&TRISH MCMILLAN, MSc, CPDT-KA, ASPCA
Animal Behavior Center, Urbana, IL

Some dogs will eliminate in the crate if it is too large. A rule of thumb is that the crate should be big enough for the dog to stand and turn around but not much larger. You can partition a large crate to make it smaller and move the partition as your dog grows. If he has eliminated in his crate, you will need to remove and thoroughly clean any padding; it's often useful to do away with all padding until your dog is keeping the crate clean. You may also want to invest in a new crate of a different type to give him a new, clean den.

&JIM BARRY, CDBC, CPDT-KA, Reston Dog
Training, Reston, VA

Clients often tell me they don't want to use a crate to give their dog a time-out because they don't want the dog to associate "bad" things with it. I tell them that when I was a child I was sent to my room for bad behavior, and I still slept in my room, played in my room, and certainly was never afraid of my room.

NICOLE JOHNSTON, CPDT-KA, Dogspaw LTD, Edmonton, Alberta, Canada

CRATE TRAINING

A proper crate training program includes: setting realistic expectations for your dog to control his bladder and bowels, based on his age and breed or breed mix; following a proper housetraining program, which includes teaching your dog to eliminate outside the house; and giving him the right amount of exercise outside the crate for his age and breed or breed mix.

TEOTI ANDERSON, CPDT-KA, Pawsitive Results, LLC, Lexington, SC

Crates are a magnificent training and living aid when used safely and responsibly. When crate training, use a collar with your name and phone number embroidered directly on the collar with no tags. Another option is to use a breakaway collar with the tags. Tags can get caught in the spaces between the wires and choke your dog.

LAURA DORFMAN, CPDT-KA, kona's touch, inc., Glencoe, IL

If you are following a proper crate training program, your dog should be able to stay in his crate, holding his bladder and bowels, for hours that equal his months in age plus one. For example, a three-month-old puppy can be in his crate for up to four hours. A four-month-old puppy should be able to stay in his crate for up to five hours. I do not recommend leaving a dog, even an adult dog, in a crate continuously for longer than the length of an average workday.

TEOTI ANDERSON, CPDT-KA, Pawsitive Results, LLC, Lexington, SC

Crates can be a useful adjunct to housetraining and can provide (if trained properly) a safe, quiet area to which a dog can retreat. However, the use of crates as a means to prevent potential destructiveness or housetraining after six months of age is a severe disservice to your dog. No dog is intended to spend most of his hours in a crate. Crating your dog while at work for eight to ten hours results in an underexercised, mentally and physically understimulated dog. Long-term crated dogs often exhibit hyperactivity when finally let out, which can include destructiveness, mouthing, and jumping as a means of attempting to get much-needed stimulation and attention. All dogs need to run, search, play, and have a challenging and stimulating environment–all of which can be created within your home to keep them engaged while you are away, rather than placing them in crates.

CHRISTINA SHUSTERICH, BA, CBC, NY Clever K9, Inc., Queens, NY

After your puppy goes in his crate, give him a food-stuffed chew toy.

DENISE DAWSON, CPDT-KA, All Breed Rescue and Training, Colorado Springs, CO

For easy crate training, throw cookies in the crate, one at a time. After your dog runs out, throw another treat in or pop it in through the back of the crate. At some point he'll start lingering in the crate. Ask for a *sit* or a *down*. Once your dog is "lingering" in his crate, start closing the door, then giving him a second cookie through the closed door before letting him out. Increase time between cookies. Feed whole meals one kibble at a time in this manner, or just place his food dish inside the crate.

TRISH MCMILLAN, MSc, CPDT-KA, ASPCA Animal Behavior Center, Urbana, IL

The best time to crate train your puppy is at night. This is because he is already sleeping, and if you keep the crate right by your bed, he will feel more comfortable. Dogs are social creatures who want to be around us–even when they are sleeping.

STEPHANIE LARSON, Lexington, NE

If your dog refuses to get into his crate, teach him to enter on cue. Set up practice time when he is hungry, and toss a tasty treat into the crate to get started. Close the crate door after your dog has entered, and give him another treat. Then immediately let him out and repeat this process until he is enthusiastically entering the crate. Next give this behavior a cue, such as the word "kennel." Say the word "kennel" before you toss the treat into the crate, and practice several times. Don't forget to give your dog a second treat after you have closed the crate door. When you have practiced several times, stop tossing a treat into the crate; instead, just say "kennel," make the hand motion of tossing a treat (but do not toss one), and wait for your dog to enter. After he enters, close the crate door and give him several treats in a row. Voilà! Your dog is learning to enter the crate on your verbal cue and hand signal. You can refine your hand signal over time to a pointing motion to the crate if you wish.

VERONICA SANCHEZ, M.Ed., CABC, CPDT-KA, Cooperative Paws LLC, Vienna, VA

One of my client's dogs hated his crate. The only thing that worked was using hot dogs in a stuffable toy and placing it inside the enclosure. When doing this with your dog, always place the food-stuffed toy in the crate first, and do *not* shut the door of the crate every time. Randomly shutting the door works best. After a couple days, show your dog the stuffable toy and walk him to the crate. At this point, the dog will usually hop in. If he doesn't, toss in the toy and he will follow.

ᥰCRYSTAL FRANKLIN, CPDT-KA,
Bethesda, MD

To teach your dog to love his crate, make sure that there are wonderful things that happen nowhere else on the planet but the crate! Any new toy should be given to him inside the enclosure. When he is calm and/ or sleeping in the crate, drop special treats into it. Toys stuffed with wonderful mixtures of treats should be given in the crate. Rewards should be so good that they really make an impression, and the fact that these extra-special things *only* happen in the crate will make a strong positive association with the crate itself.

ᥰANN WITHUN, Dog Scouts of America
Troop Leader, Fieldwood Dog Training Center,
Carlisle, PA

When your dog isn't looking, hide cookies, food-stuffed chews, or special toys in the

> **Some hotels allow dogs to stay as long as they are crate trained.**

crate so that he gets used to walking in on his own and being pleasantly surprised. Put a light piece of rope through the small hole in the stuffable chew and tie a knot before stuffing it with food, then tie the toy in the crate so that the dog can't eat the contents elsewhere.

ᥰTRISH MCMILLAN, MSc, CPDT-KA, ASPCA
Animal Behavior Center, Urbana, IL

Teach your puppy to be alone by having him sleep in his crate at night and during the day for naps. He should not think that going in the crate makes you go away.

ᥰBECKY SCHULTZ,
BA, CPDT-KA,
Becky Schultz Dog
Training and
Behavior, Golden
Valley, MN

Get a special treat like a food-stuffed toy—something your dog really likes—and shut the treat in the crate with the dog outside. Watch him scratch and whine and try to get into the crate for a few minutes. It's amazing to watch a dog who might have once not liked his crate now try to figure out how to get *in*!

ᥰTRISH MCMILLAN, MSc, CPDT-KA, ASPCA
Animal Behavior Center, Urbana, IL

To get your dog used to his crate, practice having him go into his confinement area for small, tasty food treats. Once he is comfortable going in on his own, practice having him wait a few seconds inside before getting a treat, then practice closing the door. Put the crate next to the sofa, rent a DVD, and keep your dog confined next to you while he works on a stuffed toy or other chew. Also, feed meals in the crate.

ᶜ᷈VYOLET MICHAELS, CTC, PDT, CPDT-KA, Urban Dawgs, Red Bank, NJ

Continue your crate training throughout your dog's lifetime. He will be more welcome traveling with you if he uses a crate, and it can be a familiar refuge to him while traveling. Being comfortable with confinement can help during stressful events such as grooming or hospitalization. Keep up the habit by having your dog spend short times in the crate most days. Feed him in his crate, and give gooey treats in there as well.

ᶜ᷈BECKY SCHULTZ, BA, CPDT-KA, Becky Schultz Dog Training and Behavior, Golden Valley, MN

CUES

A dog only has the mind of a two- to five-year-old child. They can understand approximately 165 words, and they don't understand sentences. So keep your cues short and try to use only one word for a cue.

ᶜ᷈ROBERT JORDAN, CPDT-KA, Pavlov's Dog Pet Dog Training, Mechanicsville, VA

If your dog is ignoring the cue, try any of the following: Move to a quieter, less distracting environment; give him some help, like a toy or food treat to refocus him; and practice with him more often. (Often a dog who "ignores" a cue really doesn't know the behavior as well as you think he does.)

ᶜ᷈LAURIE LUCK, CPDT-KA, KPACTP, Smart Dog University, LLC, Mount Airy, MD

Be consistent with cues. Make sure that you and your family are all on the same track when it comes to training your dog. If you say "Off!" when your dog jumps on you but your spouse says "Get down!" your dog will find it very hard to understand what you want. This is why a cue should be reserved for one action only. For example, if you decide to use "Get down!" for your dog to stop jumping on you, then don't use "down" for lying down. "Down" can't mean two separate things—it's too confusing for your dog. If everyone uses the same words for the same actions, your dog will find it much easier to learn.

ᶜ᷈TEOTI ANDERSON, CPDT-KA, Pawsitive Results, LLC, Lexington, SC

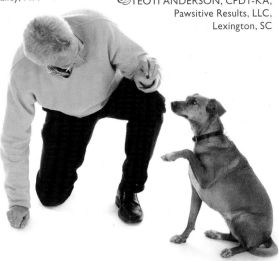

C

When training a dog who lives with multiple family members, make sure to write down and post what commands are used for what (e.g., "down" means lie down, not get down off the couch, or "here" for a recall, not "come" for a recall). If it is posted in a common place, such as by the front door or on the refrigerator, then all the family members will be on the same page and the dog will not be confused.

ॐSANDRA ENGLAND, DogBoys Dog Ranch, Pflugerville, TX

Make it easy for your dog and give each cue for a behavior a different sound. For example, if you say "Stay," choose a word other than "Lay" for your dog to get him into a prone position (use "Down" instead).

ॐCARYL WOLFF, CPDT-KA, CDBC, Doggie Manners, Los Angeles, CA

Let your dog process the information you are giving him—there is no need to repeat the cue over and over. Say the cue once and count silently in your head up to ten or more, depending on your dog. (This also helps you relax and takes some tension off the dog.) If he doesn't respond, gently say "Try again." Remember, dogs have great hearing, and they probably heard you the first time!

ॐANGIE KOBER, BS, Canine Solutions, Neenah, WI

Remember, dogs don't speak English! They are used to ignoring 98 percent of the talking we do. So when teaching a new cue word, eliminate all extraneous chatter so that the dog can focus on the new sound.

ॐJULIE HUMISTON, CPDT-KA, Puppy Love Dog Training, Minneapolis, MN

Say your dog's name before giving a cue, or he may not know you are talking to him. We talk all the time, and very little of what we have to say applies to our dogs, so they often tune our words out unless addressed.

ॐCYNTHIA EDGERLY, Bingo! Dog Training, Watsonville, CA

When putting a natural behavior on cue, say the word *as* your dog is doing the behavior. For example, when potty training him, take him outside and wait for him to begin to urinate. The instant he starts, say "Go potty" and praise him. If you say "Go potty" when he's chasing butterflies, then "Go potty" means to chase butterflies!

ॐCARYL WOLFF, CPDT-KA, CDBC, Doggie Manners, Los Angeles, CA

It's easy to assign words or cues to things your dog normally does. I started by saying "Outside" whenever I let my dogs out of the house. Soon, with repetition, your dog will understand that the word "outside" means to go out the door. You can also

then you can label the behavior with the word that describes it. For example, while your puppy is running toward you of his own free will, say "Poochie, come!" After he hears the word "come" paired with the action "running toward human" enough times, you will be able to use the cue to produce that behavior.

JULIE HUMISTON, CPDT-KA, Puppy Love Dog Training, Minneapolis, MN

Don't use a cue if you know your dog won't respond correctly. Every time you cue your dog to do something and he fails to execute it correctly, it decreases the chance he will be successful the next time. Every time you cue your dog to do something and he executes it correctly, it increases the chance he will be successful the next time.

CYNTHIA EDGERLY, Bingo! Dog Training, Watsonville, CA

Test your dog's understanding of each cue. A dog who truly understands a cue will perform the right behavior, will not perform that behavior unless you give the cue, and doesn't offer that behavior when you give a different cue.

ANN DUPUIS, CPDT-KA, Your Dream Dog, Randolph, MA

When you give cues, make sure that you don't distract your dog with movement at the same time. If you move while you cue, he will naturally focus on your movement instead, and he won't hear the sound. (The technical term for this is "overshadowing.") To avoid overshadowing your signals with extraneous movement, *hold still when you give cues*. Also, don't lure or prompt with your hand at the same time.

CARMEN BUITRAGO, MS, CAAB, CPDT-KA, Cascade Pet Camp, Hood River, OR

do this when putting him in his bed or crate. Assign a word and consistently use it whenever you do that action with your dog, and soon he will respond accordingly when you say that word.

JAMIE LURTZ, Solutions! Pet Services, Anaheim, CA

It can be very helpful to name a behavior while it's happening. For example, instead of saying "Sit" and then luring your dog into position, lure him into position, and as his butt hits the ground, *then* say "Sit" and give the reinforcer. This way, you avoid that stretch of time when you are attempting to lure the dog to sit during which he has forgotten that you gave the command. And you avoid the tendency to repeat the cue word while you are attempting to lure him into position, which may cause him to think that you need to say "Sit" five times before his butt needs to hit the ground.

ELLEN MAHURIN, MA, Clever Critters, Knoxville, TN

Dogs learn by association. If you want to teach a new cue word for a behavior, the dog must perform the behavior first and

When first teaching a dog a command, use your body language to tell him what you want. In other words, use a visual cue at first–don't use words. Wait until the dog is 80 percent efficient (completes the command eight out of ten times) before beginning to use the word command with the visual cue.

STEPHANIE LARSON, AKC CGC Evaluator, Gentle Paws, Lexington, NE

While working with dolphins at a facility in Florida, my boss did an experiment with us and the dolphins. He had each of us perform our hand signal for "jump"–just a large checkmark across the body with hand open–or so I thought. The videos of our performance were shown to us one after another, and we realized that even with this basic movement, we were all doing it very differently. This was causing some hesitation in the animals and some confusion in the young ones just learning.

Realize when you are teaching cues to an animal that you need to keep yourself consistent and your clients consistent. Body posture, tone, and word order are very important. Pick a way to do it and stick to it, and your animal of choice will learn what you want from him at a much quicker pace.

PAIGE WILLIS, CPDT-KA, DeKalb, IL

Use fewer words when training–cue your dog once and wait. Give him time to process the information and problem solve. If it is clear that your dog won't execute correctly, cue again. If he still doesn't execute correctly, stop using the cue and find another way to communicate your expectations.

CYNTHIA EDGERLY, Bingo! Dog Training, Watsonville, CA

DAY CARE

When looking for a reputable kennel or day care facility, choose a facility that you feel comfortable with and that is open to answering questions and getting to know your dog. Ask for a tour and make sure that you see where your dog will be spending most of his time. Inquire about the animal care background of the staff, the staff to dog ratio, new dog introduction procedures, cleaning protocols, and the facility's medical requirements (which should include rabies, distemper, and bordetella vaccines, as well as flea and worm preventives). Check that there is a procedure in place in the unfortunate event that your dog becomes sick or is injured during his stay. If you are boarding him for an extended period, the staff should allow you to bring your dog for a visit prior to your appointment to help with the acclimation process. Finally, make sure that the facility is licensed according to state requirements.

    JILL LYDIC, Asheville, NC

When selecting a dog day care, I utilize a tool that I always have on me: my nose. A simple sniff of the air will tell you quite a bit. A good day care has staff members on hand who are always watching for waste in the play area and clean it immediately with pet-friendly sanitizer. Even if there is an indoor potty area, that area should be cleaned and filled with fresh litter more than once a day. If the smell of animals and waste smacks you in the face when you walk into a day care facility, hygiene management may be lacking.

    LISA COLÓN TUDOR, CPDT-KA, KissAble Canine, LLC, Arlington, VA

DEAF DOGS

Training deaf dogs is really not much different from training hearing dogs. Use a penlight for a clicker. It works great, and they pick up on it quickly. Do not use a laser light because it can damage the eyes.

    JACKIE LOESER, CPDT-KA, Riverbend Agility Dogs, Stevensville, MT

To train a deaf dog to look at a human's face or hold eye contact, put some hot dog pieces in your cheek and wait for the dog to look at you. When the dog looks, spit a treat toward him. Then use a hand signal/ give the treat. At first, spit out the treat for any eye contact or head turn toward you. Raise the bar (requirement) for gazing directly at the face.

    LYNN RACHKISS, Behavior & Training Manager, Humane Society of South Mississippi, Gulfport, MS

"Dogs have four types of teeth: incisors, canines, premolars, and molars."

DENTAL CARE

Brush your dog's teeth at least once a week, but an everyday routine is the best option.

    NATALIA ROZAS DE O'LAUGHLIN, CDPT, Houston Pet Help, Houston, TX

Be sure to use a toothpaste flavor that your dog loves. Also, there are long-handled toothbrushes and small, on-the-finger brushes. You may need to experiment to see which works best for the two of you.

    PATRICIA BENTZ, CPDT-KA, CDBC, K-9 Training & Behavioral Therapy, Philadelphia, PA

Visit your vet regularly for a full teeth cleaning.

    NATALIA ROZAS DE O'LAUGHLIN, CDPT, Houston Pet Help, Houston, TX

DETECTION DOGS

Dogs who make good detection dogs don't always make the easiest pets to handle. They'll push the toy in your lap constantly, consider any guest "new meat," put the ball on your chair just as you sit on it, and sleep with the ball in their mouths and wake up looking for it. They want to play, play, play, play, play, and when they aren't playing, they are thinking about playing. Giving potential detection dogs an opportunity to channel their natural inclinations into valuable work helps both man and beast. Many languish in shelters because these qualities are not "pet-like." You cannot turn an apple into an orange, but if your dog just read that and thought to himself, "Oranges are round...somewhat ball-like...wheee!" then detection may be an incredibly rewarding life for him.

ELAINE ALLISON, CPDT-KA,
Shelter Director, Humane Society
of Wickenburg, Wickenburg, AZ

DIGGING

Dogs are going to dig, but to stop your dog from digging up your entire yard, you must give up a piece of real estate and train him to only dig in that area. To do this, pick the area that is marked as "okay to dig," and bury his favorite treat approximately 1.5 feet (0.5 m) down. Cover this up with some dirt and then put some more treats in the area. Repeat this until you have treats barely covered with dirt and then let your dog have fun. He will "dig where the gold is!"

STEPHANIE LARSON, AKC CGC Evaluator,
Gentle Paws, Lexington, NE

If your dog is digging holes in your yard, try this trick. Bury his feces in a hole where he likes to dig, and fill the hole with topsoil. Dogs do not like to play where they defecate, so he may decide to leave the area once he discovers the "surprise" left for him.

DANA COOPER, CPDT-KA, Woofers
Canine Companion Training, Round Rock, TX

Blow up small balloons and bury them in the holes your dog has dug. When he digs in the hole, he will pop the balloon.

CAROLYN KERNER, Dog Gone Right,
Amite, LA

DISTRACTIONS

Distracted, anyone? Set your dog up for success by knowing what you're up against. Dogs find certain things distracting, so you should know what those are and be prepared in advance to compete with them. Some common distractions: other dogs, strangers, food, sounds, smells, squirrels, birds, balls, children, garbage, skateboards, joggers, friends, flying discs...

JACQUELYN ENGLAND, A Dog's
Life, Sunnyvale, CA

Teaching your dog a familiar behavior in a new environment is like teaching him from scratch. Be sure to use high-value treats in new and distracting environments to help set your dog up for success.

&BONNIE KRUPA, Happy, Clean and Smart, Muncie, IN

Dogs are constantly learning what behaviors work to get them what they want, so be prepared to train wherever you go! Gradually introducing your dog to new distractions will help him learn to listen to you in all situations. Start your training at home, and only take it on the road when he is responding well. Begin with places where you can work at a distance from distractions, and gradually move closer. For example, practice in the parking lot of a pet store, a block away from a fenced schoolyard at recess, or across the street from a Little League game. Be sure to reward your dog with treats, praise, and play for focusing on you, and you'll be working closer to the distractions in no time at all!

&LAUREL SCARIONI, CPDT-KA, Pawsitive Results Critter Academy, Santa Rosa, CA

Have you ever noticed your dog give a big yawn? If you are waiting to cross the street and there is a distraction on the other side of the road but your dog gives a big yawn instead of barking or lunging, then praise him for that yawn! He just exhibited an amazing amount of self-control—and praise is one way to say thanks.

&JANE NEVE, Trainer, Canine Conduct Training Solutions, Black Creek, British Columbia, Canada

34 **DOG PARKS**

Overuse of off-lead dog parks can make it more difficult for you to control your dog on a short lead when he encounters a dog on your walks. If you are seeing this occur, talk to a trainer who uses scientific, positive, and dog-friendly training methods.

&JAMIE DAMATO, CPDT-KA, Animalsense Canine Training and Behavior, Inc., Chicago, IL

If a dog park seems overcrowded, then it probably is! Overcrowding stresses the animals and may ultimately lead to altercations. You and your dog will both be happier if you come back after the crowd has thinned out. The bigger the park, the better—always.

&JAMIE DAMATO, CPDT-KA, Animalsense Canine Training and Behavior, Inc., Chicago, IL

Dog park etiquette:

- Make sure that your dog is healthy and current on all vaccinations and has any licenses required.
- Don't bring more dogs than you can handle.
- Don't allow your dog to engage in inappropriate behaviors, such as bullying/aggressive play, jumping on other people, crowding the entrance gate, excessive barking, etc. If you are unable to control these behaviors, you and your dog should leave.
- Clean up after your dog.
- Do not bring a female dog in heat. If you have an intact male, be sure that he is social and nonaggressive before allowing him to socialize at the park.

✎JILL LYDIC, Asheville, NC

Always use your best judgment and instincts when it comes to other dogs. If you or your dog does not feel comfortable with another dog in the park, leave. Do not allow another owner to talk you into believing her dog is not a threat.

✎JAMIE DAMATO, CPDT-KA, Animalsense Canine Training and Behavior, Inc., Chicago, IL

Consider infrequent use of dog parks, such as one to two visits per week, lasting no more than 30 minutes in length. Dogs, just like kids, can behave inappropriately after extended playtime. Remember, one negative experience can create future behavioral

concerns for your pet. Using a dog park too frequently can create a dog who requires too much stimuli in order to "be tired"–you don't want to build that kind of tolerance in your dog. Stressful events that may occur in dog parks can create a strong chemical change in your dog's brain. Those chemical changes can and do interfere with his ability to process and cope with novel stimuli outside of the park environment.

✎JAMIE DAMATO, CPDT-KA, Animalsense Canine Training and Behavior, Inc., Chicago, IL

If your dog does not enjoy the style of play that occurs at dog parks, take him hiking or on long walks where he will run into other dogs in a friendly, nonconfrontational way. Not all dogs want to play with other dogs in a chaotic environment. Shy or fearful dogs may look like they are coping okay, but in fact may just be shutting down to stay out of trouble.

✎JAMIE DAMATO, CPDT-KA, Animalsense Canine Training and Behavior, Inc., Chicago, IL

DOG WALKERS

You cannot underestimate the importance of your dog walker's handling skills and knowledge of your dog. Whether your dog is with her 30 minutes a day or 3 hours a day, make no mistake—he is learning from your dog walker. I am often amazed at how people underestimate that influence, particularly in a young dog.

MARLA ABRAMS, Doggielove,
New York, NY

In the dog walking part of my business, we find that it is helpful to stand on the dog's leash if we need to pick up feces and don't want him to pull on the leash while doing this simple task.

DONNA HALL, Hot Diggity Dogs Services,
Vancouver, BC, Canada

DOMINANCE 36

Many dog owners have a misconception of what "dominance" means as it relates to their dogs. "Dominance" among canines is defined as exclusive breeding rights and priority access/control of limited primary resources. During the 1940s, studies were conducted on captive wolf populations (i.e., the animals were not in their natural environment). The captivity caused a significant amount of aggression, fighting, and other agonistic displays. The information derived from the studies of captive packs was then transferred to dog/human relationships and is primarily where the notion of "never allow your dog to be above you" came from.

Many studies have been done on free-ranging wolf populations since the earlier ones, much of which conflict with the

conclusions drawn from the captive studies. Dogs recognize that human beings are not conspecifics (of the same species). There is no scientifically valid research to support the notion that a pet dog would ever want to, or try to, dominate a human being. Most of what we see behaviorally in domestic dog/human interaction is learned, not instinctive. Pet dogs can and do learn to use behaviors to control environmental consequences. In other words, when they learn that a particular behavior "works" in gaining a desired consequence, they will continue to use it. For example, if a dog growls because someone is trying to move him off the couch or bed, it's because it's worked in the past in controlling the environmental consequence (he gets left alone where he's comfortable!), not because he's trying to be "dominant." It is our responsibility to provide structure and to teach our pet dogs how to behave to our expectations, using humane and positive training techniques. If responding to requests for behavior from you brings your dog good stuff in life, that's what he will do, simply because of the consequence it brings him.

LISA PATRONA, Dip. DTBC, CPDT-KA,
PDT, CBC, Trainers Academy, LLC,
President, Troy, MI

DOOR DASHING

A dog rushing through an open doorway can be not just annoying but dangerous. To prevent this, I teach my dogs to "back up" and "sit" as I open the door. I then open and close the door to desensitize them to the open door. When I then want to go out, I say "Okay" and they can then go through the door. I do this when entering the house also, which results in a dog who backs up and sits until invited to go through the doorway either out or in. It takes a lot of consistency and repetitions, but your pet will be safer and more polite.

℘ROSIE STEEL, Rosie Steel Dog Training, Mahaska, KS

Is your dog bursting to sneak out the door every time you exit the house? This is a potentially dangerous behavior should he sneak out the door. Here is an easy solution. Grab a handful of kibble and say "Back" right before you toss the kibble behind the dog. Then exit as he eagerly eats the treats. Practice and your dog will soon learn that the word "back" means to back up away from the doorway.

℘VERONICA SANCHEZ, M.Ed., CABC, CPDT-KA, Cooperative Paws LLC, Vienna, VA

Teach your dog to sit at the door and wait for your cue to go through. It will help prevent him from knocking you aside to get out, and it could also prevent other problems. For example, what if your dog bolts out into the yard and you then notice that your neighbor's cat has gotten in your fence? If your dog waits at the door, you can check the yard for any problems before you let him go outside.

First, your dog must know the *sit*. He must also know a release word, like "okay." The release word lets him know that he no longer has to hold a position. Take your dog to the door. Ask him to sit a couple feet (m) away from the door. Slowly start to open the door. If he breaks position, quickly shut the door, but don't close the door on your dog! Wait a few seconds. If he doesn't sit again, ask him to sit. Slowly start opening the door. If he breaks position, shut it again. Only continue to open the door if he is sitting. Once the door is open, wait a second, then use your *release* cue and encourage him to go through the door. Gradually work up to longer times when the door is open while your dog is still sitting. Shorter training sessions work best.

℘TEOTI ANDERSON, CPDT-KA, Pawsitive Results, LLC, Lexington, SC

DOWN 37

When asking your dog for a *down*, make sure that the surface is comfortable for him. Some floors are too cold, especially for breeds that have very short hair. An option is to put your dog on an elevated place, like a bed or couch. He may find the surface more comfortable, and if his head is on the edge, you could lure even below the level of that edge, which will most likely make him go into a *down*. Remember to do all the movements slowly, or your dog might jump off the furniture to keep track of the treat.

NATALIA ROZAS DE O'LAUGHLIN,
CPDT-KA, Houston Pet Help, Houston, TX

When you are luring a *down*, do it slowly! With a yummy treat in your fingers, let your dog sniff at it and get excited. Move the treat from one side to another, letting him follow your hand with his nose. This is called luring. If your dog's nose is not completely glued to your fingers *all* the time, it's because you are moving too fast. Slow down.

NATALIA ROZAS DE O'LAUGHLIN,
CPDT-KA, Houston Pet Help, Houston, TX

Dogs don't always want to perform the *down* command as readily as the *sit*. If this is the case, kneel on one knee. Extend your other leg, creating a bridge just high enough for the dog to crawl under. Now lure him under your leg with a treat. He'll have to get in the *down* position to reach the treat. When he does, click and treat.

DELTA SMITH, Dawgz Gone Good Inc.,
Leesburg, VA

If you are using the "bridge" method to teach your dog the *down* (luring him under your bent legs) and he is not comfortable going under your legs, do not force him. Start by asking him to walk under your legs while you are standing up, then while you are sitting on the floor but with a high bridge, which you gradually lower. Always have lots of treats and a fun attitude.

NATALIA ROZAS DE O'LAUGHLIN,
CPDT-KA, Houston Pet Help, Houston, TX

Teach *down* when your dog is really tired after a long walk.

SUSAN BARRETTA, Redondo Beach, CA

To teach *down* for the dog whose bottom pops up when you try to lure his head down between his front feet and for whom the luring under bent knee or chair fails, try teaching a bow. With your dog walking forward, lure his head down and back in a bow, then click and treat. Once you get a bow, say "Sit." The dog will do the body movement for *sit* (rear end hits the floor), at which point you click and treat—and you have a *down*. Repeat a few times, then say "Down" (switching the cue). You now have a dog who will do a *down*.

DEBBIE REVELL, RN, CDBC,
Pets Behave LLC, Niceville, FL

Teaching a *down* and your puppy bows instead? No problem! Mark and reward the bow, and teach her to do it when you ask "Who's the queen?"

    ✎BECKY SCHULTZ, BA, CPDT-KA, Becky Schultz Dog Training and Behavior, Golden Valley, MN

If your dog can go into a perfectly good *down* but breaks it the minute you take your hand away, try this: Use a slightly bigger treat—something the dog can lick or that takes longer to chew. Instead of giving it to him from your hand, put the treat on the floor right in front of his nose. He will most likely take a longer time finishing the treat while he is in a *down*, giving you the chance to stand up. After a few repetitions, your dog will likely stay in a *down* a little longer. Be patient—even differences of milliseconds are good improvements and deserve praise!

    ✎NATALIA ROZAS DE O'LAUGHLIN, CPDT-KA, Houston Pet Help, Houston, TX

DOWN-STAY 39

When teaching a dog the *down-stay*, I like to put my foot on the leash, close to the snap that attaches to the collar. It helps prevent him from getting up because he'll feel the pressure from the leash when he tries to rise and will go back down on his own.

    ✎LISA WHITE, FireStorm K9 Training, St. George, Barbados, West Indies

DROP IT 38

Your dog should understand that "Drop it" means that whatever he has in his mouth needs to be released immediately. This is easy to teach if you start out right. Set your dog up to succeed by using an item that he will pick up but that will also drop easily, like an old toy or chew. Let him take the item into his mouth, and then place a high-quality treat in front of his nose. When the dog drops the item for the treat, say "Drop it." Give a command like "Take it" when you allow him to hold it in his mouth. Practice only a few repetitions during each session.

    ✎SUSAN M. MILLER, CVT, CPDT-KA, CDBC, The Canine Counselor, Northampton, MA

If you are working on the *drop it* command with a resource-guarding dog, you must take necessary safety precautions. Ask your trainer for help.

ᑫ JULES NYE, CPDT-KA, Sit Stay & Play, Severn, MD

You can teach your puppy to drop what is in his mouth even before he has picked something up. Start by stashing a few yummy treats in various (puppy-proofed) places around the house in areas that your pup frequents. Then several times a day, say "Drop it" to your pup and quickly go over and hand him one of your stashed treats. Then let him go back to what he was doing—whether it was just hanging out, enjoying a chew toy, or playing with a housemate. He will quickly learn that when he hears you say "Drop it," he can expect that he will be getting a yummy treat. Pretty soon as your hand reaches toward him, he will open his mouth—even if his is holding something else.

ᑫ CERENA ZUTIS, CZ Dog Training, CA

To teach *drop it*, make a list of five to ten objects that the dog may pick up and not give back. Number ten should be the object the dog will drop most easily. Number one should be something very exciting, like a stolen object (sock, toilet paper, etc). Start with the number ten object. When the dog has it in his mouth say "Drop it" and wait. When the object is dropped, exchange it for a yummy treat. Once that object is being dropped with ease on command, move up the list. If the dog will not drop the next object, you went too fast. Avoid bribing the dog for

the object because dropping will become contingent upon seeing the treat first.

ᑫ CHERIE BEATTIE, MS, CPDT-KA, The Pet Pro, Clarksville, IN

Your dog must be taught to instantly drop whatever he is holding in his mouth. Play the "two ball game" with your dog, every day if possible, until he responds reliably to the *drop it* command. Use two identical balls. Throw the first ball. When your dog brings it to you, tease him with the other ball—show him how much fun this other ball is! While doing this, give the verbal cue "Out!" The instant he releases it, repeat the verbal cue and immediately throw the other ball. Do not use food rewards for this exercise—the reward is the other ball being thrown. Repeat for as long as the game holds your dog's interest.

ᑫ PHIL GUIDA, Director of Training, Canine Dimensions In-Home Dog Training, Marlton, NJ

Always remember that your dog is a good dog for giving up *anything* he has. If he drops his toy, you should have the same reaction as if he dropped the TV remote control he was just chewing. Be happy and reward your dog for giving things up.

ᑫ JULES NYE, CPDT-KA, Sit Stay & Play, Severn, MD

D

When your dog picks up a forbidden household item (e.g., shoe, child's toy) do not chase him around yelling at him. Instead, get close to him without making eye contact, and when you are near enough, show him a food treat he can't resist, like a piece of hot dog. Offer him the treat while giving the verbal cue "Out!" Use a happy, friendly tone—not scolding. When he releases the object, say "Out!" and give him the food treat. Then recover the forbidden item.

ᕬPHIL GUIDA, Director of Training, Canine Dimensions In-Home Dog Training, Marlton, NJ

EARTHDOG

I have a Border Terrier who is very keen on rats aboveground. However, he wouldn't go through the tunnel to work the rats in the dark. I built a little tunnel liner and covered the ends with a tarp to simulate the dark. I sent him through the tunnel each night to his dinner bowl at the other end. Using positive methods, my dog came to enjoy working earthdog tunnels.

ᕬJACKIE SHERIDAN-MOORE, CPDT-KA, Positively Obedient, MD

TOP TIDBIT

Earthdog is a sporting event that tests a dog's instincts and ability to work underground in search of quarry; this occurs in timed courses that are designed to simulate hunting conditions.

EATING TOO FAST

Scarfing down kibble is not a healthy way for a dog to eat. Here are some ideas to help your dog slow down at meal time: Mix in a few tablespoons of water with the kibble and freeze it so that he has to work the frozen bits loose to eat. Put the kibble in a food puzzle, such as a rubber treat ball. Spread the kibble out across the floor so that the dog has to pick up one piece at a time.

ᕬANN ALLUMS, CPDT-KA, Best Friends Animal Society, Kanab, UT

Because I have a hound mix, I've had to become creative in trying to slow him down when he eats too fast. The most effective technique is to use a large rubber toy embedded in the middle of the dish. As the dog eats the food, the chew toy loosens up and he has to maneuver around the object. I like this method because if he does bite down on the rubber toy, no harm is done to his mouth. This way, you avoid the additional cost of a special dish and get an extra toy out of the deal.

ᕬLISA COLÓN TUDOR, CPDT-KA, KissAble Canine, LLC, Arlington, VA

To slow down the dog who gobbles his food, use several small bowls and put a bit of food in each.

ᕬLYNETTE TATAY, Nashville, MI

EMERGENCY KIT

In case of emergency, create a "Grab & Go Bag" for your dog. It should include: grooming supplies, chew or throw toy, and a towel/blanket with your scent on it

- your basic pet first-aid kit, which should include anything rigid to use as a splint
- 14-day ration of food (pack canned food to decrease water intake or if you feed raw)
- can opener, a plastic lid to keep unused food fresh, and two bowls
- 2 gallons (7 l) of fresh water (will vary depending on the size of your dog)
- two sturdy 6-foot (2 m) leashes, along with a flat buckle collar or harness (legibly note your name and your pet's name)
- safe pain/diarrhea/antihistamine meds (consult your vet); note dosage for your dog
- current vaccination record and 30-day supply of ongoing medication; note dosage
- poop bags
- an information sheet, including photo

Store your "Grab & Go Bag" in your dog's crate. Rotate medication, food, and water every three months.

—JANE NEVE, Canine Conduct Training Solutions, Black Creek, BC, Canada

ESCAPING

The first level of intervention with a problem behavior like escaping the yard is management through prevention. If your dog escapes when left unsupervised, he cannot have unsupervised yard privileges.

—ANN ALLUMS, CPDT-KA, Best Friends Animal Society, Kanab, UT

Fence jumping is a very difficult behavior to change because getting on the other side is so rewarding to the jumper. And you don't want to chain up your dog to control fence jumping because he can get tangled in the chain, which has been known to cause strangulation and even amputation. Unfortunately, there is no magic cure for fence jumping—it requires environmental changes like supervision, securing the yard, and spaying or neutering so that the dog does not have the urge to leave. These methods are meant to prevent him from escaping but do not address eliminating the escaping behavior. You should take the time to evaluate why your dog is trying to escape. Increasing exercise and spending more time with him may make him feel more secure and eliminate the need to escape.

—CRYSTAL COLL, All Ways Pawsitive Pet Behavior and Training, Queen Creek, AZ

If your dog is escaping from your yard, you may need to fortify your fence. Often even a light-duty addition to a fence can provide enough of a visual barrier to be effective. Try adding an inward-facing ledge to the top of the fence, or perhaps try a rolling piece of PVC installed at the top of the fence that will prevent your dog from getting a foothold to clear the top.

&ANN ALLUMS, CPDT-KA, Best Friends Animal Society, Kanab, UT

To prevent your dog from escaping the yard, keep him interested in his surroundings. Leave egg cartons, paper towel centers, old tissue boxes, and even the stalks from vegetables like cabbage, broccoli, and celery in your yard. (Be careful of sweet corn husks because they can block the intestine.) Just like kids, for a dog, the wrapping or box from a chew toy is often more exciting to tear apart than the actual chew toy itself. Try putting a vegetable stalk inside a cardboard box—this makes it more exciting for the puppy. You can use rags and unwanted clothing to make rag toys and lengths of knotted material that have some pâté, cheese, or a smelly treat inside them so that the puppy has to work hard to "open" the rag toy and get the treat. Another way to keep a puppy or dog busy, and therefore happy about staying in the yard, is to make ice cubes out of the juices from meals, as well as from raw and cooked vegetables. Hide a few cubes in the yard before you leave your dog for any length of time. You can also purchase special toys that hang from a tree or a fence in the yard or kennel, and your dog can tug on them and pop treats out of them, but he won't be able to get them down. They stay interesting to a dog, helping him remain active and fit, as well as release pent-up energy.

&NINA BONDARENKO, BA, Specialist Canine Services, Croydon, Surrey, United Kingdom

Training can be used to help prevent escape behavior. Teach your dog that you reward him for staying in the yard. Start with short periods that will guarantee you catching him before he tries to escape. Enter the yard and praise him, along with awarding him a very tasty treat (roast beef, chicken, cheese, hot dog). Continue this exercise, varying the times between your appearances and gradually increasing them. Stagger them so that short ones still occur at random. The idea here is that if the rewards are of high enough value (and if other enrichment ideas are employed for the yard), your dog may be willing to forego the escape in anticipation of your return.

&ANN ALLUMS, CPDT-KA, Best Friends Animal Society, Kanab, UT

EXERCISE 42

Your dog needs daily aerobic exercise. A tired dog is a good dog; in other words, a sleeping dog can't be biting, jumping up, digging under the fence, or chewing walls. Leash walks around the neighborhood are usually not enough physical exercise; dogs need to run, explore, play with other dogs, or swim—basically, engage in any daily aerobic activity.

ᔕ ANN ALLUMS, CPDT-KA, Best Friends Animal Society, Kanab, UT

Having a large yard is not equal to having a well-exercised dog. You may see your dog dashing madly around your yard, but he is not exercising. He is doing the doggy equivalent of pacing, fidgeting, or other human forms of nervous activity. Provide your dog with fun things to occupy his time, such as a digging pit or special chew toys. Also, because dogs are social animals who need friends and companionship, a visit to the dog park daily or weekly will help him make doggy friends, as well as get in some exercise. Dogs romping around and playing together tire rapidly and will sleep happily while recovering from a hearty play session.

ᔕ CRYSTAL COLL, All Ways Pawsitive Pet Behavior and Training, Queen Creek, AZ

Most dogs are underexercised. As a trainer, I can tell you that you don't stand a chance against a dog who isn't exercised. So get out there and run around, play fetch, go hiking, and just generally have fun. Then train.

ᔕ DAYNA VILLA, IACP, Taking the Lead Dog Training, PA

The best advice for a dog who is misbehaving is to increase his exercise. The more exercise a dog receives, the less likely he is to dig in the trash and chew on valuable possessions.

ᔕ BONNIE KRUPA, CPDT-KA, Happy, Clean and Smart, Muncie, IN

Exercise is not only good for you, it's good for your dog—especially if you crate him during the day. The benefits of exercise include keeping your dog at an ideal weight, fewer behavior problems, spending quality time together, and living with a happy canine companion. So get active with him—take a walk, play fetch, play tug with a rope toy, or go to a dog park to play with other dogs. If you have access to a pond, you can even go for a swim. Or try working on commands like "doggy push-ups" (sit, down, sit…). Be creative—your dog will be glad for it!

ᔕ DARLENE KOZA, Scooter's School of Sit & Stay, Rochester, NY

E

Frustrated with your dog? Increasing his daily exercise may be the key to achieving results. The best training program in the world can fail if your dog is not adequately exercised each day. A hike in the woods, a game of fetch, or a romp with other friendly dogs in a fenced area can be just the kind of workout he needs. Leisurely strolls or time alone in a fenced backyard is often not stimulating enough to tire out your canine pal. If you find yourself short on time, call your vet and ask if there are any local dog walkers for hire in your area. Or perhaps dropping your dog off a few afternoons a week at a doggy day care is just the solution for you. Once he is properly exercised, you will begin to see your training efforts realized.

ℯ✑ADRIENNE CARSON, Harmony, NJ

Training and exercise are the best ways to keep a busy dog content and tired. Training tires a dog out mentally and exercise, physically. Playing games can be a physical energy releaser. For the mental component, work on basic obedience skills: *sit*, *down*, *come*, *stand*, and *stay*. If your dog doesn't know these behaviors, play around and see what you can come up with. If you like it, reward it! Tricks are also fantastic skills to teach and can help tire a dog out.

ℯ✑ELIZABETH LANGHAM, MS, CPDT-KA, Tree Frog Farm Dog Training and Agility, North Yarmouth, ME

FEAR

Use nonthreatening body language around shy dogs: Don't make direct eye contact, turn your side toward the dog and squat down rather than tower over him, remain silent or speak quietly, and approach by walking a curve rather than a straight line.

ℯ✑ANN ALLUMS, CPDT-KA, Best Friends Animal Society, Kanab, UT

The first thing I do with a scared dog I am going to have to handle is to bathe him. Something about the process of a slow, gentle bath changes the dog's attitude toward me every time.

ℯ✑KATHERINE ROLLINS, CPDT-KA, Kat's K9 Cadets, Greeneville, TN

A relationship built on trust and mutual respect is the most important training tool between a person and a dog. To build trust, fearful dogs need plenty of time and thousands of safe experiences. One way to build trust is by feeding the dog. A dog who takes food from the human hand learns that humans can give him good things and the hand is a safe thing, not something to be feared. If necessary, start getting him used to your presence by bringing him his food bowl and just waiting nearby while he eats. You should remove the food bowl when you leave, regardless of whether he ate or not, so that he learns that the food comes with the person. (If offered food, the dog will not starve.)

When he is readily eating in your presence, wait closer to the food bowl during subsequent feedings, with the goal of hand-feeding each bite to the dog.

    ANN ALLUMS, CPDT-KA, Best Friends Animal Society, Kanab, UT

In class, for the "scaredy dog" who is upset, backing up, and obviously frightened, have the rest of the class practice "let's go" in a pattern that takes them past (but not too close) to the handler and dog. As they pass by, each handler should toss a very small treat toward the dog. Watch the surprise on the dog's face as food drops in front of him–fun!

    CATHY BONES, CPDT-KA, Pacifica, CA

When approaching an aggressive or fearful dog, never look him in the eye and speak to him. This can anger or scare him more. If you must walk in the dog's direction, avert your eyes and do not talk to him.

    PAIGE WILLIS, CPDT-KA, DeKalb, IL

I sing to dogs during a counter-conditioning session if they are fearful/aggressive or whenever I tend to get stressed in a training session, to control my breathing and keep my stress physiology from getting away from me. This forces me to breathe! I don't sing well but can always remember the tune to the "Alphabet Song." I also often quietly sing to a dog during duration behavior training, both as a distraction and as a way to keep his focus on me without slinging a series of cues at him, like "look, watch, sit, stay, etc." It seems to keep these dogs engaged and triggers them to offer additional behaviors.

    MIRA LEIBSTEIN, CBC, CPDT-KA, Click-n-Train, Oceanside, NY

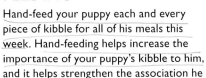

TOP TIDBIT

There are several national companies that offer pet insurance, which reimburses owners for such expenses as emergency care, prescriptions, and routine physicals.

FEEDING 43

Hand-feed your puppy each and every piece of kibble for all of his meals this week. Hand-feeding helps increase the importance of your puppy's kibble to him, and it helps strengthen the association he has toward you.

    JACQUELYN ENGLAND, Trainer, A Dog's Life, Sunnyvale, CA

If you want to avoid being hassled while preparing your dog's food, put a mat on the floor in the area you are working in but out of your way. Teach your dog to target the mat by rewarding any kind of body contact with it. When you have shaped the behavior so that he is touching the mat with two or more feet consistently, name it ("mat"). Teach your dog to sit-stay or down-stay on the mat by rewarding the right behavior often. Train duration of the *stay*, and pretty soon you won't be tripping or stepping over or around your dog when preparing meals!

    KIM WELLS, CPDT-KA, Kim Wells Companion Dog Training Services, Airdrie, Alberta, Canada

FEEDING AS TRAINING OPPORTUNITY

Forget the food bowl! Use your dog's daily ration of food for training instead of just giving it away for free. Imagine if we could just go get a bowlful of money as often as we wanted to—how many of us would go to work every day? On the days that you don't have enough training time, fill treat balls or other interactive toys with your dog's daily ration. You can even just throw his food out on the lawn for him to find as a treasure hunt. The point is to make your dog work for every bite, just like we work for every dollar.

        JACQUELYN ENGLAND, Trainer, A Dog's Life, Sunnyvale, CA

Your dog's mealtimes are terrific training opportunities. Ask for a *sit* before you put the dinner dish down. The reward for *sit* is dinner, and that's a great motivator. Get into the habit of asking for a behavior—*sit* or *down*—every time you feed your dog. It's a chance for him to practice good canine house manners, and it establishes a daily training routine for both of you.

When you're getting *sit* and *down* reliably, add *stay* to your mealtime routine. Initially, your goal is a short *sit-stay* or *down-stay* while you set the bowl on the floor. If your dog breaks the *stay* before you put the food down, say "Oops" and raise the dish back up. The reward for a successful *stay* is putting the dish down.

        MARY LEATHERBERRY, CPDT-KA, Good Dog! Santa Fe, Santa Fe, NM

Training at mealtime can be a great motivator. This can be done for training *stays* (put the dog on a *stay* while preparing his food bowl—if he breaks, put him back and start the "clock" over) and other exercises. I've used it for training *drop on recall*, *finishes* (no anticipation, and perform the finish as cued before getting the food dish), *recalls*, and *fronts* (straight, close front gets the bowl).

        NANCY TUCKER, Tamarac Tollers, Troy, NY

Your dog wants dinner? Wait for eye contact before putting the dish on the floor.

        JAMIE DAMATO, CPDT-KA, Animalsense Canine Training and Behavior, Inc., Chicago, IL

FETCH 44

Teaching your dog to fetch is a wonderful way to interact with him, and it also provides him with exercise. Use the ball exchange or the treat exchange method to encourage your dog to bring a tossed ball back to you. Wave another ball or a treat for your dog to see while backing up and encouraging him to come to you. When he gets to you, show him the other ball or treat to get him to drop the ball. Right

before he drops the ball, say "Drop it."
Then toss the ball again for him to retrieve.

ℰLUCINDA LUDWIG, Canine Connection
LLC, Dubuque, IA

FIELD TRIALS

Field trial and hunt test titles present a
broad spectrum of requirements, including
both trained skill and intrinsic talent.
A "birdy" hunting dog with some (even
minimal) trained skill might be successful
in a Working Certificate or Junior Hunting
venue. However, if handlers wish to
advance to higher levels of testing or
competition, greater levels of trained skill
are required. It is far easier to initially train
for more advanced levels than to change
expectations as the dog progresses from
title to title. For example, distance and
reliable control are easier to introduce
and establish early on than to add later.
Correctly introduced, reliable control need
not be inconsistent with enthusiasm and
drive. Research and careful consideration
of potential future goals *before* training
begins will promote success and save time
and frustration later.

ℰKRIS BUTLER, American Dog Obedience
Center, LLC, Norman, OK

FIREWORKS 45

Fourth of July can be very frightening
for dogs because of the fireworks. For
frightened animals, it is best to keep them
in a secure, sheltered environment (such
as a basement) that blocks out the noises
and sights as much as possible. Insulate
the environment by closing all windows,
drawing the curtains and drapes, and

TOP TIDBIT

A field trial is a
competitive event that
tests a dog's ability to
locate the quarry that
he was bred to hunt.

further muffling noises with a CD, radio,
or air conditioner. Put your dog in the
comfortable, sheltered environment before
he becomes apprehensive or frightened
(i.e., before the fireworks have started).
Of course, it is optimal if you can stay
with and keep him occupied with play or
obedience training. Be aware that panicked
dogs can bolt and become lost, so be
sure to lock all doors and be aware when
opening and closing doors or transporting
your animal in any way.

ℰCHRISTINA SHUSTERICH, BA, CBC, NY
Clever K9, Inc., Queens, NY

FLOORING 46

How can you keep a dog from scratching up a hardwood floor? Unfortunately, there is not a whole lot that you can do, especially if you have a big dog. You can keep his nails clipped short with weekly trimmings and filings, which will help keep contact with the floors minimal. Also, some of my clients have reported using industrial-strength finishes on their wood floors, and they say that really helps protect them. Of course, you can always throw down rugs or runners in high-traffic areas, or train him to stay out of the areas with hardwood.

ﾐ DEVENE GODAU, CPDT-KA, Trainers Academy, LLC, Royal Oak, MI

FOOD 47

Certain "people" foods are toxic to dogs. Never give your dog chocolate, onions, or grapes.

ﾐ DARLENE KOZA, Scooter's School of Sit & Stay, Rochester, NY

There are some healthy foods you can share with your dog, like carrots or some pieces of apple. If you are unsure which foods you can safely share with him, ask your veterinarian. There are also many websites that list foods and plants that will make your dog sick.

ﾐ DAINA BECKMAN, Dog Behavior Specialist/Dog Trainer, Happy Tails Dog Behavior & Training, Hornell, NY

Training is only one part of having a wonderful family pet. We owe it to our pets to feed them a diet that truly nourishes them and keeps them healthy. I use a holistic food, because in my experience, dogs with attention span and hyperactivity issues have dramatic changes in behavior when taken off low-quality commercial foods. If the old adage "We are what we eat" applies to humans, why wouldn't it also apply to our four-legged friends? It really is food for thought!

ﾐ JOAN B. GUERTIN, Common Sense Dog Training and Behavior Solutions, TX

If your dog refuses to eat his kibble, you can add some small slices of yellow cheese to the bowl to make it more enticing. You can also boil a spoonful of tomato juice with water for one minute and then pour it over the kibble. But the most powerful addition of all is canned tuna fish in water mixed in with the kibble.

ﾐ KATERINA HADZIYANNI, Humane Training, Athens, Greece

If you feed a dry dog food, always put a small, wet, mushy-type "treat" on top of the food. Something as simple as a spoonful of canned dog food or a small glob of peanut butter will work. Why? Because sooner or later in your dog's life, you will have to give him some yucky pill. If you have established this routine of a small treat with his food, the chances are high that he will scarf down his treat with the hidden pill without a second thought. And even if he never has to take a pill, he'll enjoy the extra treat and you'll enjoy giving it to him.

ꝰ PAM SHEEHAN, 4 Paws Training, LLC, Broken Arrow, OK

If your dog does not seem to be able to focus and pay attention during training, try switching dog food or introduce a raw diet.

ꝰ JOANN KOVACICH, Grateful Dog Pet Care, Inc. Penfield, NY

If you want to give your dog bones, avoid cooked bones, which can splinter. Instead, provide him with raw beef bones. Avoid anything that might splinter and puncture the gastrointestinal tract.

ꝰ LUCINDA LUDWIG, Canine Connection LLC, Dubuque, IA

FOOD GUARDING

Food guarding occurs because a dog has something valuable that he is afraid you are going to take away. The goal in working with a dog who food guards is to teach him he has no reason to guard his food from humans. To help your dog learn that he does not have to guard his food from you, start by hand-feeding him a few meals. This will teach him that having a human around during feeding is a good thing because the food comes directly from you.

ꝰ ANN ALLUMS, CPDT-KA, Best Friends Animal Society, Kanab, UT

Signs of food guarding include: tensing, lip curling, raised hackles, holding his nose in the bowl, freezing, or staring at you.

ꝰ ANN ALLUMS, CPDT-KA, Best Friends Animal Society, Kanab, UT

F

Food guarding can be a dangerous behavior that can lead to other resource guarding behaviors; it commonly escalates from growling to a bite. Keep children out of the room while your dog is eating if he growls when other dogs or people come near him during mealtimes. Owners (and more often children) are frequently bitten as a result of food guarding. If your dog shows any signs of aggression around food, there may be other factors that need to be addressed, so get a professional to help you with this problem behavior. Until you can get professional help, have him sit before you set his dish down, then give him his privacy while he is eating. You don't want the dog to practice this dangerous behavior.

DAINA BECKMAN, Happy Tails Dog
Behavior & Training, Hornell, NY

The most common mistake that I see dog owners make while raising their puppy or young dog is repeatedly taking the food away from him. This teaches him that people are not to be trusted near his food. If you want a food-friendly dog, walk up to his dish while he is eating and drop in something wonderful, such as a piece of cheese. Whatever you drop in should be better than his kibble. Now he will learn that when people come near his food, something nice happens. I only recommend this procedure for dogs who are not yet food aggressive or food guarders.

DAINA BECKMAN, Happy Tails Dog
Behavior & Training, Hornell, NY

To teach your dog that you are the source of his resources and to prevent him from being too possessive of his food, require him to sit and wait to be fed. Give him the *sit* and then the *wait* command. Lower his food bowl if he stays still. Raise it if he gets up. When he is still, place the bowl down on the floor. He should not move until you release him with a release command, such as "Okay." Practice picking up the dish while your dog is eating and returning it with a treat to teach him that having his dish removed is a good thing. Also, practice hand-feeding kibble from his dish. These exercises are best started in the puppy stage. Once a dog has a food aggression problem, it is best to consult a professional.

LUCINDA LUDWIG, Canine Connection
LLC, Dubuque, IA

Consult a behavior specialist for food guarding! A good one can help you through a fairly simple behavior modification process involving positive techniques. Some essentials include having scheduled mealtimes for your dog—do not free feed. He is more likely to perceive you as his fair leader if you are in control of all the resources. Also, resist the temptation to "test" your dog's tendency to guard during the behavior modification process or anytime thereafter—you will only give him an opportunity to practice the unwanted behavior, and thus it will be inadvertently reinforced. Once your dog has progressed, a few simple exercises added to his daily routine will be all that's required to keep mealtimes event-free.

‌LEAH GANGELHOFF, Flint Hill K-9 Training, LLC, Greater Birmingham, AL

FURNITURE 48

Decisions about whether your dog is allowed on your furniture must be made before you bring him home. To allow the cute little puppy to snuggle on the couch and then kick him off when he's 80 pounds (36 kg) is unfair and confusing to your dog.

‌CINDY STEINKE, CPDT-KA, TDI, CGC, PetTech, K-9 Elementary LLC, Mosinee, WI

Many behavior problems can be solved by meeting your dog's needs. For instance, dogs get on furniture to have a soft, comfortable place to rest and sleep as well as to be near their owners. There is nothing inherently wrong with allowing your dog on the furniture. But if in your household he is not allowed on the furniture, then provide a soft, comfortable dog bed, ideally in each room where you spend the most time or in a location in which he prefers to rest. Make sure that everyone in the family is 100 percent consistent in not allowing the dog on the furniture, if that is your house rule, so that he doesn't get confused.

‌ANN ALLUMS, CPDT-KA, Best Friends Animal Society, Kanab, UT

You may or may not want to allow your dog free access to the furniture. If you do, then teach him to get off willingly when you ask. To teach your dog to get off willingly, tell him "Off" and excitingly entice him off. When he does get off the furniture, reward him with pets, praise, play, toys, or a treat. He will learn that getting off may get him good things, so the behavior of "off" will happen more frequently.

‌CRYSTAL COLL, All Ways Pawsitive Pet Behavior and Training, Queen Creek, AZ

If your dog already has the habit of jumping on the furniture, do not allow him around the furniture when unsupervised so that you can ensure that the boundaries are consistently respected.

ANN ALLUMS, CPDT-KA, Best Friends
Animal Society, Kanab, UT

GIVE 49

To teach your puppy to release an object in his mouth, place your hand on the object, say "Give," and gently blow in his face. He should briefly open his mouth in surprise, at which point you can remove the object and praise him: "Good give!"

CAROL ROSEN, MS, Positive Dog Training
and Animal Actors, LLC, Silver Spring, MD

Teach your dog to "give," which means to release an object he has in his mouth.

When your dog has an object he is allowed to have, go to him and have a special treat in your hand. This treat must be more valuable to him than the object he already has in his mouth. Tell your dog "Give," put your hand on the object that is in his mouth, and then show him the treat. The instant he releases the object to take the treat, say "Good give," then always return the object he had in his mouth. This is a double reward for the dog–he gets a special treat and his object back. Then when he has an object in his mouth that he is not supposed to have, you can use the *give* command. In this case, you put your hand on the forbidden object, say "Give," and show him the special treat. The instant he releases the object, say "Good give" and give him the treat and an object he is allowed to have.

LISA HOLLANDER, ABC Certified,
DogGone Proud Dog Obedience/Behavior
Modification, Lexington, KY

Many owners complain that they would play more with their dog, but the dog won't give up his toy/ball. When going out to play, grab a few really good treats. When your dog returns with the toy in his mouth, put your hand on it (but don't tug). Say "Give" and then stick a treat right in front of his nose. He has to release the toy to get the treat. After enough repetitions you will not need a treat, as the dog will figure out that "Give" means that the game continues!

ELAINE COUPÉ, For Pet's Sake & Memphis
Agility, Oakland, TN

Teach your dog to relinquish food-type toys by approaching him, offering some stinky cheese, and asking "Can I see that?" When your dog drops the toy for the cheese, pick it up, look at it, and give it back, praising him and walking away. He will learn that you always have something better, that you will give the toy back, and that you'll leave if he gives it to you to check out!

🖊BECKY SCHULTZ, BA, CPDT-KA, Becky Schultz Dog Training and Behavior, Golden Valley, MN

Play the "give" game. Start out with something the dog couldn't care less about (like a plastic bottle), and place it in front of him. Then go to pick it up, say "Give," and then give him a tasty treat. Do this over and over and over again, constantly upping the value of the item and also the treat to match. When you get to toys and the food bowl, make the treat great, like roast beef or hot dog. You want the dog to think that when your hand goes in to take something, he'll get something even better! Make sure that he doesn't see what he's about to get so that he doesn't get accustomed to doing it only for the treat. Once you can take his food away easily (which may take one week or seven), then have your spouse do it, then your oldest kid, all the way down the family. Practice taking lots of things away, and reward him for giving them up nicely.

🖊DAYNA VILLA, IACP, Taking the Lead Dog Training, PA

To help prevent your puppy or dog from aggressively guarding his toys, when initially teaching the *give* command, return the toy immediately to him after he has taken the treat. This way, he will be reinforced for relinquishing the toy (by the treat), as well as taught that there is no need to guard any objects (because the toy is immediately returned).

🖊CHRISTINA SHUSTERICH, BA, CBC, NY Clever K9, Inc., Queens, NY

When teaching the *give* command, it is helpful in the beginning if you can use "life rewards" as much as possible, along with food and play. It may be that the dog loves riding in the car, so a tug game may conclude with a *give* and the dog invited to jump in the car for a trip. Or the dog may love playing with other dogs, so you can ask him for several tugs and *gives*, and as a reward, he is invited to play with other dogs.

🖊NINA BONDARENKO, BA, Specialist Canine Services, Croydon, Surrey United Kingdom

The *give* can be practiced in everyday life if you make it part of a fetch game. Once your dog learns the *give* as part of fetch, make the game dependant on him giving you the toy. If not, the fetch game ends.

🖊CHRISTINA SHUSTERICH, BA, CBC, NY Clever K9, Inc., Queens, NY

(G)

G

GO HOME 50

The *go home* command is a very basic command to teach and has helped many dogs find their way back to the nest. Each walk outside allows the opportunity to train this behavior. When you return with your dog from a walk, simply take a treat and throw it across the threshold of your door while you say the command "Go home." Your dog will be rewarded with the treat, and the command will be reinforced. Now, when you or a neighbor tells your dog to "Go home," he will graciously go home.

SUSAN M. MILLER, CVT, CPDT-KA, CDBC, The Canine Counselor, Northampton, MA

GO TO PLACE 51

Teaching your dog to go to his place can come in handy when entertaining guests or eating dinner. Select a rug or mat that will be your dog's "place." The "place" can be moved around from room to room, depending where you need it. Keep the "place" mat extra special by only bringing it out for training exercises. Use a clicker and click when your dog puts one paw on the rug, then give him a treat. Repeat until he understands what earned him the click and treat. Then up the criterion to require your dog to place two paws and then four paws on the rug, always clicking at the moment he places his paws on the rug and following immediately with a treat. Finally, require your dog to lie down on the rug, and click and treat him for going down and then staying down. Increase the time required to earn a treat. Practice increasing the time by tethering your dog to a chair leg while you watch TV and he lies next to you on his "place."

LUCINDA LUDWIG, Canine Connection LLC, Dubuque, IA

"Place" is a safe spot for your dog to relax quietly out of the way; it can be a dog bed or other comfortable location. My dog, JD, learned "place" early as I was constantly tripping over this nosy canine adolescent. Sending him to his "place" was accomplished by tossing treats to a mat. "Place" was taught for my convenience, but it ended up saving his life. JD and I were hit by a drunk driver, and my vehicle flipped and rolled several times. I was seriously injured, and when I regained consciousness I panicked, thinking the chances were slim that JD had survived. When I thought all hope was lost, my housemate appeared with JD in his arms—in shock but alive. JD had gone to his "place." Thrown from the car, suffering from injuries, JD had instinctively run to the spot where he felt safe—the mat at the kitchen door, his "place."

ELLEN TAYLOR, CPDT-KA, Community Initiatives Manager, ASPCA, Suffolk, VA

Train your dog to lie down on a rug or a mat—his "place." Pick one that your dog will lie down on comfortably. I use bathroom mats, which are plush on one side with rubber on the other, so they won't slide around. Lure your dog to the mat and click and treat him for being on it (whether he is sitting, lying down, or standing). Touch the perimeter of the mat and say "Place" or whatever your cue is going to be. Release your dog and repeat several times. Move the rug to another location and repeat the sequence. You want your dog to learn that the mat is the "place" and not a certain location. Make the mat the best place for him to be. Offer all-new treats and toys on the mat, and reward your dog any time he lies down there on his own. Place the mat next to your favorite chair, and encourage your dog to lie on the mat next to you. Periodically praise, pet, and offer treats.

You will be able to use "place" as an anchor command for your dog. For example, put the mat in your dining room and have your dog lie there while you are eating. Use "place" when company comes so that he doesn't bother your guests. The

place can become "the crate without the crate" for your dog.

> BARBARA LONG, CPDT-KA, Paw in Hand
> Dog Training, Chapel Hill, NC

GREETINGS

For dogs who are overexcited to greet visitors, keep a food-stuffed chew toy ready in the freezer. As soon as the guests arrive, give him the toy. By the time he has finished eating the food in the toy (approximately 20 minutes), the guests will be settled, the situation will be less exciting, and the dog should be a bit tired from all of the "de-stuffing!" The key is giving the toy *before* the dog gets too excited by the guests.

> JESSICA JANOWSKI, Puppy Please! Dog
> Training, LLC, Goffstown, NH

Dogs greet with all they have: sight, sound, smell, touch, and the ever-popular big, slobbery tongue. Teaching good manners is as easy as counting 1-2-3...or 60. By giving your dog one whole minute to take in the sight, sound, and smell of the person standing there, you give him the chance of a better greeting because a lot of it is done before he has actual physical contact. Buy your furry friend some time by counting to 60. Then look at him—if he is calm, he can greet the person; if not, count again. What you will find over time is that your dog will calm down quicker because his senses aren't being overwhelmed by the fabulousness of well-meaning dog lovers. Put the greeting on cue—"Go say hi!"—and praise him calmly if you want him to greet calmly. Teach your pal a calm meeting routine and he will have a greeting disorder no more!

> ELAINE ALLISON, CPDT-KA,
> Shelter Director, Humane Society
> of Wickenburg, Wickenburg, AZ

One way to train your dog to sit to greet guests is by training him to sit before you and your family greet him each time upon returning home. Simply do not greet or pet your dog upon returning home until he sits (of course, provided he knows the *sit* command!). The *sit* command can be combined with a *stay* command if your dog repeatedly jumps.

           ℰCHRISTINA SHUSTERICH, BA, CBC, NY
Clever K9, Inc., Queens, NY

G

Inappropriate greeting behaviors include rushing the door, jumping up, alarm barking, etc. The key to stopping all unwanted behaviors is to give the dog something else to do instead. For greeting, the most common alternative behavior is the *sit*. *Sit* may work well out in public or with strangers but can be extremely difficult for many dogs when greeting their own families. It is often much easier to teach a dog to retrieve a toy and greet family and visitors with a toy in his mouth.

      ℰMICHELLE DOUGLAS, CPDT-KA, CDBC, The Refined Canine, West Haven, CT

To help eliminate excited welcomes, walk into the house and completely ignore the dog—no talking or eye contact. Make believe that the dog is not there. Go to the kitchen, get a treat, and then wait or ask for calm behavior (like a *sit*)—then treat the dog. This will teach him that calm behavior will bring attention, and it will also redirect him from the excitement of the greeting. If all arrivals and departures are low key, this can help with greeting excitement and separation anxiety.

      ℰANGEL ROBINSON, Angels Tailwaggin Training LLC, Blairstown, NJ

Make it a house policy to reward only for "four-on-the-floor" greetings. If you're consistent, your dog will learn that he can get your attention (and a food reward) by greeting you politely.

      ℰMARY LEATHERBERRY, CPDT-KA, Good Dog! Santa Fe, Santa Fe, NM

To prevent overexcited greetings, occupy your dog. Find an awesome treat that you will only give him when company is over. My favorite options are pig ears or a hollow chew stuffed with peanut butter, but any type of edible chew item will do.

      ℰJENNIFER SCHNEIDER, CPDT-KA, Pick of the Litter Dog Training, Seattle/Tacoma Area, WA

If you take a group training class, ask your instructor to greet your dog at the beginning of every class so that he can practice proper greetings. The instructor may even choose a different person in class each session to practice greetings with all of the dogs.

      ℰANN WITHUN, Dog Scouts of America Troop Leader, Fieldwood Dog Training Center, Carlisle, PA

Does your dog get too excited when guests come to your house? Does he jump, bark, or maybe even growl at visitors? Just because you have a dog doesn't mean that one of his jobs is to greet everyone who comes to your door. Too many times I've found dogs who just can't handle the stress of greeting visitors, and their owners can't handle the stress of it either! The simplest solution is to not let your dog be the greeter. If he is crate trained, you can put him in his crate to relax with a nice food-stuffed toy or other favorite item. Otherwise, you can put him in any room that keeps him from the main activity of the house, and give him a food-stuffed toy to play with. This will let both you and your dog relax. Once your guests have settled in, you may find that your dog can now visit with people in a calm and stress-free manner.

‹ LENORE SMITH, CPDT-KA, Downward Dog Companion Dog Training, LLC, NH

GREETINGS, DOOR

Working on polite door-greeting behaviors? Put treats and a clicker near the door so that when the doorbell rings, you have the tools you need to teach your dog to be polite right at your fingertips!

‹ DAWN ANTONIAK-MITCHELL, Esq., CPDT-KA, BonaFide Dog Academy LLC, Omaha, NE

Does your dog go crazy when visitors come to your door? Decide specifically what you would like him to do instead. Make the doorbell the signal to perform this alternate behavior, and practice many times before a real visitor comes. For example: Ring the doorbell, walk the dog over to a specified place (a rug or his bed), put him in a *sit/stay*, and give him a treat. Use a leash/tether and a helper if necessary. Expect backsliding with real visitors, but persist and you will get polite behavior.

‹ JULIE HUMISTON, CPDT-KA, Puppy Love Dog Training, Minneapolis, MN

Is your dog rushing the door when visitors come over and embarrassing you? Keep his leash on the doorknob. Only allow your visitor in when the dog is on leash. Practicing with five new people every day will make greetings at the door much less exciting for him, and he'll know what to do when visitors come. Practice every day instead of just when someone shows up!

‹ BECKY SCHULTZ, BA, CPDT-KA, Becky Schultz Dog Training and Behavior, Golden Valley, MN

G

Place a bath mat or small rug away from the door but convenient enough to walk to when the doorbell rings. Walk to the mat and face it. The puppy will automatically go to where your shoes and face are pointing. Once the puppy is on the mat, give him loads of attention, petting, and praise. He will quickly learn that this mat is "magic" and is where all the fun begins. The "magic mat" will make it much easier for you and your guest to get into the house without tripping over a pet.

ꙮ ANN ISENHOUR, Bow Wow Boutique, Gastonia, NC

Dogs are startled by the sound of a doorbell. We all experience a sense of anticipation (good or bad) of who might be on the other side. Training a dog to have appropriate door manners can curb barking in addition to the well-intentioned "mugging" of guests or even escaping the house. Work on the *sit* and *wait* commands near the door with your dog. Once he can do a reliable *sit/wait* at the door, repeat the training process with a family member or a friend ringing the bell or knocking on the door. Do not allow the person entering the house to greet the dog in the entranceway. Reward your dog for holding the *sit/wait*. Have greetings in another room, but only allow petting if your dog is in a *sit*. Keep a leash at the front door so that you can put it on him when the doorbell rings until he is perfect at holding a *sit/wait*.

ꙮ JEANNE HAMPL, Hampl's Dog Obedience, Gig Harbor, WA

To keep your dog from jumping up when people come into the house, keep a leash by the door. When the doorbell rings or someone knocks, put the leash on your dog and step on it. When he sits and is polite, the guest can reach down and pet him. However, if the dog is antsy, ask the person to turn around and ignore him for a few minutes.

ꙮ BONNIE KRUPA, CPDT-KA, Happy, Clean and Smart, Muncie, IN

Keep a treat jar near the front door so that when guests arrive, you can hand them a treat and tell them to command your dog to sit for the treat. Repeating this activity with each guest will train your dog not to jump on them.

ꙮ KAREN COTTINGHAM, Primetime Pet Services, Salisbury, MD

Grab a handful of treats before you open the door for your guests to come inside.

Immediately after allowing guests inside, start rewarding your dog for appropriate greeting behaviors: Say your dog's name and reward him with a treat for looking at you; reward him with a treat whenever he has all four paws on the floor; ask him for a *sit* (it doesn't matter who the dog sits for) and reward with a treat; reward him with a treat for offering a *sit* instead of jumping.

ぜJENNIFER SCHNEIDER, CPDT-KA, Pick of the Litter Dog Training, Seattle/Tacoma Area, WA

GROOMER, CHOOSING

Finding a reputable groomer is as simple as contacting your local shelter or rescue group. Many groomers donate their time and resources to humane organizations to help animals feel better and find homes. A groomer found this way not only comes as a somewhat known entity skill-wise but is also a generous person who truly cares about animals and their needs.

ぜMARNI EDELHART, CPDT-KA, Pioneer Pets LLC, Easthampton, MA

GROWLING 53

A dog's growl means that something is wrong; he is either uncomfortable, scared, feeling threatened, or feeling that something he has is threatened. Never punish a growl, as it is an important form of communication from your dog and serves as a warning that something is wrong. If you suppress the growl, you may succeed in suppressing the warning so that the dog has no other recourse but to escalate to a snap or even a bite.

ぜANN ALLUMS, CPDT-KA, Best Friends Animal Society, Kanab, UT

Never punish a dog for growling. A growl is a dog's way of saying "I'm very uncomfortable with what is happening, and if it continues, I may have to bite someone to make it stop!" This is a very good warning system, and you don't want to eliminate it. Dogs who aren't allowed to growl may go straight to the bite. Rather than forbidding the growl, calmly figure out what is making your dog uncomfortable and eliminate the cause of the growling instead.

ぜJULIE HUMISTON, CPDT-KA, Puppy Love Dog Training, Minneapolis, MN

GUILT

It is a common misunderstanding to think that a dog shows guilt when you return home to find that he has dumped over the trash in your absence. Many people think it's guilt that causes a dog to tuck his tail, lower his head, and look contrite. Actually, this is just a dog's way to try to calm his owner, who is clearly not happy about something. It's called "appeasement behavior." A dog often shows appeasement behavior even before an owner has seen any evidence of wrongdoing simply because he has learned to associate the return of the owner with corrections or punishment.

ॐTERRY LONG, CPDT-KA, DogPACT Training and Behavior Services, Long Beach, CA

He didn't do it for revenge! A dog may look "guilty" when you come home, but it's just because he is reading your body language. Here's what your dog is thinking: "I don't know what I did, but look at how mad she is. I think I'll hide over here until she calms down." Dogs don't do bad things out of spite. They do things because the rules are unclear or they have not been taught what they are supposed to do.

ॐDARLENE KOZA, Scooter's School of Sit & Stay, Rochester, NY

HAND SIGNALS

Dogs aren't verbal animals, so when teaching any new behavior, teach a hand signal first and add a verbal cue later. If you start with a reliable hand signal (for *sit*, *down*, and *come*), you will always be able to get the dog to do it, even with distractions.

Then, when you start teaching the word, say the word first once, then use your hand signal as your back-up plan to make it happen. The word should predict the hand signal.

ॐJULIE SONTAG, CPDT-KA, One Smart Puppy, New York, NY

Dogs are visual and masters at reading body language. For clear commands, use hand signals along with your verbal commands.

ॐDARLENE KOZA, Scooter's School of Sit & Stay, Rochester, NY

When hiring a dog trainer, ask her if your dog can be trained to obey hand signals as well as verbal commands. This will help in a noisy environment or when your dog is too far away to hear you.

ॐJIM FIORINO, Jim's K-9 College, Albany, NY

HANDLING 54

Handling is very important. Slowly, gently, consistently, persistently, and pleasantly handle every part of your dog in short, relaxing sessions. This builds trust in your relationship so that you can handle him in stressful situations.

~KATHERINE ROLLINS, CPDT-KA, Kat's K9 Cadets, Greenville, TN

Sitting with your dog or puppy between your legs and touching him all over his body every evening for about 15 to 30 minutes is a great way to calm him down before bed. With him either on his back or tummy, start by running your hands down his back or tummy from head to tail. Talk calmly to him during this time. Include playing with his toes, ears, mouth, and tail. Touching everything will help him get used to the feeling. Remember not to let him get up if he is whining, struggling, or complaining. He will relax if you keep rubbing and petting him. Then put him in his crate for the night.

~ROBIN CARROLL, Trainer/Instructor, GAP dogs, Inc., CO

Handle your puppy's feet, ears, and mouth early and often, and make sure that your dog is comfortable with having these areas touched. As soon as you get your puppy or young dog, introduce him to the positive benefits associated with having you handle these areas. Take a yummy treat and gently touch the top of his paw, and give him a tiny piece of the treat. Each time he allows you to do this without licking or mouthing your hand or retracting his paw, give him a big piece of treat. When he is successful several times and over many sessions, gently lift his paw slightly off the ground in your hand and give him a treat while holding his paw. Do this for a few seconds, then release and praise. Slowly increase the duration until he is comfortable having his paw thoroughly examined and handled. You can use the same basic technique for the ears, mouth, and other areas on the body. Your veterinarian and groomer will thank you, and you will be able to check your dog if he is injured.

~TONIA WHILDEN, Houston Dog Ranch, Houston, TX

Having a bit of trouble grooming and handling your pup? Placing him on a raised surface usually has a significant calming/subduing effect that can make any handling tasks much easier. The top of the washing machine or the dryer are handy spots.

~CERENA ZUTIS, CZ Dog Training, CA

H

> **Petting a dog can lower blood pressure and reduce stress.**

Teach your puppy to learn to accept restraint by holding him in the crook of your elbow, with the other arm over his rear. Hold him snugly until he relaxes. Don't expect him to like this. Hold him up to half an hour each day. This isn't cuddling but teaches your puppy to allow restraint. Have other family members restrain him while giving him a treat. Then ask friends to do it too. Your puppy will learn that being restrained doesn't always mean that he's going to get a shot or have something scary happen.

BECKY SCHULTZ, BA, CPDT-KA,
Becky Schultz Dog Training and
Behavior, Golden Valley, MN

HANDLING, COLLAR

Get your dog used to your taking him by the collar. Oftentimes, dogs are sensitive to this maneuver and may even turn and bite when they are not used to being handled this way. When teaching your dog to come, put your fingers through his collar when he comes back to you. Give him lavish praise and treats whenever he comes to you and when you take hold of him by the collar. It will likely be necessary at some time in your dog's life to grab his collar and pull him away from something. Practicing this under favorable conditions will desensitize him and help prevent any accidental biting.

LUCINDA LUDWIG, Canine Connection
LLC, Dubuque, IA

At some point in a dog's life, he may need to be led by the collar. Many dogs are startled when their collars are grabbed, or they dislike being held by the collar because they have been handled roughly. So a dog may bite, try to pull out of his collar, or avoid the reaching hand if not trained to enjoy it. Accustom your dog to enjoy having his collar grabbed by teaching "gotcha." To do so, first prepare tasty treats for him. Then touch his collar while saying "Gotcha," followed immediately by giving him a treat. Start out as gently as you need so that he allows it, and work up to the point where you can grab his collar and lead him by it. The dog should enjoy every moment of this training, or else you're moving too fast for his comfort level. When he starts to look to you expectantly for a treat when you touch his collar while saying "Gotcha," then you know he's ready to move on to a closer approximation of the collar grab.

Remember to reward your dog with a treat each time that he allows the collar handling.

ℰ ANN ALLUMS, CPDT-KA, Best Friends Animal Society, Kanab, UT

HANDLING, FEET 57

To get dogs accustomed to having their paws touched and held for nail trimming, owners should paint their dogs' toenails. Clear polish is fine. Paint two or three nails a day for a week or more until the dog relaxes.

ℰ CATHY HAWKINS, CPDT-KA, Cathy Hawkins Dog Training & Camp Jigsaw, Springfield, MO

Teach your dog "paw" or "shake." If the only time you handle your dog's feet is to cut toenails or to clean them off when they're muddy, he will likely not enjoy having his feet handled. Teaching him to play with his feet with you will make handling them less stressful.

ℰ TINA M. SPRING VAN WHY, Sit Happens Dog Training & Behavior, Athens, GA

As a groomer as well as a trainer, I like to teach my clients to include a foot massage as part of their affection routine with their puppies and dogs. It may sound silly, but the animal becomes very relaxed and is much more cooperative to vets and groomers alike when nail trimming time comes around! I did this with my now 6-year-old Lab-cross, and when the time comes, she is quite happy to roll onto her back and give me a paw at a time so that I can do her nails.

ℰ WENDIE PATRICK-PRIDE, T.O.G.S. for Dogs, Bridgewater, Nova Scotia, Canada

Train the *feet* command to stop your dog in his tracks before coming in with muddy paws. Start with wiping the paws (whether clean or dirty) and giving him a treat when finished *before* he enters the house. Add your command (I use the word "feet"), and continue giving the positive reward before entering the house. Soon, say "Feet" as your dog approaches the door. He should stop and wait for you to wipe, at which point you can give your *release* command to come into the house.

ℰ JOYCELYN SCHEDLER, CCTS, Tail Town Training, Bastrop, TX

HARNESSES 58

I have found that in certain breeds, such as Bulldogs, Pugs, and Corgis, that if the harness is put on upside down (that is, the belly strap over the dog's back and the back strap under the belly), sometimes it will actually fit much better, since it can be hard to fit those "odd-shaped" guys!

ℰ CATHY BONES, CPDT-KA, Pacifica, CA

range of motion. The result will be a puppy who doesn't pull and has no aggression issues caused by constant leash correcting.

~ANDREA CARLSON-CARTER, Courteous Canine, Inc., Lutz, FL

HEAD HALTERS

For dogs who have a difficult time walking on a loose leash, try using a head halter. This is especially helpful for elderly or frail owners or for kids. Always pair the head halter with a positive reinforcement (such as a treat) while getting the dog accustomed to it. Later, the head halter will be a signal for going for a walk, and the walk itself can be the reinforcement.

~CYNTHIA FORD, Yuma, AZ

If you need to use a tether line around your house on your harness-wearing dog and you notice he keeps tangling/tripping on the line, on the right or left shoulder area of some harnesses there is a metal loop—just thread the end of the line through this loop and the line will now hang above the dog's shoulder. However, if you are using the harness for walking, don't thread the line through this loop because it will not allow the correct use of the harness for leash walking.

~KATHY FARDY, MA, Dog's Time, It's Their Time!, Billerica, MA

Use only a tracking harness on a puppy for the first six months of training. A collar should be for ID tags only, and no leash should ever be attached to it until the puppy is over six months old. Do not use a head collar, a chest harness, or any type of device that interferes with his normal

If a dog is not taking to a head halter, I like to hook the leash to the metal piece under the chin instead of the ring. This relieves the pressure from across the nose while still allowing head control. The dog takes to the head halter more quickly without stress.

~REBECCA ENGLE, MA, CPDT-KA, First Steps & Beyond Canine Obedience, Plano, TX

To wean your dog off a head halter, after attaching it, put the leash on the collar rather than the head halter and go for a walk. Eventually you can loosen the head halter until you don't need it anymore. The dog won't realize that the leash isn't attached to the head halter, and you will actually be loose leash walking with your dog. This is a great way to wean your dog off of a training aid.

~BONNIE KRUPA, CPDT-KA, Happy, Clean and Smart, Muncie, IN

HEALTH 59

Your dog needs regular visits to the vet, just as humans need checkups from a physician. Vet exams can also diagnose or rule out any physiological issues that could be contributing to a particular behavior issue.

ANN ALLUMS, CPDT-KA, Best Friends Animal Society, Kanab, UT

Taking good care of your canine companion is extremely important! Visit your veterinarian as needed but at least once a year. Keep your pet up to date on vaccinations and/or an alternative. Regular grooming and bathing are also important for your pet's health, as is an appropriate diet.

JACQUELYN ENGLAND, A Dog's Life, Sunnyvale, CA

It can be difficult to get a urine sample from small female dogs. An easy way to collect it is to use a large, long-handled plastic spoon. You probably already have one in your utensil drawer in the kitchen.

Simply press the spoon down into the grass and slide it under the dog once she has started the flow. The size of the large plastic spoon is just right to collect a 5 ounce (14— ml) sample, and the plastic slides easily in the grass and does not seem to be as intrusive as metal. Simply transfer the liquid to a sealed container and transport to the vet.

ANN ISENHOUR, Bow Wow Boutique, Gastonia, NC

Puppies should be wormed at every vet visit until age 12 to 16 weeks.

ANN ALLUMS, CPDT-KA, Best Friends Animal Society, Kanab, UT

Recently needing to get an immediate urine sample, my vet instructed the tech to "get the ladle." It's a great idea! Use a cheap plastic long-handled ladle to neatly capture a dog's urine without getting it all over your hands or a cup. It can then be transferred to the necessary receptacle.

TERRY CUYLER, CPDT-KA, M.Ed., Pawsitive Results In Home Dog Training, Lake Mary, FL

HEEL

Heeling doesn't have to be a chore; it can be your dog's favorite game! With your dog off leash in a safely enclosed area, walk briskly around and ignore him completely. When he happens to end up by your side, say "Yes!" and toss him a treat. Take off in another direction and wait for him to reappear at your side. When your dog is quickly returning to your side, delay the "Yes!" and treat until he has taken a few steps with you.

Continue to toss him rewards and then move away so that he has to try to catch you again. As you add more steps, feed your dog some treats as he walks with you, then toss one and move quickly away. Soon your dog will be working to stay in *heel* instead of you working to keep him there!

> *LAUREL SCARIONI, CPDT-KA, Pawsitive Results Critter Academy, Santa Rosa, CA*

If your dog is trained on a solid *watch me* cue with distractions, you can use that to train a solid *heel* as well. Ask for the cue and take one step; if eye contact is maintained, click and treat. Stay at one step until your dog seems comfortable, then build up to several steps all while he is beside you in a *heel* position watching you. Once this behavior is solid, add the new *heel* cue followed immediately by the *watch me*, and start walking. Your dog will quickly learn what the *heel* is, and then you no longer have to say "Watch me" for the heeling behavior.

> *HEATHER MOHAN-GIBBONS, MS, RVT, CPDT-KA, ACAAB, Collected Wisdom Animal Behavior, LLC, Milwaukee, WI*

When first training your dog to loose-lead walk and heel, begin the training off lead (in a safe area). Owners can get into the trouble of using the leash as a crutch and using it incorrectly to teach a dog the *heel* position. By starting the training without a leash, the dog will more effectively learn the position he should be in. The leash can come in later when training to correct his position, and the voice command ("Heel") will also be more effective.

> *STEPHANIE LARSON, AKC CGC Evaluator, Gentle Paws, Lexington, NE*

HERDING

When it comes to herding, it can be very helpful to train a solid *lie down* at home and in your own yard so that when you need your dog to lie down while working stock, he has had numerous repetitions and is more likely to comply.

> *SUE STERNBERG, Animals for Adoption and Great Dog Productions, Accord, NY, and Moab, UT*

HERDING BREEDS

If you have a herding breed and no livestock, teach him a serious toy habit when he is young. Whenever he begins to exercise his instinctive herding behavior by biting at moving heels or pants, wiggle a toy in his view and insert that in his mouth instead. Tell him "Get your toy!" and play for a few seconds. With praise and repetition, he will learn to grab a toy (keep lots of them handy!) when he feels that irresistible need to use his mouth.

ॐJULIE HUMISTON, CPDT-KA, Puppy Love Dog Training, Minneapolis, MN

HIGH FIVE

"High five" is a very simple variation of "shake." One your dog has fully learned "shake," you can teach "high five" by saying "shake, high five" and using the hand signal for "shake" (your hand palm up in front of your dog). As he lifts his paw, switch your hand to the "high five" hand signal position (your palm facing your dog) and make contact with his paw as he lifts it, and treat him simultaneously. As your dog learns, say "Shake, high five" but say "Shake" in a progressively quieter voice until he can follow just the words "high five." Simultaneously, progressively change your hand signal from the palm up position for "shake" to the palm facing your dog position of "high five" by gradually lifting your palm higher until he understands the position of your palm facing him as "high five."

ॐCHRISTINA SHUSTERICH, BA, CBC, President, NY Clever K9, Inc., Queens, NY

HIKING

All the caregivers at my work carry canned citronella spray. Citronella is a smell that dogs and animals find distasteful but causes no pain or harm. While it is very useful for interrupting inter-dog and dog–human aggression, it can also be used to deter snakes or other loose animals while hiking with your dog. It fits in a pocket, so it can be easily carried on hikes and walks.

ॐANN ALLUMS, CPDT-KA, Best Friends Animal Society, Kanab, UT

HOT WEATHER

Basic guidelines for summer safety include taking your dog for walks early in the morning or later in the evening to avoid the hottest parts of the day. This also prevents painful burns on footpads because he won't be walking on hot blacktop or asphalt. It's important to remember that brachycephalic breeds (dogs with short, pushed-in faces) and older or younger dogs are most susceptible to heat exhaustion.

JAMIE DAMATO, CPDT-KA, Animalsense Canine Training and Behavior, Inc., Chicago, IL

In hot weather, dogs can overheat quickly. Stay out of high-energy environments when the temps are high!

JAMIE DAMATO, CPDT-KA, Animalsense Canine Training and Behavior, Inc., Chicago, IL

HOUSE RULES

Owners should decide on the "house rules" (what they want their dog to do) and focus on reinforcing him regularly for everything that is appropriate behavior (e.g., chewing on his toys, greeting owner without jumping up, paying attention to owner, etc.). In other words, don't primarily react when your dog does something undesirable; be proactive by looking for the good in him and rewarding that. Catch him in the act of doing something good! Be a benevolent leader by meeting your dog's needs and giving him what he wants in exchange for doing what you want.

ANN ALLUMS, CPDT-KA, Best Friends Animal Society, Kanab, UT

You and your family should decide right from the start what the house rules are going to be for the new dog or puppy. Decide where he will sleep and eat. Ask yourself questions like: Will the dog be allowed access to furniture and other rooms of the house? Predetermining things like manners around the kitchen table is also a great idea. These rules should be consistent with each family member right from the start. The shock of enforcing rules after the dog or puppy settles in may

cause confusion and unacceptable behavior outbursts.

CRYSTAL COLL, All Ways Pawsitive Pet Behavior and Training, Queen Creek, AZ

HOUSETRAINING

Lack of housetraining is a common reason that pet owners relinquish a dog or banish him to the backyard. Yet housetraining is a straightforward process, as long as you understand that your new pet is like a toddler without a diaper and needs to be housetrained appropriately.

ANN ALLUMS, CPDT-KA, Best Friends Animal Society, Kanab, UT

When housetraining, be gentle, be patient, be consistent, and most of all, set your puppy up to be successful.

TRISH MCMILLAN, MSc, CPDT-KA, ASPCA Animal Behavior Center, Urbana, IL

Supervision and consistency are the keys to housetraining success.

JIM BARRY, CPDT-KA, CDBC, Reston Dog Training, Reston, VA

Imagine this: Inside your house you have a wonderful bathroom—it's clean and temperature controlled, the toilet seat is heated, and there's a guy standing outside the bathroom door waiting for you to finish so that he can clean and sanitize the area. Outside about 100 feet (30 m) away from the back door is an outhouse that's old and rickety, there are splinters in the seat, and you only have newspaper sheets for toilet paper. It stinks in the summer, it's freezing in the winter, and there are cracks in the walls; it's horrible. Now, how much would I have to pay you to get you to go outside and use the outhouse every time? Think about your dog in the same situation—he can go in an inside area where it's nice, soft, and temperature controlled, with someone standing by at all times to clean up, deodorize, and sanitize the area; or he can go outside to his toilet area where it's not sanitized, where it's dirty, wet, cold in winter, hot in the summer, and where it stinks. There is nothing nice about the outside toilet area. So how much do you think you have to pay your dog to use his outside toilet area?

SANDRA L. WIRE, K9 FunTime, LLC, Indianapolis, IN

It can be helpful to take a long weekend to devote to housetraining. Stay home with your dog and go out every hour, generously rewarding each success. If you can keep it up for three or four days, progress is often very rapid.

JIM BARRY, CDBC, CPDT-KA, Reston Dog Training, Reston, VA

Most dogs prefer to have specific potty areas and like to avoid soiling their eating and sleeping places, so they respond well to an organized housetraining plan. You will need to prevent accidents in inappropriate areas and reward the dog for eliminating outside (or on a wee-wee pad). Of course, as we all know, pulling that off day in and day out until the dog is fully housetrained will take some time, effort, and careful attention to detail.

ɛ⁄VYOLET MICHAELS, CTC, PDT, CPDT-KA, Urban Dawgs, Red Bank, NJ

Housetraining is simply teaching your puppy where you want him to go to the bathroom and where you don't want him to go. To do this, you need to supervise and reward him when he does it right (giving him lots of opportunities to be right!); supervise and interrupt him when he does it wrong (then take him to where he's supposed to be and reward him when he does it right); and prevent him from accidentally making mistakes when you're not able to supervise.

ɛ⁄TRISH MCMILLAN, MSc, CPDT-KA, ASPCA Animal Behavior Center, Urbana, IL

During housetraining, ensure that the dog is in one of three situations at all times during housetraining: 1. outside with you; 2. inside with your constant supervision (tethered to you if needed); or 3. confined in a small, dog-proofed space such as a crate or exercise pen.

ɛ⁄VYOLET MICHAELS, CTC, PDT, CPDT-KA, Urban Dawgs, Red Bank, NJ

A puppy's bladder is very small (and his brain isn't much bigger!). By the time he realizes he has to "go," it's too late. With all of the exploring and playing that a puppy does in a day, it's easy for him to get off track. Because of this, frequent outside breaks are a must.

ɛ⁄LAURIE ROBINSON, Valparaiso, IN

Take a very young puppy outside every time he wakes up, after every meal, and every hour on the hour otherwise. Take him out more often if he's playing very actively. Don't wait for him to "ask"—he doesn't know how!

ɛ⁄TRISH MCMILLAN, MSc, CPDT-KA, ASPCA Animal Behavior Center, Urbana, IL

You may find it helpful to put elimination on a verbal cue, uttered calmly and quietly just as the dog is beginning to eliminate. Once the cue is paired with a good reward history, it often helps keep the dog focused on the task at hand.

ɛ⁄JIM BARRY, CDBC, CPDT-KA, Reston Dog Training, Reston, VA

Teaching a dog to potty outside takes time and devotion. If you get your puppy out every hour or two, reward for good behavior, watch him carefully when he is inside, and crate him when you can't watch him, you will have a dog who learns quickly.

eJANE BRYDON, M.S.Ed., M.Ed., CPDT-KA, Jane Brydon, Dog Training Coach, LLC, Clifton Heights, PA

When initially housetraining your dog to eliminate outside, you should accompany him to his potty area. This is because your puppy needs to learn that in addition to going potty outside, peeing and pooping in front of you is a good thing. When he eliminates on the correct spot, praise him and maybe even give him a small treat right away. Sending your dog outside alone to go potty might teach him to go potty "away from you" instead of in front of you. Your dog might conclude that sneaking off to another room also qualifies as "away from you," and you will not be able to catch him in the act to interrupt an accident.

eADRIENNE CARSON, Harmony, NJ

Because dogs return to eliminate in the same area, you may find it useful to take some of your dog's feces or urine and use it to "seed" an outside area. Then take him out and encourage him to go in that place.

eJIM BARRY, CDBC, CPDT-KA, Reston Dog Training, Reston, VA

Dogs naturally like to relieve themselves in a spot where they have gone once before. Use this natural tendency to help you with potty training.

When your dog is not watching, wipe up a urine accident with a paper towel and take it outside and rub it on the grass where you want his potty spot to be. For convenience, this spot should be only a few feet (m) from your front door. For solid mistakes, simply pick one up a piece of the feces and put it in the same spot outside. You have now successfully marked the spot for your dog!

eCOLLEEN B. HURLEY, Orlando, FL and Gainesville, FL

When you're outside with your new pup, keep a yummy treat hidden in your pocket. When he starts looking like he's going to potty (sniffing, circling, etc.), say your cue. (I use "Hurry up.") As soon as he starts eliminating, praise him quietly for the entire duration and when he's done, give him that treat. Soon your pup will be in a hurry to "perform" as soon as he gets outside.

eTRISH MCMILLAN, MSc, CPDT-KA, ASPCA Animal Behavior Center, Urbana, IL

H

When you take your dog outside for a walk, wait until he eliminates and then use the walk as a reward, not the other way around. And be sure to have other high-value reinforcers for your dog, like treats or favorite toys, available after—and only after—proper pottying.

JIM BARRY, CDBC, CPDT-KA, Reston Dog Training, Reston, VA

of his habits throughout the day. Indicate the time that you take him outside and whether he went to the bathroom. If the dog eliminates inside, indicate when and where this occurred. Be specific (for example, on the rug in the bathroom). Keeping a log may help you determine a pattern in your dog's elimination schedule. It will also help you accurately assess if he is making progress or not.

KRISTINA N. GAGE, CPDT-KA, SmartDog Dog Training, Saratoga Springs, NY

Always accompany your dog to eliminate so that you can reward with praise and small, delicious food treats just as he finishes. Be careful not to interrupt him in the middle of eliminating. Start praising and treating when the dog is still eliminating but finishing the last drop.

VYOLET MICHAELS, CTC, PDT, CPDT-KA, Urban Dawgs, Red Bank, NJ

Escort your dog outside every couple of hours for a potty break. Yes—go *with* him to make sure that he goes potty, and don't try to pressure him to go potty, which will only make him tense. Help him succeed by taking him to the same spot each time and rewarding him (with praise, treats, play, etc.) as soon as he relieves himself.

ANN ALLUMS, CPDT-KA, Best Friends Animal Society, Kanab, UT

Dogs can develop a preference for eliminating on certain types of surfaces. If this has occurred in your home, you may be able to obtain a sample of that surface—say, a carpet—and put it outside so that your dog learns to go there. You can then gradually reduce the size of the sample.

JIM BARRY, CDBC, CPDT-KA, Reston Dog Training, Reston, VA

Don't take your puppy on a long or adventurous walk until *after* he does his business. Go directly to one area where you want him to eliminate. When he is done, go for a fun walk. That is his reward. If you let him wander first, he may get distracted.

ANGEL ROBINSON, Angels Tailwaggin Training LLC, Blairstown, NJ

A conscientious breeder can help prevent housetraining issues by working with the pups prior to selling. This means that the puppies won't be leaving as early as some people would like. (I never sell a Corgi under ten weeks of age.) By then I have them crate trained, paper trained, and box trained. After they are sold, the owner who is home to let them out can set the outdoor habits.

ℰ JOAN B. GUERTIN, Common Sense Dog Training & Behavior Solutions, East Texas

When housetraining your dog, keep a log Many of my clients still think methods like paper training, rubbing the dog's nose in accidents, or spanking are okay for housetraining–but they aren't! Instead, take your dog out on a schedule. Start with once an hour. As soon as you get to the place you want him to go, say "Go potty" repeatedly. As soon as he starts to squat (or lift his leg), begin to praise him; when he is finished, give him a treat while continuing the praise. Take him right back in the house. When you take him out for exploration and play, don't say "Go potty." If he does go, praise him with "Good boy, go potty." If he goes in the house, ignore it; don't let him see you clean it up. If you see him going, stop him with a clap of your hands, take him out to his spot, and give the command "Go potty." If you want him to pee outside, don't teach him to pee in the house.

ℰ DAINA BECKMAN, Happy Tails Dog Behavior & Training, Hornell, NY

If your puppy is having a hard time transitioning from paper to the outdoors, leave a bit of soiled paper in his potty area so that he has a scent cue to show him the place to go.

ℰ TRISH MCMILLAN, MSc, CPDT-KA, ASPCA Animal Behavior Center, Urbana, IL

Rescue dogs, strays, or any dog who was housed in an unclean environment will fail at housetraining if given too much freedom in the new home because he has had little chance of understanding what is expected of him. The secret to clarifying the routine and preventing mistakes is to structure the living environment and to monitor the dog's behavior as closely as possible.

ℰ JOAN B. GUERTIN, Common Sense Dog Training & Behavior Solutions, East Texas

Some dog owners have had success with pads or litter boxes, even when their dogs didn't get the knack of going outside. And some dogs can learn to use doggy doors to manage their own trips to the potty. Even so, dogs must be trained to use these aids, using sound management and reinforcement. As a last resort, you can try doggy diapers!

ℰ JIM BARRY, CDBC, CPDT-KA, Reston Dog Training, Reston, VA

If your dog has been housetrained for years and suddenly starts eliminating in inappropriate areas, start with a vet check. Although some dogs do have training regressions, medical issues, such as a bladder infection, urinary tract infection, or canine cognitive dysfunction (CCD), can also be the cause of changed behavior.

ᴇᴥLISA PATRONA, Dip. DTBC, CPDT-KA, PDT, CBC, Trainers Academy, LLC, President, Troy, MI

Any time your puppy is out and about, you must keep your eyes on him. Baby-gate him in the room with you, follow him around, and keep the corner of your eye on him at all times for signs he needs to go out, like circling or sniffing the ground. You cannot supervise an unhousetrained puppy too closely! If you give him free run of the house too early, he will learn that it's perfectly fine to potty anywhere if there's no human watching. Uh-oh! If you are not actively supervising your puppy, he must be in a puppy-proofed area, in a crate, or tethered to your belt by a leash.

ᴇᴥTRISH MCMILLAN, MSc, CPDT-KA, ASPCA Animal Behavior Center, Urbana, IL

Supervise, supervise, supervise! Supervision means just that—your incompletely housetrained dog must be under constant observation between potty trips. That means in a crate, on a leash attached to you, or in the same room and within a few feet (m) of your location. Otherwise, you won't be able to detect those signs of imminent elimination, like circling or sniffing, and respond promptly. And every event that you miss makes your task more difficult.

ᴇᴥJIM BARRY, CDBC, CPDT-KA, Reston Dog Training, Reston, VA

Provide constant supervision. This helps prevent accidents during the learning stage so that the dog doesn't learn undesirable habits that are more difficult to change. Set up the environment to help the dog (and you) succeed: Block access to other rooms (so that the dog doesn't go to the dining room to do his business, which doesn't seem like living space to her), feed her on a regular schedule (what goes in regularly comes out regularly), and clean previous accident sites with an enzymatic cleaner.

ᴇᴥANN ALLUMS, CPDT-KA, Best Friends Animal Society, Kanab, UT

If your dog has continuing housetraining problems or has a relapse after having been successfully housetrained, your first step should be a trip to the vet. Ask your vet to check for a urinary tract infection, an intestinal parasite, a congenital deformity, or another medical problem that could contribute to difficulty in controlling the bowels and bladder. Also, be aware that some medications can affect elimination patterns; your vet can provide more information.

ᴇᴥJIM BARRY, CDBC, CPDT-KA, Reston Dog Training, Reston, VA

HOUSETRAINING, ACCIDENTS

Keep an "accident log" when you are housetraining a puppy. Note the day and time, what type of accident (pee or poop), and where it was found. This will help you determine if you need to adjust the puppy's schedule of feeding and walks and whether you need to restrict his access to certain areas. For example, if your puppy has an accident every day between 5 and 6 p.m., you may need to schedule an extra trip outside during that period. You will also be able to tell if your housetraining efforts are working. If you note two accidents every day the first week and only one accident every other day the second week, you know that your puppy is improving.

    ~BARBARA LONG, CPDT-KA, Paw in Hand Dog Training, Chapel Hill, NC

If your puppy/dog makes a mistake in the house and you don't catch him, forget about it—there is nothing you can do or say that he will understand if you don't catch him in the act. If you do catch him, yell "No" or "Stop" or something to startle him and immediately carry or escort him out to his spot and stand there.

    ~JANE BRYDON, M.S.Ed., M.Ed., CPDT-KA, Jane Brydon, Dog Training Coach, LLC, Clifton Heights, PA

If your puppy has an accident in front of you, say "Oops!", pick him up mid-squat, and run him outside. Picking puppies up generally causes them to stop eliminating. Reward him when he "finishes" outside.

    ~TRISH MCMILLAN, MSc, CPDT-KA, ASPCA Animal Behavior Center, Urbana, IL

Elimination is an inherently reinforcing behavior because it reduces the physical discomfort that your dog feels. Be sure not to add to that reinforcement by giving him attention after an accident. Even negative attention can be reinforcing, so don't yell at your dog; just try to interrupt if possible and relocate outside.

    ~JIM BARRY, CDBC, CPDT-KA, Reston Dog Training, Reston, VA

Clean all accidents thoroughly with an enzymatic cleaner to get the smell completely out. If it smells like a potty spot, it *is* a potty spot.

    ~VYOLET MICHAELS, CTC, PDT, CPDT-KA, Urban Dawgs, Red Bank, NJ

If you find an accident in the house, clean it up with paper towels or toilet paper, then take it and the dog to the desired outside elimination area. Drop the poop (or if it's pee, rub it into the ground) and then move aside. Let the dog smell it, praise, praise, praise, and give the command word for potty, "Good potty! Good potty!" By redirecting where the dog wants to "go," I've had great success.

    ~SHEILA LIEBERMAN, Loving Obedience Dog Training, Miami, FL & Metro, DC

H

People sometimes get the idea that dogs leave droppings for them out of spite. Nothing could be farther from the truth! Dogs, unlike people, find smelly stuff very attractive. And they know you do too because they see you pick it up and take it away. So it sometimes helps to ensure that your dog is elsewhere when you are cleaning up accidents.

    JIM BARRY, CDBC, CPDT-KA, Reston Dog Training, Reston, VA

Expect confusion and mistakes. Be ready to catch your dog in the act. Interrupt him ("Outside!") at the start of any mistakes indoors, then hustle him outside to finish. If he finishes outside, praise and reward this behavior. Note: Interrupt, don't punish. If your dog makes a mistake unsupervised, never, ever punish him— there is zero connection to the act that happened many dozens, hundreds, or even thousands of behaviors ago. Also, if your interruption is too scary, you may end up with a dog who no longer eliminates in front of you, which can make the housetraining process very difficult.

    VYOLET MICHAELS, CTC, PDT, CPDT-KA, Urban Dawgs, Red Bank, NJ

Use an enzymatic cleanser from the pet store to clean up accidents—products formulated for humans won't fool a canine nose!

    TRISH MCMILLAN, MSc, CPDT-KA, ASPCA Animal Behavior Center, Urbana, IL

If there have been a lot of accidents in your home, you may need to go to great lengths to find and clean up the entire residue. To do this, buy an ultraviolet lightbulb, put it in a small lamp, and plug it into a long extension cord. Wait until nighttime, turn off all of the other lights, and close the shades. Carefully inspect your entire home with the blacklight. Thoroughly clean any areas that glow, always using an enzyme-based cleaner, until there is no more sign of stains. (Be sure to consistently use an enzyme cleaner; standard household or carpet cleaners will not completely remove odor and may attract dogs back to the same area.)

    JIM BARRY, CDBC, CPDT-KA, Reston Dog Training, Reston, VA

Don't believe the old myth about never cleaning up an accident in front of your dogs because it will reinforce their behavior, give them the attention they crave, and indicate your approval for continuing with their elimination behaviors. In reality, what does cleaning up urine or fecal matter have to do with giving your dog attention? Behaviorists have clearly established that dogs have no moral codes when it comes to their behaviors. Therefore, they simply repeat behaviors that have been reinforced (i.e., been successful—for them) in the past. In addition, reinforcement (for a dog) only

occurs at the time of the behavior, not an hour or even a minute after, which is usually when you have discovered the mess. So scrub away! Your actions or even your grumbling (as you clean up the mess) will not reinforce the actual act of eliminating. Your time will be better served applying the principles of a sound housetraining program.

℘LISA PATRONA, Dip. DTBC, CPDT-KA, PDT, CBC, Trainers Academy, LLC, President, Troy, MI

This tip is what I call the "Martha Stewart scoop on poop." When a dog has an accident or throws up in class, I cut a paper plate in two and use the two halves to easily pick up the waste and toss it in a plastic grocery bag. This method works well on softer varieties of carpeting and makes sure that the mess doesn't get ground deeper into the carpet.

℘LYNNE YOUNG, CPDT-KA, PetsRx and Dog Training Club of Chester Co., Wilmington, DE

Clean up any accidents with a cleanser containing liquid enzymes that eliminate stains and odors. Once the area is dry, feed or play games with your dog in the spot where he had the accident. Dogs don't like to eliminate where they eat or play, so this can help prevent them from resoiling the same area.

℘DANA COOPER, CPDT-KA, Woofers Canine Companion Training, Round Rock, TX

HOUSETRAINING, CRATES

A crate can be invaluable in preventing housetraining accidents when you cannot supervise your dog, and it has the added benefit of reducing destructive chewing. Dogs do not tend to soil their sleeping area, but they should not be crated for more than two to four hours at a time without a potty break. Being crated too long can actually undermine housetraining.

℘ANN ALLUMS, CPDT-KA, Best Friends Animal Society, Kanab, UT

During housetraining, it is vital to use a crate (and/or dog-proofed confinement area such as an exercise pen) when you are not able to constantly supervise the dog. Bring him directly outside to eliminate first thing whenever you take him out of the confinement area. Do not allow him to roam around while you are getting ready to go out because this is a common time for a dog who is not housetrained to have an accident. Increase the size of the crate (or confinement area) every two weeks as your dog is successful (meaning no accidents within the area) by adjusting/removing the crate divider and eventually using an exercise pen to provide additional space. If an accident occurs, reduce the confinement area to the last successful size. As your dog continues to successfully learn where to eliminate and what to chew, you can start increasing his confinement space by using baby gates or exercise pens to provide extra dog-proofed room.

&VYOLET MICHAELS, CTC, PDT, CPDT-KA,
Urban Dawgs, Red Bank, NJ

A canine of any age who was left for too long in a crate and developed the habit of eliminating in it may look at crate time as the time to repeat that behavior. Instead of crating him, tether him to you as you go about your business—this will keep you apprised of his actions. Use the tethering rather than crating as the basis for retraining.

&JOAN B. GUERTIN, Common Sense Dog
Training & Behavior Solutions, East Texas

HOUSETRAINING, FEEDING

Housetraining issues? Don't free-feed (leave food out all the time). Feed your dog at the same time(s) every day. If he doesn't finish eating within 10 to 15 minutes, remove the food bowl. Be consistent with feeding times.

&LYNETTE TATAY, Nashville, MI

Take into consideration your pet's feeding habits. It could be that you are feeding too much too often. Free-feeding is counterproductive if you want to cultivate good potty habits. At night, particularly if crating your dog, feed early enough so that he can eliminate thoroughly before bedtime. Also, withdraw water mid-evening.

&JOAN B. GUERTIN, Common Sense Dog
Training & Behavior Solutions, East Texas

Keep your puppy on a regular feeding schedule; if things go in at regular times, they'll likely come out at regular times too.

ॐTRISH MCMILLAN, MSc, CPDT-KA, ASPCA Animal Behavior Center, Urbana, IL

Be sure that you are feeding your dog a high-quality food, preferably one with natural and organic ingredients. Some dogs have sensitivities to particular foods or to chemicals used as preservatives or as color or flavor enhancers. These sensitivities can affect a dog's digestive system and contribute to housetraining problems. Also, make sure that your dog gets plenty of exercise—at least half an hour of vigorous activity each day—to keep him physically fit.

ॐJIM BARRY, CDBC, CPDT-KA, Reston Dog Training, Reston, VA

Frequent meals equal more frequent elimination. Feed your dog two times per day (or as recommended by your vet). Whatever is not eaten within 30 minutes should be pulled up (unless the dog is actively working to obtain food from a work-to-eat stuffable toy, which should be stuffed according to his individual abilities—

not so hard that he gives up). Weather and activity permitting, pull up water by 8 p.m.

ॐVYOLET MICHAELS, CTC, PDT, CPDT-KA, Urban Dawgs, Red Bank, NJ

HOUSETRAINING, "HOLDING IT"

A rough rule of thumb is that a dog can physically "hold it" for one hour per month of age plus an hour. For example, a two-month-old dog will likely be able to hold it for three hours. This can of course vary among individual dogs. It is reasonable to expect an adult dog to hold on four to six hours. Of course, many can hold on longer, but is it humane to make them?

ॐVYOLET MICHAELS, CTC, PDT, CPDT-KA, Urban Dawgs, Red Bank, NJ

How long can a puppy hold it? First, think about how long you can hold it. If you are eating, drinking, and moving around, the answer is probably a shorter amount of time than if you were not doing those things. The same goes for your puppy. Limit his movement and access to food and water, and he can hold it for longer than if he has a bowl of food and water plus the whole room or house in which to play. Keeping these things in mind, I still like to suggest that you shouldn't expect your puppy to be able to hold it longer than you can!

ॐCOLLEEN B. HURLEY, Orlando, FL and Gainesville, FL

Puppies need a puppy-proofed area like an x-pen with a water dish, a bed or crate, some legal chew toys, and a potty area if you're going to be away for more hours than the pup's age in months.

—TRISH MCMILLAN, MSc, CPDT-KA, ASPCA Animal Behavior Center, Urbana, IL

Avoid leaving your dog confined for longer than he can physically hold it. Arrange for a professional pet sitter or family member to provide a relief visit. If you must leave the dog for longer than he can physically hold it and have exhausted all options for scheduling someone to give a relief visit, set him up in a larger dog-proofed confinement area (maximum area of an exercise pen) with wee-wee pads on one end and toys, water, and a bed on the other. This should especially be avoided (except in emergencies) if your goal is outdoor elimination only. If your dog is wee-wee pad trained, you may be able to leave for longer periods, but be sure to consider his mental and physical stimulation needs.

—VYOLET MICHAELS, CTC, PDT, CPDT-KA, Urban Dawgs, Red Bank, NJ

During the first weeks, your puppy may not be able to hold it all night. But be boring during midnight potty trips so that he doesn't start waking you up for playtime!

—TRISH MCMILLAN, MSc, CPDT-KA, ASPCA Animal Behavior Center, Urbana, IL

HOUSETRAINING, PUNISHMENT

Never punish your dog for having an accident in the house. Punishment may suppress behavior, but it does not teach the dog what is acceptable behavior and can create fear and mistrust within him. Punishment may inadvertently train a dog to go out of sight to potty, not because he is acting out of spite or anger but because he has learned that his person can be very unpleasant to be around. For example, I adopted a one-year-old dog who, for several weeks, did not go potty anywhere outside if I was watching. In her prior home, she had been harshly punished for having potty accidents but not been shown, much less rewarded, for pottying in appropriate areas, so she learned to fear and avoid the presence of people when she eliminated.

—ANN ALLUMS, CPDT-KA, Best Friends Animal Society, Kanab, UT

Don't punish your puppy for housetraining mistakes. Puppies are good at looking guilty but not so good at remembering events in the past. It's your fault, really—why weren't you supervising an untrained pup? Roll up a newspaper and swat *yourself* over the

nose three times while repeating "I will supervise my puppy."

≈TRISH MCMILLAN, MSc, CPDT-KA, ASPCA
Animal Behavior Center, Urbana, IL

Some dog owners cling to the myth that taking a dog to his mess, rubbing his nose in it, and scolding him sufficiently will teach him not to go potty in the house. In truth, dogs can only associate their behaviors with consequences that fall within two seconds of an occurrence. Taking the dog to the mess after the fact and introducing this type of punishment may create an even larger problem: coprophagia (poop eating).

≈LISA PATRONA, Dip. DTBC, CPDT-KA,
PDT, CBC, Trainers Academy, LLC,
President, Troy, MI

I often hear "My dog knows that he shouldn't potty in the house because he looks guilty when I scold him." But believing this will only weaken your chances at helping your dog build solid housetraining habits, not to mention the damaging effects on your relationship because you believe that somehow he's doing this on purpose to upset you. Your dog looks "guilty" because you are frightening him. He is simply trying to make you stop your scary behavior toward him using displays that, in a dog's mind, should work. Submissive displays, like cowering, or as we humans call it, "looking guilty," have nothing to do with your dog "knowing that he's done something wrong." His submissive postures should tell you that he is recognizing your anger and potential for continued aggression toward him, and he's asking you to please stop. Whether the scolding happens during the behavior or after the fact is not the important factor; the response from the dog will be the same because of your aggressive behavior toward him. Serious problems resulting from punishments during the housetraining process will develop if you continue to use punishment based on your belief in the myth that "he knows he shouldn't potty in the house because he looks guilty."

≈DEVENE GODAU, CPDT-KA, Trainers
Academy, LLC, Royal Oak, MI

HOUSETRAINING, SIGNALING

Want to know when your dog wants to go outside? Teach him to "ring a bell." Hold a bell in front of his nose. When he touches it, click and treat or praise and treat. Repeat many times so that he is always successful. Then hold it so that he has to take a step to touch it, then two steps, etc. Then hang it on the doorknob and ring it every time he goes out. Then start to point to it and get him to ring it before he goes out. Soon you will have a bell-ringing dog! You can also put a bell on the outside so that he can ring it to get your attention to come back inside.

≈DEB WALKER, K9-Behavior Company,
Lake Oswego, OR

No signal to go out? Is your dog's signal too subtle for teenagers or spouse to notice? Get a pet chime and teach your pet how to use it. Rub a little peanut butter on the pet chime pad and reward and treat again when he licks or nudges it hard enough to make it ring. Put one on either side of the door so that your pooch can signal to come in again. This will save your carpets and your doors!

eꝯBECKY SCHULTZ, BA, CPDT-KA,
Becky Schultz Dog Training and
Behavior, Golden Valley, MN

Hang a bell from the door handle of the door that is normally used to let your dog outside. Ring the bell just before letting him outside, each and every time. Most dogs will learn to ring the bell on their own after several weeks of training.

eꝯJENNIFER SCHNEIDER, CPDT-KA,
Pick of the Litter Dog Training,
Seattle/Tacoma Area, WA

You need to teach a clear signal so that your dog can let you know he needs to go out. Routine will help him get started, but without a clear signal, often the owner is trained but not the dog. Possible signals include: a bell on a rope hung on a doorknob; a hotel-type desk bell made especially for dogs; a wireless electronic chime; the use of "targeting" by having the dog tap a human body part like a foot; teaching the dog to sit in front of you and give you eye contact; dog goes to the door and stands or scratches; or dog comes and pesters to get your attention.

eꝯJILL SCHATZ, CPDT-KA, 121 Dog Training, Bondurant, IA

Learn to read your dog's signs that he has to go potty. Common signs are circling, sniffing, pacing, and squatting. When you see these signs, immediately get his attention and redirect him to the door. Then say something in a happy, excited tone, such as "Outside!" and take him out. With repetition, this exercise will help him associate the feeling of having to potty with going to you and to the door.

eꝯANN ALLUMS, CPDT-KA, Best Friends Animal Society, Kanab, UT

Watch your dog's body language—a simple flick of the head toward the door may mean potty time.

eꝯLYNETTE TATAY, Nashville, MI

HUGGING

For the most part, dogs instinctively do not like to be hugged, even though most family dogs with good relationships tolerate it. Most people hug their dogs because they themselves need it! But if hugging is uncomfortable for your dog, minimize this activity unless you are conditioning him (with rewards) to accept it. Your dog's body language will tell you whether he likes a hug. During the embrace, look for signs of stress, which include freezing, looking away, lip licking, yawning, ears back, cowering, pulling away, or rolling over to avoid the hug. After the hug, observe if your dog leaves your space or shakes off, signs that he may not like the embrace.

ANN ALLUMS, CPDT-KA, Best Friends Animal Society, Kanab, UT

IDENTIFICATION

IDs, please! Always make sure that your dog has proper identification. If for any reason he escapes and becomes lost, a collar and tags and/or a microchip will increase the chances he will be returned to you.

JAMIE DAMATO, CPDT-KA, Animalsense Canine Training and Behavior, Inc., Chicago, IL

INDOOR EXERCISE

As dog owners, how can we get our dogs' energy out when we're cooped up inside during bad weather? Try playing some indoor games that will engage your dog—and if you have kids, let them participate too!

ELIZABETH LANGHAM, MS, CPDT-KA, Tree Frog Farm Dog Training and Agility, North Yarmouth, ME

For rainy day fun, create an "obstacle course" in your home. Write different

Licensing your dog is required in most states.

exercises (like "sit-stay for 10 seconds," "down," "find the hidden treat under a cup," etc.) on sticky notes. Post them around your house (in doorways, on the refrigerator, on the coffee table, etc.). Then put your dog on leash. Walk with him from note to note, performing the exercises you have written for yourself. Remember to reward your dog for each exercise or at the end with a big treat or his favorite game. You've just trained, exercised, and bonded with him!

TRACEY SCHOWALTER, Puppy Adept, Inc., Gainesville, GA

Play hide-and-seek with your dog. Dogs love to be with their people, so this game comes fairly naturally and can also teach a dog each family member's name. Let's call the family members Sam and Jane. Jane will hide and Sam will say "Where's Jane?" Jane will take this as a cue and call the dog's name. Once the dog finds Jane, she will offer heaps of reinforcement. Keep repeating the game. Jane should change locations to keep the dog interested. Eventually, she can stop calling him because he will understand what to do when Sam says "Where's Jane?"

ELIZABETH LANGHAM, MS, CPDT-KA,
Tree Frog Farm Dog Training and Agility, North
Yarmouth, ME

Dogs need daily exercise year round. Unfortunately, bad weather, illness, and a host of other things sometimes make it impossible for us to take our buddies for a run in the park or a game of fetch. When you can't get your dog out for physical exercise, give him mental exercise instead. Spend a little time teaching a new trick or behavior, or run him through a repertoire of behaviors he already knows (*sit*, *down*, *stand*, *stay*, *speak*, *come*, etc). There's no substitute for a long run in the fields, but when outdoor exercise is not an option, try working your dog's mind with creative indoor games.

VALERIE CASPERITE, WonderDogs,
West Berlin, NJ

"Find it" is a great indoor game. Use an item that is rewarding to the dog, such as a tennis ball, a bone, or a dog biscuit. Have him get into in a *sit-stay*, and place the item about 5 feet (1.5 m) from him. Say "Find it." He should get up and move to get the reward. Tell him how brilliant he is while he eats or brings back the item. Repeat this a few times. Increase the distance between the dog and item, and slowly make the game more challenging by hiding the item or putting it in another room.

ELIZABETH LANGHAM, MS, CPDT-KA,
Tree Frog Farm Dog Training and Agility,
North Yarmouth, ME

"Back n' forth" is a great rainy day boredom buster. Toss a piece of your dog's kibble down the hall and say "Get it." While he is eating the kibble, say "Daisy, come" (replace "Daisy" with your dog's name) in a bold voice. Toss a treat in the opposite direction and say "Get it." Repeat a few times. Not only have you released a lot of physical energy, but you have also had successes and repetitions of the all-important *come* command!

ELIZABETH LANGHAM, MS, CPDT-KA,
Tree Frog Farm Dog Training and Agility,
North Yarmouth, ME

Introduce a new dog to a resident cat by keeping the dog on leash for several days. Let the cat go where she wants to go, ensuring "safe passage" to her litter box, food, and water. When kitty learns that you won't let her be assaulted by the new dog, her curiosity will get the best of her and she'll start showing up and checking out the new kid in town. Never let the dog chase the cat—not even once—so that your cat will trust you and believe she's safe.

BECKY SCHULTZ, BA, CPDT-KA, Becky Schultz Dog Training and Behavior, Golden Valley, MN

INTRODUCTIONS, CAT-DOG

Cats often adjust slower to new things than dogs do. Don't be alarmed if your cat and new dog or puppy do not act like best buddies. Your cat may simply just learn to tolerate the dog. Time is often the best behavior resolution for your friendly feline. In the meantime, always supervise dog–cat interactions. Watch all interaction around food, toys, litter boxes, and sleeping areas. Always make sure that your cat has a safe place to retreat from the dog. Be quick to distract or interrupt any aggressive or overly playful behavior. Do not punish either the dog or the cat; instead, redirect attention elsewhere. Each pet should learn that when the other pet is around, good things happen. Give them lots of positive associations in the presence of one another.

CRYSTAL COLL, All Ways Pawsitive Pet Behavior and Training, Queen Creek, AZ

To prevent a dog from chasing a cat during the introduction process, attach a leash or drag line to his collar so that he can't practice the chasing behavior. (Don't leave him unattended with the leash attached.) The leash is a management tool to use to limit his ability to chase and should never be used as a correction. You may want to tether the leash to you or near you to limit your dog's options.

ANN ALLUMS, CPDT-KA, Best Friends Animal Society, Kanab, UT

INTRODUCTIONS, DOG-DOG

When introducing a new dog to your household, introduce the two dogs on neutral territory, not in your home. Do not interfere in how the dogs work out their relationship unless there are serious aggression issues. At that point, it would be wise to contact a behavior specialist to help.

CHRISTINA SHUSTERICH, BA, CBC, NY Clever K9, Inc., Queens, NY

If you have decided to add a new pet to your home, have a place for new and existing pets to meet outside the house. You want them to meet on equal turf, not in the original dog's house that he may want to protect from strangers.

ᏋᎫ ANE BRYDON, M.S.Ed., M.Ed., CPDT-KA, Jane Brydon, Dog Training Coach, LLC, Clifton Heights, PA

To help set the stage for a positive first meeting between two dogs, start by conditioning them to associate each other's presence with good things. There should be a handler for each dog, and each handler should have a supply of tasty treats. Gradually move the dogs into each other's presence, and as soon as each dog becomes aware of the other, immediately begin feeding tasty treats to each dog. In this way, both dogs will learn to associate the other with something pleasant right off the bat.

ᏋᎫ ANN ALLUMS, CPDT-KA, Best Friends Animal Society, Kanab, UT

Prepare a large crate as the temporary safe house for the new pet. A sturdy wire crate may be best because it allows the new animal to see and study his environment while remaining protected from the other pet or pets. Cover the top of the crate and two sides with a blanket and place the crate against a wall, facing outward into the room. Supervise all interactions among the new and existing pets, and gradually let the new pet out of the crate for supervised interactions. Gradually increase the time the new and existing pets are allowed to interact. Leave leashes on the pets while they interact under your direct supervision so that you can quickly pull them apart if necessary. Don't leave the pets alone at home together until you are certain they will not harm one another.

ᏋᎫ LUCINDA LUDWIG, Canine Connection LLC, Dubuque, IA

Most dogs are more than willing to help us raise the puppy we bring home. It is the established pet's duty to let the puppy know the rules about toys, space, and food. A growl or a snarl is a dog's way of warning that something worse is coming if the pup doesn't back off. If you scold the older dog for this behavior, you are giving all the wrong signals and minimizing the established dog's status. You need to stay out of this communication and see if the puppy responds politely to the warning by backing off, or whether he responds inappropriately by demanding to take the toy, space, or food even after a growl or snarl. If the pup doesn't back down, honor the older dog's status by giving the pup a quick and sudden time-out. This involves picking up or quickly taking him to an isolation area (bathroom, bedroom) with a phrase that is only used in this situation, such as "You blew it!" or "Time-out!" Close the door and count to 10 or 15 seconds. When the pup is not whining or barking, he can come out and join the family again. Dogs hate isolation and will learn to avoid it by stopping the behavior that brings it on.

&TERI THOMAS, CPDT-KA, Angels in the Making, LLC, Grand Junction, CO

If it's not possible for the new pet to meet the current resident on neutral territory, place a towel in your dog's bed, then find a way to take that towel to the location where the new dog currently resides. If you do not have that luxury, at least use the towel when transporting the new dog home. This will help the new dog become familiar with your dog's scent.

&HEDDIE LEGER, The PawZone, LLC, Liberty, MO

When introducing dogs who have never met, have them take a walk next to each other before putting them in the yard together.

&MELANIE MCKEEHAN, Assistant Director of Operations, Red Dog Pet Resort and Spa, Cincinnati, OH

When your dog is meeting another dog on leash, make sure that you keep tension out of the leash. The leash can be short, for control, but still loose. If it's safe, drop the leash and let the dogs interact naturally. If your dog feels strangled every time he sees another dog, he will start to dislike other dogs. Tight leashes and restricted body language lead to leash aggression.

&JULIE HUMISTON, CPDT-KA, Puppy Love Dog Training, Minneapolis, MN

It's not a good idea to let your dog approach another dog without asking permission from his owner first. If the other dog is shy, fearful, or aggressive, he could lash out at your dog. If the dog is at the veterinarian's office, he could have a contagious disease. Always ask permission from the dog's owner before you go near to make sure that it's okay for your dog to say hello.

&TEOTI ANDERSON, CPDT-KA, Pawsitive Results, LLC, Lexington, SC

INTRODUCTIONS, DOG—HUMAN

Even if a dog approaches you, this doesn't necessarily mean that he's friendly. Wait for him to curl his body in front, almost touching you. Then drape your hand gently along his back. Avoid approaching dogs to say hello—let them come to you and look for the curl.

&MAUREEN SCHOOLEY, Blue Paws, Inc., New Port Richey, FL

When you are approaching a dog you don't know very well, try not to look him directly in the eye, as this is a threatening approach. Look at his ears instead. Also, approach the dog at an angle instead of a straight line. When you pet him, don't bring your hand over his head. Instead, pet him under the chin.

&DARLENE KOZA, Scooter's School of Sit & Stay, Rochester, NY

JOGGING

I have a Collie who loves to jog with me. I'm working on interval training, where I walk for a short time and then jog for a short time. When I change pace, I sometimes surprise her and she jumps up to give me a herding-dog nip. By giving her a cue (I use "Move it!"), she gets a warning and is much more relaxed about pace changes.

&JILL MILLER, CPDT-KA, Mad City Dog Training, Madison, WI

JUMPING UP

To prevent jumping up on guests, start by training your dog not to jump up on your family. Do not reinforce jumping up behavior in any way, either by petting, looking at, or pushing your dog away. Just ignore him and step sideways. When your dog has all four paws on the floor, verbally praise, pet, or treat him.

&CHRISTINA SHUSTERICH, BA, CBC, NY Clever K9, Inc., New York, NY

Dogs jump up to greet you. They want to smell your face and your breath. But depending on their size, they might tip you over, rip your stocking, or put muddy paw prints on your business clothes that you just had dry-cleaned. Stopping this behavior is easy. You just have to make sure that from this day forward, you will never allow the dog to jump up on you again. Arm yourself with treats before you enter the house. You end this annoyance by turning your back on your dog when he jumps up on you. Don't give him any attention—no eye contact, no talking. Simply fold your arms across your chest and turn away from him. Now here is the important part: The second he stops jumping on you, say "Good dog!" and immediately put a treat in his mouth. He can be sitting or just standing there—it doesn't matter. You are going to reward *anything* that is not jumping on you. If he jumps again, repeat the exercise. He will quickly learn that jumping gets him nothing, but not jumping gets him attention and a wonderful treat.

ℰJANE BRYDON, MS.Ed., M.Ed., CPDT-KA, Jane Brydon, Dog Training Coach, LLC, Clifton Heights, PA

Teach your pup that jumping means that you remove your attention altogether. He only gets attention when all four paws are on the floor. Practice switching quickly from "Yay, good puppy!" to "Humph!" so that you can deliver effective feedback. Work on teaching no jumping for the first five minutes after you come home each day this week, and remember to practice no-jump greetings even if your pup has stopped jumping. Success is a muscle that should be exercised. You should notice your puppy's jumping steadily decrease over time!

ℰJACQUELYN ENGLAND, A Dog's Life, Sunnyvale, CA

For jumping up on people, I tether the dog with about 6 feet (2 m) of leash and walk out of jumping range. With a fistful of treats, I walk back up to the dog, say "Hi" in a happy, excited manner, and then if he starts to jump, I abruptly turn away and walk out of range of the leash. I then turn back for another trial, and if the dog either sits or keeps four on the floor (even for just a moment), I say "Yes!" (or click) and treat. With a few repetitions, dogs get this game very quickly. Even children can be the greeters, with adults marking the moment the child should give the treat.

ℰJANIS DOLPHIN, Mendocino DogSports, Gualala, CA

Make sure that anyone who comes in contact with your puppy is not rewarding jumping behavior. Even one person rewarding jumping will cause the bad behavior to continue.

ℰDARLENE KOZA, Scooter's School of Sit & Stay, Rochester, NY

Strangers unwittingly sabotage your no-jumping rule in short order by giving your pup attention with only two paws down. You can still deliver "Humphs" even though your dog isn't jumping on you. Simply step away from the stranger with your pup in tow as soon as he jumps up. Ask people to only pet your pup when he's on the ground, or lure him into a *sit* for all greetings.

ℰJACQUELYN ENGLAND, A Dog's Life, Sunnyvale, CA

J

If your dog is jumping on you, most likely he wants your attention. Therefore, the best way to stop the behavior is to not give attention for it. When your dog jumps up on you, simply step away from him—he can't stay up on a moving target. Never say anything or look at him during this exercise, or it could be perceived by him as attention. After you step away and the dog's four paws are back on the ground, then praise him. The jumping may get worse before it gets better, but the jumping will start to subside on its own.

✍STEPHANIE JUHASZ, Smarter Than The Average Dog, S. Londonderry, VT

Are you having trouble with your dog jumping up on you? Dogs jump because they want attention, and they will continue to jump if it is working for them. Some of us may think that we are not paying attention to our dog, but if the behavior exists, the dog is getting reinforced for it. Try turning your back on the dog who is jumping on you. If that still doesn't work, while he is jumping on you, say a word or phrase that communicates to him "you blew it," and leave the room. Take a minute break from the dog. Return to the room, and if he jumps again, say the "you blew it" phrase again and leave the room

once more. Continue until the jumping has stopped. Teach your dog that the consequence of jumping on you leads to your removal.

✍NICOLE CORSON, CTC, CPDT-KA, Wag This Way™, Salt Lake City, UT

If your dog is jumping to solicit your attention, keep in mind that *any* form of attention might be enough incentive to keep him jumping. If you think what you are doing is negative or punishing to your dog, look at how he reacts to what you are doing. If you push him down and say "No!" but he keeps jumping, he is being rewarded. If he does jump, do *not* talk to, touch, or make eye contact with him. Ask him to perform an incompatible behavior, such as a *sit* or *down*, *before* he has a chance to jump.

✍SUE BROWN, CDBC, CPDT-KA, Love My Dog Training, Littleton, CO

Is your dog jumping up? The best way to stop a behavior you don't like is to replace it with one you want. Teach your dog that sitting gets him everything he wants, and he'll be too busy sitting to jump!

✍LAUREL SCARIONI, CPDT-KA, Pawsitive Results Critter Academy, Santa Rosa, CA

You can teach your boisterous puppy an alternative to jumping on people in greeting by teaching him to "hand target" instead. By teaching him to touch his nose to an outstretched palm, you give him something specific to do instead of jumping. Start by presenting your flat hand, palm toward his face, just a couple of inches (cm) from his nose. When he looks at it or sniffs it, say "Yes!" and give him a treat. Gradually, only reward him when he actually touches his nose to it. Now you can add the cue "Say hello!" This is also a great behavior to teach to shy dogs who are afraid of people reaching for them.

TERRY LONG, CPDT-KA, DogPACT Training and Behavior Services, Long Beach, CA

Giving your dog a lot of attention for jumping up rarely solves the problem. When you say "No" or yell "Off," you are still giving him attention, and that's what he wants. Ask yourself what you want your dog to do instead. Most people want the pup to stand or sit—not jump! Ignore the behavior by folding your arms and putting your fists into your armpits. Don't look at him or say a word. Turn around and face away from him if necessary.
The very second the pup has four paws on the floor, say "Yes" or click. Then give a treat. Have others do the same. Remind them that you are training your dog, and you don't want him to jump on anyone, ever!

GLORIA J. WHITE, CPDT-KA, Pawsitive Waggers Training, Cincinnati, OH

You can't always control the behavior of other people who may undermine your training by petting your jumping dog. Until your dog can control himself, help him out. Ask him to sit, but if he can't, just calmly stand on the leash or (for tall dogs) hold the leash near the clip. If the dog sits, the leash will be short but loose. If he starts to jump, the leash will prevent it. You can stand calmly and ignore him until he sits, and he won't be able to jump enough to put his paws on the visitor.

JULIE HUMISTON, CPDT-KA, Puppy Love Dog Training, Minneapolis, MN

Does your dog jump up? Train yourself: When he jumps, shut your mouth, cross your arms, and turn your back. If your dog jumps on your back, step away. When he has four feet on the floor or offers a *sit*, you can now talk to and pet him. But be prepared—if you start to pet him and he jumps up again, cross your arms, shut your mouth, and turn your back. As the dog learns that jumping up gets him ignored, the behavior will gradually go away.

ELAINE COUPÉ, For Pet's Sake (& Memphis Agility), Oakland, TN

Is your dog jumping up on people? Use a head harness for maximum control of him. Have him meet five new people every day and practice "sitting politely for greeting." Quietly praise and treat him for sitting for greeting. Keep the leash short enough to prevent his feet from touching a person. Remind him to sit, then reward. If you do this with five new people every day, your dog should learn this behavior very quickly!

BECKY SCHULTZ, BA, CPDT-KA, Becky Schultz Dog Training and Behavior, Golden Valley, MN

Jumping up is one of the most common complaints I hear from dog owners and one of the easiest to eliminate. Ignore the behavior. Every time you push your dog, or say "Off," or even yell at him, you are rewarding him by giving him just what he is jumping up for: your attention. Ignore the dog while he is jumping, and once he has "four on the floor," be quick to reward him. Be consistent and practice with different people, making sure that they follow your training rules.

◠ANN W. FIRESTONE, CPDT-KA, DogSense In-Home Training and Behavior Service, South Acworth, NH

If your dog jumps up on you the instant you walk through the door or let him out of the crate, plan to arrive home and ignore him for a few minutes. This will give your dog time to calm down and also reinforce the idea that he does not get your attention until he settles down and stops jumping. After a few minutes, approach your dog, ask for a *sit*, and reward him with your attention. You may also reward him with a food treat for sitting–this can decrease the amount of time it takes for him to learn to sit for your attention when he is excited.

◠JENNIFER SCHNEIDER, CPDT-KA, Pick of the Litter Dog Training, Seattle/Tacoma Area, WA

Dogs jump up to greet us and to get our attention. However, not everyone likes it when they jump up, and because dogs don't generalize well, we need to teach them not to jump up unless they are expressly invited. Dogs are reinforced for jumping every time we give them any attention for this behavior, especially if the attention is occasional. When a dog jumps up, you can help him learn polite greetings if you:

- Don't pet him.
- Don't touch him to push him off.
- Don't talk to him or say "Off."
- Don't look at him.
- Don't knee or step on him.

Teach a dog not to jump by consistently taking away your attention for the behavior and by reinforcing him for not jumping.

◠ANN ALLUMS, CPDT-KA, Best Friends Animal Society, Kanab, UT

KEEP-AWAY — Green

To prevent your dog from playing keep-away, try the two-ball retrieve. Start with two identical toys/balls. Throw one of them. As the dog returns with his ball, show the second one. Bounce your "fun" ball, and make it seem so much more interesting that he *has* to drop his. Your dog may try to convince you that his is really the fun ball, but don't fall for it. The second he drops his ball say "Yes!" and throw your "fun" ball past him, nice and low, so that he has to chase it. Pick up the first ball while he's getting the second one. When he returns, show him that *you* have the fun ball again and he has the boring ball.

ᴇ✑TRISH MCMILLAN, MSc, CPDT-KA, ASPCA
Animal Behavior Center, Urbana, IL

KITCHEN MANNERS

Are you tripping over your dog when preparing meals? Place a mat where he can see you and be near you in the kitchen but not in the way or under your feet. Teach him to target the mat by rewarding him when any part of his body contacts it. Next, teach your dog to sit-stay or down-stay on the mat. Reward him for staying on the mat often at first, then introduce a random reward schedule. Soon you'll have a dog who waits quietly on the mat while you're preparing meals for a small tidbit every now and again.

ᴇ✑KIM WELLS, CPDT-KA, Kim Wells
Companion Dog Training Services, Airdrie,
Alberta, Canada

LARGE BREEDS

If you have a puppy who will grow up to be a big dog, consider getting a crate that will fit him when he's full grown that comes with a divider. You can move the divider as he grows. Most puppies will not soil their dens. For the purpose of housetraining, a crate should just be big enough for your puppy to stand up, stretch out and turn around in. A larger crate will enable him to pee in a corner and still remain dry, so it may not teach him to hold his bladder. If you purchase a crate with a divider, you'll achieve the goal of confinement for housetraining without having to buy different-sized crates as your little puppy grows into a large adult.

ᴇ✑TEOTI ANDERSON, CPDT-KA, Pawsitive
Results, LLC, Lexington, SC

Giant breeds are not considered adults until about the age of three. If you have a large- or giant-breed puppy, just because his body is big doesn't mean that his development has reached adulthood. So if your 75-pound (34-kg), one-year-old Golden Retriever is still chewing your couch, this isn't unusual. He's still a baby! Be patient.

ᴇ✑TEOTI ANDERSON, CPDT-KA, Pawsitive
Results, LLC, Lexington, SC

K
L

Don't start your giant breed puppy on a giant-sized leash. When your puppy leans into his collar and pulls, you won't even notice—then the puppy learns to pull! Start your giant breed puppy on a new 1/4-inch-wide (6-mm) leather leash. You'll definitely notice when your puppy pulls even a little. You won't allow your puppy to pull, because the leash will hurt your hand. You'll be cognizant of every move your pup makes on his leash and you will remember that all of your pup's time on his leash is training time. A pup who learns to walk nicely on his 1/4 inch (6 mm) leash grows into a dog who doesn't pull on a 1/4 inch (6 mm) leash. The big payoff comes when you can walk your 150 pound (6– kg) dog on his 1/4 inch (6 mm) leash. Everybody will be amazed at what a great dog trainer you are!

⌒MARTY SWINDELL, BS, CPDT-KA,
LickSkillet Dog Training, Lee's Summit, MO

I once worked with a six-month-old Rhodesian Ridgeback who had been expelled from his puppy class during the first week. He was absolutely panic stricken to the point of attempting to crawl right up his owner's body, digging in with his nails all the way. It didn't take long to recognize that this very large puppy was also very immature. He was so awkward that he stumbled over his own feet every few steps. His confidence level was so low it's no wonder he panicked when asked to keep up with the older dogs in regular class. We worked privately for several weeks to teach the dog how to get in touch with his own body. Teaching him to do turns, back up, and move forward at his own comfortable pace soon had him feeling more comfortable and moving zmore confidently. Then I moved him into the puppy class, where he had a chance to socialize and be the puppy he was. At about eight months, he was confident enough to move easily and very successfully into the regular obedience class. Lesson learned—don't rush the giants!

⌒JOAN B. GUERTIN, Common Sense Dog
Training and Behavior Solutions, East Texas

A swing finish isn't just for competition obedience. Students with large and giant breeds often struggle with trying to maneuver their dog to their left side to practice heeling exercises or just to get the dog out of their way. The formal swing finish gives them a tool to manage their big dog and is easy for students and dogs to learn with a lure. Mastering this particular command also gives beginning students a lot of confidence and pride in

Genetic evidence suggests that an evolutionary split of dogs and wolves occurred about 100,000 years ago.

their training abilities, as well as their dog's ability to learn. Young puppies can learn this exercise easily. It's really a necessity for large- or giant-breed pups.

ᴇ⁄MARTY SWINDELL, CPDT-KA, LickSkillet Dog Training, Lee's Summit, MO

LEADERSHIP — Purple

Dogs need a sense of security, to know that someone is in charge. Dogs, like most of the rest of us, function best in a world that makes sense, one that has clear rules. In fact, if a dog is uncertain about the rules, he will often take it upon himself to make them up and enforce them. This is not a bad trait; it is his effort to help things go smoothly and make life predictable. The downside is that we can end up with a dog who makes rules that don't fit in our human household very well. So be a good leader. Establishing leadership does not mean establishing dominance through "alpha" posturing or manhandling. Clarifying leadership merely requires that there be no doubt that you and other humans are the source of all good things, that your dog can always look to you for direction and structure, and that the rules are predictable and consistent.

ᴇ⁄ANN ALLUMS, CPDT-KA, Best Friends Animal Society, Kanab, UT

Dogs have behavior problems not because of "dominance" but because of a lack of clear communication between dog and owner. Sometimes dogs engage in objectionable behaviors because they simply weren't trained and they don't know what we want them to do. Other times behavior problems can be based on fear and frustration, and these issues need to be addressed with the assistance of a behavior professional. The old-time belief that a dog is trying to "be the alpha" and dominate you is incorrect and often leads to fear, anxiety, and / or aggressive behaviors from the dog.

ᴇ⁄MYCHELLE BLAKE, MSW, CDBC, Las Vegas, NV

Dogs need to feel secure to be truly happy. This means that they need to feel secure that you will be their leader and that they can count on you to take charge. As leader, your duties are to establish the rules, enforce the rules, and maintain social order.

⁊LISA HOLLANDER, ABC Certified, DogGone Proud Dog Obedience/Behavior Modification, Lexington, KY

The role of decision maker must be held by the humans in a family (or pack, as understood by the dog). The following simple game clears up any questions as to who is making decisions. The humans are always "Simon." So when a family member initiates something, such as play, calling the dog over for attention, or making a request (like sit), then it's okay because "Simon says." When the dog (who is not Simon) initiates something, such as bringing over a toy to play or demanding attention, he should be ignored because "Simon didn't say." The Simon is always in charge. I find this a particularly good illustration when I'm teaching children how to display leadership every day.

⁊PENNY LOCKE, Dog Listener, All About Canines, Novato, CA

LEASHES

Leashes keep your dog safe, and not just from the obvious dangers, like cars. Leashes will help prevent him from devouring garbage, drinking contaminated water, and eating animal feces, which can lead to diseases like parvovirus. Dogs might also find dead animal carcasses— gourmet cuisine for Fido! You want to be able to prevent all access to these things.

⁊DEVENE GODAU, CPDT-KA, Trainers Academy, LLC, Royal Oak, MI

When you are training your dog in a public area, use a leash. This is important for his safety, as well as the safety of other dog or people present. A 6- to 8-foot (2- to 3-m) leash is ideal when training basic commands that require you to be near your dog.

⁊NATALIA ROZAS DE O'LAUGHLIN, CDPT, Houston Pet Help, Houston, TX

Leashes are excellent tools to use in the house as well as outside. They can be used to work on polite leash walking, to prevent jumping on guests or children, and also to help you monitor your pet.

⁊TINA M. SPRING VAN WHY, Sit Happens Dog Training & Behavior, Athens, GA

When training your dog, use a regular 4- to 6-foot (1- to 2-m) leash. Avoid using retractable leashes to train. Even if you lock them, they're still bulky to hold. They also provide constant tension on your dog's collar, which may cause him to learn that there should always be tension on his collar; when you put a regular leash on him, he'll pull to get that same sensation. Save retractable leashes for exercising your dog or for walking him after he learns how to walk politely without pulling.

⁊TEOTI ANDERSON, CPDT-KA, Pawsitive Results, LLC, Lexington, SC

Leashes give you more control when meeting up with other dogs. Your dog may love other dogs, but can you be sure about the other dogs you meet?

&DEVENE GODAU, CPDT-KA, Trainers Academy, LLC, Royal Oak, MI

Using retractable leashes on walks allows dogs room to explore and get more exercise than by just walking alongside the owner.

&KAREN COTTINGHAM, Primetime Pet Services, Salisbury, MD

When training your dog, keep him on leash, but drop the leash to the ground and step on it or tether it to a fence or tree. This will prevent you from tugging on the leash unnecessarily if you hold it in your hand. I see people who automatically tug on the leash when they get frustrated or the dog gets distracted or nonresponsive, and this only confuses your dog instead of helping him learn.

&NATALIA ROZAS DE O'LAUGHLIN, CDPT, Houston Pet Help, Houston, TX

When training a dog to walk on a loose leash, the first thing he needs to learn is the length of the leash. To do this, make sure that the length of the leash is always the same. This means, at least at first, that you must not use an expandable leash. Choose a certain-length leash and always walk with it. Hold the leash properly. Put your whole hand through the loop and hold on to a part of the length of the leash. Choose a section close to the loop so as to not shorten the leash too much. Now make sure that you don't change the length of the leash by extending your arm in front of you. You also do not want to shorten it by wrapping it around your hand a million times. I suggest putting your hand in your pocket or looping a finger or two through a belt loop.

&COLLEEN B. HURLEY, Orlando, FL, and Gainesville, FL

If you take your dog to a dog park or other enclosed large running area, you may find that he doesn't come when he sees the leash in your hand. The reason is that he has learned that "leash in mommy's hand means play ends." Do not let the leash in your hand become an indicator that fun stops. When you are playing with your dog in an area where he can run free, sometimes let him play while dragging his leash, then remove the leash and play, put the leash on and play, put the leash on and play another game, or take the leash off and continue playing. Avoid establishing a pattern that you *only* put the leash back on the dog when you are done and going home.

&PAM SHEEHAN, 4 Paws Training, LLC, Broken Arrow, OK

L

A leash telegraphs information. Through its vibrations, your dog can tell where you are and how you feel. If you're anxious, that will travel down the leash to him. To help maintain control of a reactive dog, step on the leash! Find the spot that will give him some slack but keep him close. This breaks the angle of force if your dog pulls and gives you more control. Your weight on the leash secures him, stops tension from radiating down the leash to him, and partially frees your hands to do other things (wave clueless people off, click and treat your dog, etc.).

ᥲ ANN DUPUIS, CPDT-KA, Your Dream Dog, Randolph, MA

Except in areas where it is unsafe or unwise to do so, trainers should train off leash. Nothing will show you quicker the effectiveness of your training/reinforcement schedule than a dog who can walk away! If your dog is leaving you to go and do something more interesting, chances are your criteria are unclear and your reinforcement schedule is too low. Working without a leash forces you to find ways to be interesting, reinforcing, and a clear communicator. Because if you're not, most dogs will walk away to find something more interesting to do. Use that information to change your behavior.

ᥲ PAM SHEEHAN, 4 Paws Training, LLC, Broken Arrow, OK

Many areas have local leash laws—keep your dog leashed if you want to avoid fines.

ᥲ DEVENE GODAU, CPDT-KA, Trainers Academy, LLC, Royal Oak, MI

Never tie your dog out on a leash on a balcony. He can easily hang himself when trying to go after a squirrel or other attraction.

ᥲ LUCINDA LUDWIG, Canine Connection LLC, Dubuque, IA

LEAVE IT

Teaching your dog the *leave it* command is very useful for the times when you want him to leave a small or dangerous animal, food dropped on the floor, or other things or people. With your dog on leash, flex your foot with your heel on the floor, and place a treat on the floor near your foot. Move your foot nearer the treat if necessary so that you can lower your foot over the treat if your dog lunges for it. Command your dog to "leave it." He will most likely try to get the treat until he learns the meaning of the command. When he attempts to get the treat, simply lower your foot over it, then pick up your foot and try again. When your dog leaves the treat, reward him with a tastier treat, such as a hotdog, from your other hand. At first, practice for a short time and then gradually increase the time you ask your dog to "leave it."

ᥲ LUCINDA LUDWIG, Canine Connection LLC, Dubuque, IA

I find that when some clients teach *leave it* to their dog, they reward him with the treat that they just asked him to "leave." I teach that *leave it* means that the dog can't *ever* have whatever the item may be.

≈LISA L. SICKLES, CPDT CDBC, WagWag Enterprises, Englewood, CO

LITTER BOXES

How to stop your dog from eating "Kitty Roca" out of the litter box? I sprayed bitter apple, hot sauce, pepperoncini juice, and mint (separately) in the box and along the insides and roof, as well as in the droppings, once a day for a week, then weekly for a month. Enough residual scent remained in the roof of the box to deter any more "visits." Help your dog safely associate "yuck" to litter waste, and the job is done.

≈CYNTHIA KURTZ, The Pet Geek, West Linn/Sandy, OR

A dog is going to eat cat poop. Unfortunately, there is no humane way to stop this behavior because cat poop is very tempting to a dog. It is disgusting to us, but a dog has different tastes—accept this fact!

Most dogs tend to be lactose intolerant.

The best solution is a prevention strategy—keeping the cat box out of your dog's reach. Make sure that it is still convenient for the cat, but perhaps put the litter box in a closet with a narrow opening, in another room that only cats can access, on a shelf, or in a privacy box.

≈ANN ALLUMS, CPDT-KA, Best Friends Animal Society, Kanab, UT

People ask me all the time, "How do I stop my dog from eating kitty krunchies from the litter box?" Sometimes a little management is all you need. Raise the litter box to a shelf or counter that the dog cannot reach but that the cat can still jump to. Or get a covered litter box so that the dog can't graze at an open box.

≈PAULA KELMAN, CPDT-KA, Eagle Ridge Kennels, Buffalo, NY

LITTERMATE SYNDROME

When littermates become too aggressive with people or animals, separate them completely for 21 days with the guidance of a trainer. They'll start to think as individuals, not a pack, and in turn the aggression will diminish.

≈SANDRA ENGLAND, DogBoys Dog Ranch, Pflugerville, TX

LOST DOG

If your dog is lost and you are looking for him, bring along one of his best buddies if you can. One dog may pick up the scent of the other.

≈CERENA ZUTIS, CZ Dog Training, CA

The timing of your marker word is very important in training. Because it "marks" the behavior the dog was doing at that instant, the better your timing, the faster he will learn what brings rewards and what you want.

ANN ALLUMS, CPDT-KA, Best Friends
Animal Society, Kanab, UT

Don't confuse marker words with rewards. For instance, "Good boy" is generally said as praise, which is a reward. Rewards always come after marking the behavior.

ANN ALLUMS, CPDT-KA, Best Friends
Animal Society, Kanab, UT

LURING

Use lure reward training to train your dog to sit and lie down by luring him into those positions and then rewarding him. Because dogs do what works and because they get rewards for completing those behaviors, they'll start offering them for you. You can use this technique to teach your dog anything you can lure him to do, like play dead, roll over, spin, sit pretty, take a bow, etc.

JACQUELYN ENGLAND, A Dog's Life,
Sunnyvale, CA

MARKER

A marker is a sound or short word that, when consistently followed by a treat, tells the dog he did something you like. It predicts a reward, and it bridges the gap between the behavior and the reward. The marker word should be said the instant the dog does what you want and is always followed by some kind of reward. When training, use one marker word consistently. Examples of marker words are "yes," "good," and "right."

ANN ALLUMS, CPDT-KA, Best Friends
Animal Society, Kanab, UT

MEDICATING

If your dog refuses to eat a bitter pill, crush it and add it to a small bite of tuna fish. Dogs seem to love tuna fish, so you can use it for many "difficult" situations.

KATERINA HADZIYANNI, Humane
Training, Athens, Greece

Desensitize your puppy or dog to syringes for giving liquid medicines and dewormers. Fill a syringe with chicken broth. Let your dog lick the syringe, and squirt a small

TOP TIDBIT

Marking a correct behavior means that you are making it clear to the dog which behavior he has performed correctly.

amount into the side of his mouth. Repeat this several times. He will associate the sight of the syringe with a delicious taste and will not avoid the medicine.

ꙮBARBARA LONG, CPDT-KA, Paw in Hand Dog Training, Chapel Hill, NC

For ease in administering a pill to a dog, hide the pill in a very palatable piece of food, such as a tidbit of hotdog, butter, steak, chicken, or canned dog food–items that the dog can and is willing to swallow readily. A long-handled spoon makes it easy to deliver a bite of canned food to the dog.

ꙮANN ALLUMS, CPDT-KA, Best Friends Animal Society, Kanab, UT

Eventually, we all have to give our dogs medication, short or long term. You can avoid having to force pills or capsules down your dog's throat by teaching him to take them willingly. Start by rolling a moist treat in the shape of a pill. Have your dog sit in front of you. Let him see that you have a treat (pill) to give him. Say "Open" and gently lift his upper jaw by the top front teeth. As soon as his mouth opens, drop the treat in the back of his mouth. Be sure to praise him when he swallows it. Practice this often, and when you do have to move to medicine or vitamins, always follow with a treat. If your dog understands that "open" means something good (a tasty treat), you'll both be less stressed when it matters most.

ꙮHELENE KOBELNYK, My Lifelong Friend K-9 Academy, Capitan, NM

When trying to give a dog a pill or vitamin, instead of shoving it down his throat, push the pill through a small piece of bread and tell him it's a treat.

ꙮSHANNAN BESSEY, The Well Trained Dog, Omaha, NE

MEDICATIONS — Pink

Understand what the side effects are of all medications prescribed for your dog. You have the responsibility of informed consent where your dog has no say.

ꙮKATHERINE ROLLINS, CPDT-KA, Kat's K9 Cadets, Greenville, TN

MENTAL EXERCISE —

Obedience training is a great mental exercise. Thinking is a tiring activity for dogs, just as it is for humans. Most dogs really enjoy a rapid-paced, exciting game of "come here," "sit," "heel," "sit," "heel," "down," "stay"… You can play "come here" and reward with hugs, a massage, a celebration of praise and treats. Don't allow training to be a boring, tedious routine.

ꙮCRYSTAL COLL, All Ways Pawsitive Pet Behavior and Training, Queen Creek, AZ

> **Mental stimulation can be as exhausting as physical exercise.**

Give your dog something mentally stimulating to do while you're at work. Dogs get bored when they are left alone for long periods (and some for short periods). If you don't give him something to do, he will figure something out on his own. Usually, a dog's first choice is to chew. After that it goes something like: lick, dig, shred, and bark. You get the picture, and it's not pretty. Try distributing his morning breakfast into several different treat toys, and place them throughout the house (or in a crate for crate-trained dogs). Your dog will enjoy the variety, the challenge of the task, and the reward.

ℰ TONIA WHILDEN, Houston Dog Ranch, Houston, TX

MOTIVATION

It's hard to motivate a dog if you don't know what he likes. Make a list of your dog's favorite foods, activities, and toys. Then decide which ones you will reserve as reinforcers during training. Update the list as he matures. He may find playing with toilet paper super reinforcing at five months old but less so at five years old.

ℰ DIANE PODOLSKY, CPDT-KA, CTC, The Cultured Canine, LLC, White Plains, NY

Always, always, always make yourself think "What is motivating this dog?" whenever attempting to train or otherwise modify a behavior.

Remember that each and every dog is an individual, so what works for one may not necessarily work for another. The key is to motivate the dog and figure out how to make him *want* to respond (and not out of fear either). If you crack that code, you will be halfway there.

ℰ LORENA B. PATTI, MS, CPDT-KA, ABCDT, AKC CGC Evaluator, Waggers Doggie Daycare & Training, Orlando, FL

MOUNTING

Mounting is a common behavior in dogs (both male and female), and although embarrassing, it's usually nothing to worry about. Usually, it's a much bigger problem for us than it is for our dogs! If your dog is mounting other dogs during playtime, keep an eye on the interaction, and give them a break from the play before the mounting starts. Work to keep the excitement level down and allow brief and frequent

If your dog is mouthy or rough when taking a treat from a human hand, then you need to make sure that you do not reward this behavior by letting him have the treat. Hold the treat in such a way that he has to use his tongue instead of his teeth to get it. If this isn't working and you are concerned, seek the help of a certified trainer or behavior consultant.

ePATRICIA BENTZ, CPDT-KA, CDBC,
K-9 Training & Behavioral Therapy,
Philadelphia, PA

interaction, but be sure to stop it before he's started to mount. If you are unable to stop it before it starts, remove him from play immediately (as soon as the behavior starts) for a brief 20- to 30-second time-out and then let him interact again. If your dog starts mounting again, repeat the time-out. It shouldn't take more than a couple of time-outs for him to get the message that if he wants to continue to play, mounting makes the play stop and is not a good idea!

eLISA PATRONA, Dip. DTBC, CPDT-KA,
PDT, CBC, Trainers Academy, LLC,
President, Troy, MI

MOUTHING

If your puppy is mouthing you, redirect him immediately to a rawhide or other interesting chew, and praise him for chewing on those items.

eANN ALLUMS, CPDT-KA, Best Friends
Animal Society, Kanab, UT

If your puppy is mouthing or nipping hard during play, end the session. He will learn that mouthing you during play has consequences, and he will eventually stop doing it.

eMYCHELLE BLAKE, MSW, CDBC,
Las Vegas, NV

For mouthing/teething problems with puppies, get two rope toys with knots on the end. Put them in a bowl and pour a can of low-sodium beef or chicken broth over them. After an hour, shake off the excess broth, put the toys into two baggies, and freeze. When your pup starts mouthing something, get the frozen rope and then clap your hands and say "No." When your pup looks up, give him the rope and lots of praise.

ePETER GOBEL, Training-U to train your pet,
Randolph, MA

Try emitting a short, startling "OUCH" the instant your dog's teeth touch your skin. The goal is for him to stop biting on you or learn to be gentle, at which point you can then praise him for *not* biting you the instant the behavior stops or praise him for behavior like gentle licking instead. If your dog doesn't react to the "OUCH," then still say the word "OUCH" to mark the behavior that causes it, and follow by immediately turning your back on him for 30 seconds, leaving the room for 30 seconds, or giving him a 30-second time-out in another room. Then come back for more interaction until he learns that teeth on skin cause you to immediately go away, which is the opposite of what he wants. Be consistent, and do not let the mouthing or biting to escalate. It's important to react instantly when you feel your dog's teeth on you so that he doesn't get any more practice engaging in this behavior.

℅ANN ALLUMS, CPDT-KA, Best Friends Animal Society, Kanab, UT

MOVING

To make moving less stressful, ensure that your dog is in compliance with local legal and health requirements. Keep a health certificate handy if you are moving across state lines.

℅MARGARET JOHNSON, CPDT-KA, The Humane Trainer Inc., Austin, TX

Consider boarding your dog or having him stay with a friend to avoid being lost during the move. If you do keep your dog at home during the move, keep him in a crate or a secure room to which only you have access. Placing his familiar bedding, water, and toys with him may help him feel more comfortable.

℅MARGARET JOHNSON, CPDT-KA, The Humane Trainer Inc., Austin, TX

Taking a few minutes during the moving process to give your dog a little extra exercise can significantly reduce his stress level (and yours!). A nice, relaxing walk with your best furry friend could be just what the doctor ordered for both of you during this time.

℅MARGARET JOHNSON, CPDT-KA, The Humane Trainer Inc., Austin, TX

Dogs can get lost during the confusion of moving day. Make sure that your dog's identification tags include your name, address, and a phone number where you can be reached, and securely attach them to your dog. Microchips are a safe and more permanent way of ensuring that he can always be identified. Carry a current color photo of your dog, and have a detailed written description of his height, weight, age, sex, and any other distinguishing characteristics in case he does get separated from you.

୧୬MARGARET JOHNSON, CPDT-KA, The Humane Trainer Inc., Austin, TX

If you are moving to a different environment (i.e., suburbs to city), remember that this change may seem drastic to your dog. If possible, take him to visit your new home prior to your move to help ease him into this change. Remember that dogs are not toasters, and they don't just "plug right in" to a new environment. Until your dog acclimates to his new home, it is best to keep him safely confined or supervised.

୧୬MARGARET JOHNSON, CPDT-KA, The Humane Trainer Inc., Austin, TX

Help your dog make the transition to a new home by having many of his belongings out for him in the new residence. If possible, place these items in locations similar to where they were in your old house.

୧୬MARGARET JOHNSON, CPDT-KA, The Humane Trainer Inc., Austin, TX

Stress and change in a dog's environment often lead to behavioral changes. Remember that your dog will need some time to learn that rules for the old house also apply to the new house. If he is having trouble adjusting after you move, contact a professional trained in animal behavior to help you through the rough patch.

୧୬MARGARET JOHNSON, CPDT-KA, The Humane Trainer Inc., Austin, TX

MULTIPLE DOGS

When selecting a second or third dog, it is best to consider the gender and breed of your current dog. Dogs of the opposite sex often pose less potential for conflict than dogs of the same sex. Carefully research the breed characteristics; different breeds react differently to other dogs.

୧୬LUCINDA LUDWIG, Canine Connection LLC, Dubuque, IA

Do you have a multi-dog household where one dog steals from the others? Whenever I gave my three dogs rawhide chews, one attempted (often successfully) to steal from the others as well as keep his own. When this happened, I took the thief's rawhide away and put him in his crate with nothing while the other dogs enjoyed theirs. This has been extremely effective in extinguishing the thief's stealing behavior, and it has also allowed the other dogs to enjoy their treat or toy in peace in the meantime.

୧୬ANN WITHUN, Dog Scouts of America Troop Leader, Fieldwood Dog Training Center, Carlisle, PA

Some multi-dog households suffer from excessive barking. When one or more dogs start barking, resist the urge to focus on the barking dogs and instead identify the dog or dogs who are not barking. For every dog who is not barking, say "Good quiet" and deliver a treat. Continue praising and treating the quiet dogs, and gradually the barking dogs will stop barking. Maybe they'll think to themselves, "Hey! Why is that other dog getting a treat while I'm not?" For whatever reason, it works. Once you've done this a number of times, you can probably stop any dog from barking by calmly saying "Quiet." Then you can distribute the treats for the quiet behavior.

ANDREA ROBINSON, Positive Pet Training and Supply, Madera, CA

Although many dogs do enjoy the company of another dog, the owner should still plan to spend time with each dog separately for training, socialization, and play. Otherwise, the dogs may bond more to each other and less to the human. We want dogs to view humans as the leaders and providers of all good things, including companionship. Training builds such a bond, as well as ingrains appropriate behaviors in the dogs' repertoire, behaviors that have been well rewarded. By focusing the dogs more on looking to you for leadership and guidance, they will feel more secure and not like they have to try to control each other. This will help reduce tensions and anxieties that may arise in some situations because of a dog's uncertainty of who is in charge.

ANN ALLUMS, CPDT-KA, Best Friends Animal Society, Kanab, UT

MUZZLES

Muzzles tend to be associated with upsetting events, like preventing a dog bite when a dog is injured or scared, but using one can help caregivers save your dog's life without endangering themselves. To help your dog remain calm when wearing a muzzle, start by relaxing! Dogs don't know that muzzles are used during upsetting times if they have not had that experience. A muzzle is just an object to them. Teach your puppy or dog to insert his nose into the muzzle to receive a tasty treat. Play "put your nose in" until he eagerly shoves his nose into the muzzle to get the treat. Add the muzzle strap to the game—put nose in, get a treat; stand still while I fasten strap, get a treat—and you're there! Your dog will be very willing to wear a muzzle if it is ever needed. Be sure to practice often so that the memory of the game remains strong.

DIANE PODOLSKY, CPDT-KA, CTC, The Cultured Canine, LLC, White Plains, NY

When might you use a muzzle? At the vet's, when an unpleasant procedure is anticipated (like cleaning an infected ear); at the groomer's, when something is likely to be uncomfortable (working out a stubborn knot in the hair); or when your dog is injured and you need to take a close look at the problem. Using a muzzle prevents him from learning that biting (a very natural reaction to all of the above situations) can cause people to stop doing whatever they are doing. While no one wants to upset their dog or cause him discomfort, sometimes we need to do so temporarily to care for them.

꘠DIANE PODOLSKY, CPDT-KA, CTC, The Cultured Canine, LLC, White Plains, NY

NAIL CLIPPING — *Dark Blue*

Always look at the bottom of toenails rather than the top before cutting so that you can see exactly where the quick is located.

꘠P.J. LACETTE, the original Best Paw Forward, Osteen, FL

If you are physically unable to sit on the floor to cut your dog's toenails, have him lie on his side on your bed. Then you can sit on the bed next to him, and it will be easy to cut his toenails.

꘠MARY ANN RIECKE, Tail Waggers Dog Training Club, Chicago, IL

Trouble cutting toenails? A gob of peanut butter worked into the crevices on the roof of your dog's mouth can buy you enough time to do one toenail each night.

꘠P.J. LACETTE, the original Best Paw Forward, Osteen, FL

To my knowledge, there is no law—federal, state, or local—that states that all of a dog's toenails must be cut on the same day. Take your time and work with your dog to make toenail cutting as stress-free as possible. You won't go to jail, and he will be grateful for the improved relationship. Over time, work up to being able to get them all done at once.

꘠TINA M. SPRING VAN WHY, Sit Happens Dog Training & Behavior, Athens, GA

Cut toenails after a walk on wet grass, a swim session, or a bath, when the nails are soft.

꘠P.J. LACETTE, the original Best Paw Forward, Osteen, FL

Put an outline sketch of your dog's paws on your refrigerator door. Spread some positive reinforcement in the form of peanut butter on the lower portion of the door. Clip one nail each day while your pup licks the peanut butter off. Mark off which nail you clipped on the outline. By the time you get to the end, it will be time to start over.

꘠LOIS JEAN PIVA, MS, CPDT-KA, Blooming Grove, NY

> **The "quick" is the blood vessel that runs down the center of a dog's toenails.**

For a dog who is goosy about having his nails done, take him into the bathroom and close the door, smear some whipped cheese (garlic and herb works well) or cream cheese on the door at the dog's eye level, and encourage him to lick the cheese off the door. While he does this, pick up his foot and clip the nails.

ᕔCATHY BONES, CPDT-KA, Pacifica, CA

One thing that can be very difficult for dogs at the vet clinic is toenail trimming. You can help by desensitizing your dog at home. Start by handling each foot in gradually increasing increments of time. Then work up to tapping each toenail gently with a spoon to simulate the sound and feel of the toenail clippers.

ᕔCYNTHIA FORD, Yuma, AZ

NAME

Choosing a name for your dog is a big decision. Try to select pleasant-sounding names with at least two syllables (even when you are using your "annoyed voice"), and try to avoid names like "Squirt," "Barkley," "Digger," "Chewey," "King,"

"Caesar," and other monikers that can have behavioral meanings that may not be positive.

ᕔTINA M. SPRING VAN WHY, Sit Happens Dog Training & Behavior, Athens, GA

After adopting a dog, many owners wonder if they should change his name. I always recommend changing the name immediately for several reasons. First, dogs do not process their names like humans do. To them it's only a sound. It may be significant and it may not, depending on their experiences upon hearing it in the past, which brings me to my next point. In most cases, we have no idea what kind of lasting associations the dog has made between that sound (the name) and his environment. Sometimes terrible things have happened upon hearing it. So changing it and immediately establishing that the new sound (the dog's name) means only good things to follow helps ease traumatic memories associated with his life before you came along—and that can only be a good thing for everyone!

ᕔLISA PATRONA, Dip. DTBC, CPDT-KA, PDT, CBC, Trainers Academy, LLC, President, Troy, MI

Changing the name of a dog who has been rescued is very easy to do. Simply decide on a name and click/treat as soon as you say it. This way, your dog will learn to love the sound of his name because it has been paired with yummies! Additionally, this starts to build an orienting response in him when he hears it. In no time flat, when you say his name, he will look at you, happily anticipating the click/treat. Responses to cues from you can only be accomplished if he's focused on you in the first place. Teaching him to happily orient to you when you say his name is where it starts. If you don't have that to begin with, you're not likely to see him respond to what you're asking of him from there either (e.g., a *sit*, *down*, or *come*).

LISA PATRONA, Dip. DTBC, CPDT-KA, PDT, CBC, Trainers Academy LLC wPresident, Troy, MI

Be careful not to overuse your dog's name. Prefacing every command and interaction with his name will teach him to immediately tune out as soon as he hears it because it is said so frequently and for every situation.

CHRISTINA SHUSTERICH, BA, CBC, NY Clever K9, Inc., Queens, NY

Your dog's name should be the "power word" in his vocabulary. To keep it this way, try not to use it in anger, frustration, or while he is actively engaged in

something else. Call your dog's name, and reward him for coming to you. Take small steps in achieving the bigger picture!

NANCY TANNER, CPDT-KA, Paws & People, LLC, Bozeman, MT

NAME RECOGNITION

One cue that every dog needs to know is name recognition. The purpose of name recognition is to teach the dog to pay attention to you when you say his name, which means looking at you and giving his full attention to you. Practical applications of the name recognition cue are to get his attention before giving him another cue and to use when working with multiple dogs.

ANN ALLUMS, CPDT-KA, Best Friends Animal Society, Kanab, UT

Teach "attention to name" by saying your dog's name sweetly, then marking and giving a treat. You can use this to get his attention away from everything else and back to you! This helps with dogs who bark out the window, are distracted by other dogs, or are considering "illegal" behaviors like counter surfing.

BECKY SCHULTZ, BA, CPDT-KA, Becky Schultz Dog Training and Behavior, Golden Valley, MN

The steps to teach name recognition are to have treats ready, say your dog's name, and immediately as he looks at you, mark the behavior, followed by a treat. Through repetitions of this lesson, the dog will learn that it pays to look at you when he hears his name.

ANN ALLUMS, CPDT-KA, Best Friends Animal Society, Kanab, UT

Teach your dog that his name means "look at me." Charge the clicker. Wait until he looks at you. (Flashing glances are okay.) Click/treat. Brief glances will make you faster and more accurate. You must capture the behavior of "looking at me," not "looking away," in order to proceed. Sit quietly—don't lean forward to catch his eye, whistle/call his name, move your hands/body, etc. Wait for the eye contact from him, then click/treat. When he is looking at you consistently, click/treat for longer looks (one second, then two, three, etc). Name it (say the dog's name) as he looks steadily at you. Click/treat. Cue it (say the dog's name) when he isn't looking. Does he look confidently at you? Click/treat. Now he knows that his name means "look at me!"

ᐁKATHERINE BRYCE, CPDT-KA, The Family Dog, Santa Fe, NM

If your dog doesn't look at you when you first say his name, make an attention-getting noise (e.g., kissy sound) so that he does look. This will prevent you from repeating his name (which dilutes the effectiveness of the sound) and will help him succeed. You want your dog to succeed so that he can be rewarded, which will make him likelier to respond correctly the next time. Don't assume that he is being stubborn or ignoring you. Also, never use your dog's name in a harsh tone. That will undermine your training in teaching him that his name is a good thing and is meant to get his attention.

ᐁANN ALLUMS, CPDT-KA, Best Friends Animal Society, Kanab, UT

NAPS

Just as kids need nap time or downtime, so do our dogs. It's important that we give our dogs adequate time to play, as well as adequate time to rest in between. Dogs (like kids) who play too long end up playing too roughly, hurting one another, or bickering. Let your dog enjoy his playtime, interspersed with time left to nap, chew on a bone, or engage in another activity.

ᐁRUTH BRUNETTE-MEANS, CPDT-KA, All Breed Rescue & Training, Colorado Springs, CO

NIPPING

Fix nipping behavior by using the "switching" technique. First, teach your dog a nice fast *sit*. Then play with him by running around and hyping him up a little. Abruptly stop and ask for a *sit*. Praise, treat, and repeat. If he can't sit, try again but be less excited. If he can sit, repeat five times and then get just a bit more excited and begin to do the things that make him nip. Then stop, ask for a *sit*, praise, and treat as soon as he does. Repeat and escalate.

ᐁDEB WALKER, K9-Behavior Company, Lake Oswego, OR

NO —

"No" is only a word! The word "no" is often overused, and its actual meaning and function are misunderstood. "No" does not tell a dog how to behave; rather, it acts as a startle to interrupt unwanted behavior. "No" can function well as a startle; however, it lacks the power to inform the dog of the correct behavior. The word "no" in and of itself usually fails to get rid of the unwanted behavior, causing the owner to use it more and more frequently. Thus, "no" is robbed of the startle ability it had, leaving the owner feeling frustrated and misunderstood and the dog unsure of how to behave. To truly get rid of the unwanted behavior, "no" can be used as a startle, but it is up to the owner to instruct the dog on how to behave (e.g., teach the *quiet* command, reinforce it, and use it to turn off unwanted barking.)

  CHRISTINA SHUSTERICH, BA, CBC, NY
Clever K9, Inc., Queens, NY

Never tell a dog no without also telling him the preferred behavior. Think of this scenario: You are in your kitchen doing dishes and your husband comes to you and says "No" and walks away. You'd think "Okay, well what then?" Always teach your dog the alternate behavior when saying "No."

  DONNA SAVOIE, CPDT-KA, Pack of Paws
Dog Training, Charlton, MA

NOISE PHOBIA

Very briefly, some tips for treating noise-phobic dogs are: Test for any possible contributing medical conditions, including diminishing eyesight; identify all noise triggers; and desensitize and countercondition to noise triggers. These tips are not a treatment program or a substitute for a treatment program! If your dog has a noise phobia, seek a full behavioral treatment program.

  CHRISTINA SHUSTERICH, BA, CBC, NY
Clever K9, Inc., Queens, NY

To help keep puppies from becoming sensitive to loud noises, I make a point of knocking their stainless steel dog bowls into each other, knocking them against crates, and even deliberately dropping them so that the youngsters associate loud noises with good things to come. This is especially important in all-adult homes, which tend to be quiet.

  VICTORIA HYNES, The Educated Canine,
The Colony, TX

NOTHING IN LIFE IS FREE (NILF)

Make sure to implement the nothing in life is free (NILF) policy. Your dog should earn all rewards, including food, treats, petting, etc.

  BONNIE KRUPA, CPDT-KA, Happy, Clean
and Smart, Muncie, IN

Start a "nothing in life for free" policy for your dog. There are millions of everyday ways you give your dog reinforcements, like walks, games, pats, belly scratches, access to toys, and play. Ask him to do something for you before getting anything. Have him do a command, such as a *sit*, before you put on his leash, or take off his leash at the dog park, or put down the food bowl.

  JACQUELYN ENGLAND, A Dog's Life,
Sunnyvale, CA

A simple leadership exercise is what I call a NILF program (Nothing in Life Is Free). It is important to expect your dog to do something in exchange for what he wants. Even a simple *sit* for food or treats will suffice. This exchange works best if you employ it in all interactions with your dog. My dogs have to sit and wait to be released before eating, going out to play, and even occasionally during our fetch games. They must perform something for each treat and even for affection that they are trying to get from me, which I haven't offered. If you think about it, you can find dozens of ways to implement this into your daily routine. You can practice all of your basic commands (as well as tricks) while constantly reminding your dog that you are the pack leader without actually having to do anything special.

BRAD JONES, ABCDT, Pettis County K9
Academy, Sedalia, MO

OBEDIENCE — Dark purple

You can teach the retrieve over the high jump (for American Kennel Club [AKC] open obedience) inside your house. Purchase a tension-mounted curtain rod to fit across your hallway (or in a doorway if you don't have a hall). Place it just high enough so that it is easier for your dog to jump over it than step over it. Throw your retrieve article down the hall and say "Over" just as he jumps over the rod and again on his way back. After a few repetitions, say "Over" before you throw the article. Soon have him sit at heel while you throw, waiting for the command. That's the whole open routine! Gradually

raise the rod to the required height. Master the exercise in your house before you try it with real jumps.

MARTY SWINDELL, CPDT-KA, LickSkillet
Dog Training, Lee's Summit, MO

Here's a tip for getting the cookies out of your hand for heeling in obedience. When you are ready to wean from treats in the hand and begin using the air cookie or invisible cookie step, give your dog two to ten times as many treats or yummier treats. In other words, when you take away the lure, deliver extra goodies until the new behavior of working for an empty hand is well established. I also do the same thing—extra and yummier treats—when I first go to the obviously empty signal hand.

P.J. LACETTE, the original Best Paw
Forward, Osteen, FL

OBSESSIVE-COMPULSIVE DISORDER

My team and I once had an obsessive-compulsive Border Collie, Telly, residing at our shelter. She attacked shadows, especially her own. She was difficult to walk because she lunged and attacked any shadows cast in our path, despite attempts to minimize the problem by avoiding walks when the sun was brightest. Whether due to the resulting arousal level or specific shadows, she could not pass other dogs without becoming reactive. Our solution? In combination with increased physical and mental stimulation, the key was a pair of "Doggles." By putting sunglasses on, shadows were dimmed enough for Telly not to react to them. Her level of anxiety was reduced significantly, and within a week or so, she was able to take longer walks and pass by dogs quietly. Her overall stress dropped enough that she was able to meet other dogs—as long as the Doggles were on. Once she'd played for a few minutes, we could take them off, and she was able to herd, run, or wrestle with her doggy friends without incident.

〜SHAYNA STANIS, CPDT-KA, Berkeley, CA

OFF

To keep your dog off the couch and off Aunt Martha, you must teach him that he will be rewarded if his paws stay on the floor. Make sure that you are not rewarding him when he does jump on people or furniture. Start by sitting on the couch or on the bed, and when your dog approaches, "click" and treat him on the floor. If he gets up on the couch, say "Off" in a calm, happy voice and lure him to the floor with a treat in your hand. As he follows the treat and jumps off, "click" and treat. Soon your dog will get the idea that being on the floor is rewarding, while being on the bed or couch is not. At first, only encourage him off the bed and not on it. Once you are sure that your dog will jump off the bed when asked to, you can then give a cue like "up, up" to get him on the bed with you.

〜AGATHA WEISZ, CPDT-KA, The Not Naughty Dog, Houston, TX

If your dog jumps on the couch, calmly lead him off. Don't get mad or frustrated, and don't say more than a simple "Off." Then once all four feet hit the floor, say "Good off!" and give him attention. Just a few pats on the head will do. If he jumps back up, do the same thing. You may have to do this 100 times, but if you continually show him that you are not getting mad, but at the same time you're not backing down, he will give up. Many times with dogs it's about who is most patient! Always remember to praise with "Good off!" once he's actually off the couch, and give him attention while he's off. The attention you give him must be on your terms, not his.

〜DAYNA VILLA, IACP, Taking the Lead Dog Training, PA

O

OFF LEASH

Should you let your dog off leash? Consider what his breed was developed for. Sighthounds (such as Greyhounds, Whippets, and Borzoi) were bred to hunt by sight, and that drive can be so strong that they will take off at the sight of a squirrel or sometimes even a leaf floating through the air. Scenthounds (such as Beagles, Basset Hounds, and Coonhounds) were bred to track by scent, so again, the job they were bred to do will often be more motivating than their owners. Consider that hundreds, and in some cases thousands, of years of breeding for these jobs may not be compatible with your dreams of letting your dog off leash in an unfenced area.

DEVENE GODAU, CPDT-KA, Trainers Academy, LLC, Royal Oak, MI

Dogs should never be allowed to run loose in an unfenced area. Even dogs with acres to roam have been known to find the highway and be killed by traffic. There are also stray dogs who may not be as friendly as your dog. And unfortunately, not every human your dog meets will be kind either. Don't risk your dog's life! If you do not have a fence to contain him, then try alternate forms of exercise. Attend a reward-based training class to teach him to walk politely by your side—then you can exercise together. You can also try visiting a local school or recreation complex with outdoor fenced-in areas to exercise your dog. Call your local pet sitters to see if they offer dog walking services too. There are just too many dangers out there to let your dog run free.

TEOTI ANDERSON, CPDT-KA, Pawsitive Results, LLC, Lexington, SC

If you've taken care to diligently train your dog and decide to unleash him, please make sure to:

- Keep both eyes on your dog. You want to be able to call him away from anything he might attempt to eat or play with.
- Clean up after your dog. People not picking up after their dogs is the biggest reason dogs are banned from public areas, so bring plastic baggies with you to clean up after him.
- Keep a leash handy. If your unleashed dog is making other dogs or people uncomfortable, put him on leash and take him out of the situation.

When in doubt, use a leash. It is always better to be safe than sorry! Your dog's life depends on it.

DEVENE GODAU, CPDT-KA, Trainers Academy, LLC, Royal Oak, MI

> **Dogs can be allergic to dust, mold, pollen, grass, flea bites, and certain foods.**

OUTDOOR ACTIVITIES

If you are planning to spend the whole day doing outdoor activities, remember to pack a picnic basket for both you and your dog. Bring a water dish, bottled water, treats (which can include cheese cubes or peanut butter-stuffed bones), sandwiches, and during the winter months, fill a thermos with beef stew (for both of you) along with some hot chocolate or hot coffee (for just you).

    SUSAN M. PARKER, Dynamic Dog Training Services, LLC, President, The Little Rhodie Bully Breed Club Inc., RI

PESTS

Brewer's yeast is good for keeping bugs and mosquitoes off your pet (and you). For a 40- to 90-pound (18- to 41-kg) dog, give two pills a day. For a smaller dog, give only one pill a day.

    SHANNAN BESSEY, The Well Trained Dog, Omaha, NE

TOP TIDBIT

The most common type of flea to afflict dogs is the cat flea, *Ctenocephalides felis.*

PHOBIAS

When training a service dog, I found that a trainee was frightened of the sounds, scents, and movement of the drive-through car wash. To change this behavior, I packed the car full of kids, each equipped with treats, and tried again. We went through the wash four times, each time cheering, laughing, smiling, and giving treats like it was a big party. By the fourth run-through, the dog was wagging his tail, and his ears were perked with joy. He associated the car wash with happy times, and we never had a problem again. Plus, my car was never cleaner!

    CYNTHIA KURTZ, The Pet Geek, West Linn/Sandy, OR

PLAY - Red

When you are ending play with your dog, use the cue "last one" before you are about to give his last ball toss, etc. This way, the dog knows it wasn't his behavior that ended the play but merely the cue.

    JILL HALSTEAD, BA, CTC, Follow the Leader Dog Training Services, Richmond, VT

Your dog wants you to throw the ball? Wait for eye contact. Praise and then throw the ball.

    JAMIE DAMATO, CPDT-KA, Animalsense Canine Training and Behavior, Inc., Chicago, IL

PLAY BETWEEN DOGS

If you are having trouble recognizing if your dog is engaged in appropriate play, just look at the other dog(s). Is everyone having fun?

    JOANN KOVACICH, Grateful Dog Pet Care, Inc., Penfield, NY

A "play bow" is an invitation to play—the dog lowers his front end and his back end will be up in the air, and his ears will stand up.

All dog owners need to educate themselves as to what real inter-dog play looks like. If you have one of the really lively breeds (e.g., a pit bull, Doberman Pinscher, etc.), this is especially important. At the dog park, I often see owners express fear of dogfights when they are witnessing dog play. They try to break it up when actually that inter-dog play is one of the most important components of a socialized, friendly dog.

MARLA ABRAMS, Doggielove, New York, NY

Some dogs are so boisterous when playing with other dogs that people wonder if they're really playing at all. Are they actually aggressive? In general, "no blood, no foul." If both dogs are enjoying themselves and willingly participating in the game, then things are probably fine. You may have an issue if:

- one dog yipes and the other dog does not stop engaging
- one dog tries to escape or get away from the other
- one dog looks unhappy (Is the tail tucked? Ears down? Is he cowering?)
- one dog keeps coming to you in a pleading manner—he may be trying to tell you to end the game for him (Not every dog is assertive enough to stop another dog from coming on too strongly.)

Even if the dogs are having a blast, you may find the play action disturbing. It's okay for you to set limits on your dogs' play behavior. If things get too rough in your opinion, stop the game. Say "Time-out!" and clap to get their attention. Then ask each to sit for a treat. Have them settle down separately for a while, then let them play again if you wish. It's always a good idea to supervise dog play so that you can be ready to step in should things get out of hand.

TEOTI ANDERSON, CPDT-KA, Pawsitive Results, LLC, Lexington, SC

PLAY BITING

To help your puppy control any mouthy play behavior, avoid playing too roughly with him and never encourage mouthing or biting during play.

CRYSTAL COLL, All Ways Pawsitive Pet Behavior and Training, Queen Creek, AZ

To help stop roughhouse play biting, use a leash on the puppy in the house and in the yard when you are supervising him. When the puppy wants to playfully roughhouse, gently pick the leash up and hold him an arm's length away from you. Hold the leash straight up from the puppy's head. (You are *not* raising him off his feet.) Do not say anything. He will bite at the leash and struggle to get at you. Calmly wait until he stops struggling, and then you can release the hold on the leash. Repeat each time the puppy is out of control. Soon you will begin to see him approach you more calmly or settle easier instead of wanting to roughhouse with you.

ꞓSANDY OTTO, Puppy Preschool, Inc., Bowling Green, KY

Teach your puppy "bite inhibition" to help stop play biting. As puppies play together, they learn from other puppies how forceful their bite is. When a puppy yelps from the bite of another, the puppy who did the biting will back off. Your job is to teach your puppy bite inhibition toward humans in a similar manner. First, you must teach your puppy that when he puts his mouth on your skin, he must not apply pressure. When interacting with your puppy, if you feel any mouth pressure on your skin, loudly say "OUCH" and remove your attention by pulling away just as a puppy would do in play. You should adjust the intensity of your voice when saying "OUCH" according to the temperament of your puppy. A shy puppy will respond to a softer voice, but a rowdy puppy may require a more emphatic tone. You must then take the last step and make him understand that he should *never* put his mouth on humans. So now say "OUCH" loudly every time he puts his mouth on your skin.

ꞓCRYSTAL COLL, All Ways Pawsitive Pet Behavior and Training, Queen Creek, AZ

PROBLEM BEHAVIORS

Any time there is a sudden change in behavior in your dog, first visit your veterinarian for a thorough checkup. The change could be illness related. Make an appointment immediately, if possible, and be sure to inform the vet of the exact behaviors he is exhibiting. Barring a medical problem, there may have been a change in routine or environment to which your dog is having trouble adjusting. A dog will mirror your emotional state, so if you are feeling stressed, he may feel insecure because his pack leader is worried about something.

ꞓANN ALLUMS, CPDT-KA, Best Friends Animal Society, Kanab, UT

behavior modification programs. Not looking at a behavior like it is a "problem" opens new pathways to change it.

&DANY GROSEMANS, mAPBC, All Dog Training, Heusden-Zolder, Belgium

Ignore it! Sometimes completely ignoring what your dog is doing will make the behavior stop. Ignoring will prevent you from rewarding him by mistake. If it's safe and reasonable, don't look at your dog, touch him, or talk to him. ("Safe" means the behavior won't injure your dog, house, or family; "reasonable" means the behavior doesn't involve something like your most expensive shoes!)

&KATE GORMAN, CPDT-KA, Gentle Spirit Pet Training, Basking Ridge, NJ

If you are seeing concerning behaviors in your dog that are new, seek help right away. Many medical problems can be first noticed by behavior changes, and most reputable behavior professionals will require you to go to a veterinarian to rule out medical causes. It is generally quicker to change a behavior if it has not been practiced and reinforced for a long time. Think about smoking—if you just started, it will be easier to stop now than after several months. The sooner you seek help, the easier it is going to be for you and the behavior professional to change your dog's behavior

&HEATHER MOHAN-GIBBONS, MS, RVT, CPDT-KA, ACAAB, Collected Wisdom Animal Behavior, LLC, Milwaukee, WI

If your dog is displaying a behavior that upsets you, don't wait to contact a qualified trainer or behaviorist. In many cases, dogs will not outgrow these behaviors. In addition, the longer you wait to address the problem, the more time and effort it will take to fix it. Some signs that you should contact a behaviorist include avoidance of some (or all) people or other dogs, barking and growling, and snapping or biting.

&KRISTINA N. GAGE, CPDT-KA, SmartDog Dog Training, Saratoga Springs, NY

A problem behavior is distinct from any other behavior by just one quality: We call it a problem. For the dog, it is just a normal behavior. Looking at it as if it is a normal behavior makes it easier to find ways to influence it. It is not necessary to "cure" or "solve" a normal behavior. One only has to determine what motivates the present behavior and start trying to find ways to change the motivation. Normal behavior can be influenced by normal

Dogs don't consider any of their behaviors a problem—humans do. Dogs are perfect at being dogs. If there are "problems," don't allow the dog to keep practicing them. For example, if your dog is raiding the garbage can, avoid putting food in the garbage can, or secure the lid on the garbage pail, or use management tools such as gates and tethers to keep the dog away from the garbage.

ꝏLYNETTE TATAY, Nashville, MI

The first thing that must be assessed with problem behaviors is the management of the dog. Many (if not most) problem behaviors are rooted in an issue of the dog's basic needs not being met. Ensure that he is receiving adequate nutrition, medical care, exercise, and mental stimulation. The last two items in that list are the ones I most often find deficient. The problem behaviors that result can range from destruction and aggression to shyness and withdrawal.

ꝏMAUREEN PATIN, CPDT-KA, What a Good Dog!, Prosper, TX

Generally speaking, there are two steps in addressing your dog's undesirable behaviors, and you must do both steps:

1. Remove the reward of the undesirable behavior.
2. Teach your dog what you want him to do instead.

ꝏJERRY D. PATILLO, CPDT-KA, Happy Human Happy Dog, Richardson, TX

If your dog has a problem behavior, such as jumping or barking, you need to understand what will increase the behavior. You may be surprised that a dog can be reinforced by eye contact, telling him to be quiet, or pushing him back down. Some dogs will continue the problem behavior if they are getting negatively reinforced.

ꝏLISA L. SICKLES, CPDT-KA, CDBC, WagWag Enterprises, Englewood, CO

There are essentially only two steps needed to stop most problem behaviors. The first step is to make the undesirable behavior nonrewarding or less rewarding. The second step is to teach the dog something else to do in a given situation that is not compatible with the unwanted behavior. Such are the components of counterconditioning.

ꝏMICHELLE DOUGLAS, CPDT-KA, CDBC, The Refined Canine, West Haven, CT

To assume that your dog will grow out of his bad behaviors is unfair. Our canine family members must be taught what we expect of them.

ꝏCINDY STEINKE, CPDT-KA, TDI, CGC, PetTech K-9 Elementary LLC, Mosinee, WI

Don't ever forget that your dog is a dog (even if he will never be "just" a dog)! Reminding yourself of this will truly help in eliminating training and behavior problems.

ꝏANN KING, CPDT-KA, Canine King, Westchester, NY

P

A dog only does what works for the dog—he'll only repeat effective behavior. In his eyes, what is effective is that which gets him food, affection, or play. Be careful not to provide any of these when he exhibits unwanted behaviors, such as jumping or barking. Frequently, we inadvertently reinforce what we don't like by scolding the dog or brushing him away, which he actually views as reinforcement. Turning away from the dog is effective at stopping unwanted behaviors. However, this must be very quickly followed by reinforcement of the desired behavior.

ᕫJANE YOUNG, AKC CGC Evaluator,
Foxfield Dog Training, Mansfield, MA

If you have a dog who is having trouble with something, such as behavior with other dogs, do something different! Many times we continue at the one thing our dog has a problem with, which can be very stressful. For example, if your dog is difficult around other dogs, take a break and try tracking or a "sniffer dog" class. These scent games are great fun and will allow you and your dog to build your relationship on something positive. Then slowly add in a challenge. You will most likely see a totally new outlook on life!

ᕫVICKI WOOTERS, CPDT-KA, Wooters
Dog Training, Malvern, PA

I have my clients ask themselves two questions: 1. What is the dog getting out of his unwanted behavior (i.e., what is reinforcing the behavior)? 2. What would I rather the dog do instead? The second question is where most of the work is done through positively reinforcing the wanted behavior. I find asking these questions most helpful in teaching owners

about how dogs learn and why positive reinforcement is the way to go.

ᕫNORA ANDERSON, ABC Certified,
Anderson Canine Training LLC, Skillman, NJ

If your dog's behavior is trying your patience, take a few slow, deep breaths. Not only will this help you relax, but it will also show your dog that you are calm, as you lead by example. This will also take some pressure off you and your pooch and give you some clear thinking about how to handle the circumstances.

ᕫNAN ARTHUR, CDBC, CPDT-KA,
KPACTP, Whole Dog Training, Lakeside, CA

PROOFING

Everyone's goal is a dog who consistently obeys commands. It is absolutely essential that you can ensure your dog's behavior in order to enjoy dog parks and other public venues. The best way to attain this goal is through "proofing," which gradually increases the level of distraction under which your dog performs. When proofing, be sure that you very gradually add to the level of distraction and only after success at the preceding level.

ᕫMAUREEN PATIN, CPDT-KA, What a Good
Dog!, Prosper, TX

Once your dog has learned a command, "proof" his behavior by asking him to follow the command in different settings. Proofing tests your dog's ability to perform under distraction and in different circumstances and demonstrates his understanding of the command.

    ぞLUCINDA LUDWIG, Canine Connection LLC, Dubuque, IA

Save your absolute yummiest food treats for proofing. Good items to try are bits of cooked liver, chicken, or beef. This is definitely a time to pull out the people food! Your dog needs to get the message that you (and your rewards) are even more interesting than that cute little Pug at the dog park.

    ぞMAUREEN PATIN, CPDT-KA, What a Good Dog!, Prosper, TX

When proofing, increase your dog's ability to sustain a behavior by adding a distraction, such as a bouncing ball, another dog, or food on the floor. When he can maintain a behavior such as the sit under distracting circumstances, increase the distance and practice in different settings.

    ぞLUCINDA LUDWIG, Canine Connection LLC, Dubuque, IA

PULLING ON LEASH 90

Pulling back when your dog pulls ahead on a leash will only cause him to pull harder. Dogs have an oppositional reflex that causes them to pull in the opposite direction when they are pulled back, so pulling on a leash can actually create harder pulling ahead by your dog. The best way to train a dog to walk correctly is by verbal commands and proper leash techniques that do not involve pulling.

    ぞCHRISTINA SHUSTERICH, BA, CBC, NY Clever K9, Inc., Queens, NY

Why does your dog continue to pull on leash? Well, walking on leash is fun and naturally reinforcing for him. Without proper training, over time your dog has learned that if you do not move the way he wants to move, all he has to do is pull. He has also learned that the harder he pulls, the more likely the chance that you will move. Most owners try to correct this pulling by pulling back on the dog. Not only does this not work, but it actually teaches a dog to pull even harder. Sometimes your dog may also be stronger than you, such as when you are not paying attention or when your center of gravity is off because your arm is too far out in front of you. With all of this combined, you have inadvertently become a very well-trained owner, following obediently behind your dog wherever he wants to go!

    ぞCOLLEEN B. HURLEY, Orlando, FL, and Gainesville, FL

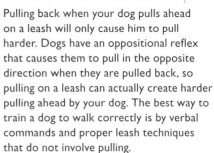

To prevent your dog from pulling on the leash, anything more than a standard buckle or snap collar is rarely needed. Use a 4- or 6-foot (1- or 2-m) leash rather than a retractable one. The first step, and often the only method needed to stop pulling, is to simply stop whenever your dog pulls. No jerking or reprimand is needed. Whenever he pulls, stop and he will learn that he gets nowhere. Call your dog back to you with a food treat in your hand held at the position near your leg where you would like him to walk. Click with your clicker at the instant he arrives at that magical spot and give him a food treat; then resume walking. Vary the direction of your walk, changing directions without any verbal cue so that your dog has to watch you to see what direction you are heading. This will teach him to pay attention to keep from being bumped or stepped on. You can also wrap your leash around your waist to avoid the yo-yo effect of a tug of war with your dog while walking. This also frees your hands to enjoy your walk, click when your dog is in the right position at your side, and give him food treats as reinforcement. Eventually he will learn that pulling is not rewarding, but walking at your side with a slack leash gets him where he wants to go. At first, this will make for a very long walk, but consistency will pay off with a dog who learns to walk well on what is called a "loose leash."

&LUCINDA LUDWIG, Canine Connection LLC, Dubuque, IA

If your dog is a leash puller, purchase a head halter or harness to control the pulling in the short run. This will prevent him from continuing to practice the behavior. In the meantime and for the long run, contact a qualified trainer who can teach you positive methods for teaching your dog not to pull.

&KRISTINA N. GAGE, CPDT-KA, SmartDog Dog Training, Saratoga Springs, NY

Exercise your dog off leash before working on lead to burn off excess energy that may be used to pull.

&ANN ALLUMS, CPDT-KA, Best Friends Animal Society, Kanab, UT

PUNISHMENT

Punishment often causes more problems than it solves. Many studies in the psychology of learning demonstrate that, whether rearing children, teaching students, or training animals, punishment causes unwanted behavioral fallout—like aggression, fear, escape, avoidance, tantrums, rebellion, loss of trust, destructiveness, apathy, and clinginess.

&CARMEN BUITRAGO, MS, CAAB, CPDT-KA, Cascade Pet Camp, Hood River, OR

P

Positive training tries to avoid punishment as much as possible. Punishment can have serious effects on the human–dog bond, destroying the trust that is an important part of all relationships.

ᛒᏗCOLLEEN B. HURLEY, Orlando, FL, and Gainesville, FL

Proper punishment of bad behaviors includes three steps. First, reward your dog when he is good so that he will know what you do like. Second, calmly stop bad behaviors with a sharp "No" and little fuss. Last, quickly redirect him to a behavior you do like, and praise him when he does the new behavior. Redirecting your dog is called counterconditioning—you are informing him what good behaviors are and giving him a chance to succeed so that he doesn't have to guess what you want. By combining these steps and giving lots of rewards for being good, he will start to choose good behaviors over bad ones.

ᏗWENDY ANASTASIOU, BA, CDBC, CPDT-KA, Life With Fido, Spotsylvania, VA

Many dog owners who come to my class are already punishing their dogs for unwanted behaviors. I like to emphasize to them that we are the humans and the dogs are a species that doesn't speak our language, so we should never assume that they understand unless we have spent lots of time and patience teaching them the new behavior. While teaching, don't punish, but rather set your dog up for successful situations. Anticipate that some unwanted puppy/dog behavior is going to occur, and practice successful setups of real-life situations so that your puppy will know what to expect when put into the situation. It is all about teaching your dog, anticipating his actions, and preventing

unwanted behaviors using positive-based training—and I know it works.

ᏗDONNA HALL, Certified Dog Trainer, Hot Diggity Dogs Services, Vancouver, BC, Canada

Did you know that when you get angry with your dog when he is acting up, you can be aggravating the behavior? For example, let's say you are scared of spiders and you start screaming. Then your friend comes over and yells at you, maybe even smacking you in anger. Now, not only are you still scared of spiders, but you have to be worried and maybe even defensive that you might get hit and yelled at. So if your dog is growling at someone or something because of fear, anger, or frustration, getting mad at him can actually make the behavior worse, not better. Think about changing the association. If every time you see a spider, I gave you candy, you would eventually realize that the spider equals something great, not fear.

ᏗHOLLY BRAND, RVT, Certified Dog Trainer, West Coast K-9 Training, Brentwood, CA

PUPPIES

If you are purchasing a puppy from a breeder and have the opportunity to visit the litter before the take-home date, bring a stuffed squeaky toy and a blanket with you. Leave the toy and blanket with the breeder, and ask her to allow the items some exposure to the litter (not too much or the toy and blanket can get too soiled). The items will help keep your puppy calm on his first day in the new home away from the litter. If you can't make the early visit, make the request by phone—any good breeder will accommodate you.

ᴥTHOMAS JACKSON, Baltimore, MD

Do not bring home a puppy until he is at least eight weeks old. Some breeders have been letting puppies leave their mother and siblings as young as six weeks—that is too young! These puppies do not learn bite inhibition, and you could end up with a puppy who does not know how to control his mouth, biting you with his razor-sharp puppy teeth. These puppies may also have other behavior issues that could have been corrected by staying with their mother for those additional precious weeks.

ᴥDARLENE KOZA,
Scooter's School
of Sit & Stay,
Rochester, NY

When bringing a new puppy home, make a schedule for feeding, potty breaks, and attention. This will help prevent you from forgetting to take him out or overwhelming him with play and attention.

ᴥCRYSTAL COLL, All Ways Pawsitive Pet Behavior and Training, Queen Creek, AZ

To help set the stage for success, owners should puppy-proof every place the puppy will be allowed *before* bringing him home. Look at the world from your puppy's perspective by crawling on the floor and observing potential temptations and hazards. Assume that if it can be chewed or played with, it will be. Keep small objects out of reach, secure electrical cords, pick up remotes, cover trashcans, close closet doors, discard poisonous houseplants, and fence off garden patches. Help your puppy stay safe and out of trouble!

ᴥANN ALLUMS, CPDT-KA, Best Friends Animal Society, Kanab, UT

When bringing home a new puppy, pretend that he's an alien being from another planet where everything in our world is different and new. Puppies really don't understand English. I tell clients that an 8-week-old puppy has only been on earth for 64 days—this helps bring in some clarity of how "new" he is to his new home environment. Enjoy his explorations, and try to see the humor in his antics as he watches and learns from humans.

ᴥDONNASUE JACOBI, Just Like Home Pet Sitting and Training, Menlo Park, CA

Having a puppy in the family can be a wonderful experience, especially when he knows what his boundaries are. You need to teach rules and impulse control so that your puppy can be successful. Exercise, training, and nutrition are critical components for making a puppy a whole dog.

ELIZABETH LANGHAM, MS, CPDT-KA,
Tree Frog Farm Dog Training and Agility,
North Yarmouth, ME

New puppy keeping you up all night because he is afraid or lonely? Stuff the crate with oodles of plush toys. He will feel safe and happy with "littermates" next to him.

REBECCA ENGLE, MA, CPDT-KA, First
Steps and Beyond K-9 Obedience, Plano, TX

When bringing home your new puppy, you can expect some sleepless nights ahead. Try this: Elevate the puppy's crate next to your bed so that he can see you. This will help with separation from the litter and will calm him down as he learns to integrate into his new home.

SHA NEWMAN, Training With Love for
Canines, Valley Glen, CA

Puppies need two two-hour naps a day or they will get punchy. These naps should be uninterrupted and in their "zone." Having a zone that your pup can call his own will help him learn to self-soothe and not need to be with you 24-7. The family can be around the pup, but he will not be following you around while you're cooking, doing laundry, going to the bathroom, etc.

ELIZABETH LANGHAM, MS, CPDT-KA,
Tree Frog Farm Dog Training and Agility, North
Yarmouth, ME

When will your puppy be considered an adult? With toy breeds, such as Papillons, Chihuahuas, or Yorkshire Terriers, puppies are usually considered adults when they turn one year of age. Small dogs, such as Cocker Spaniels or Shetland Sheepdogs, are considered adults at around one and a half to two years of age. With large dogs, such as Labrador Retrievers, Siberian Huskies, or Collies, puppies are usually considered adults at two to two and a half years of age. The giant breeds, such as Great Pyrenees or Saint Bernards, are not considered adults until they reach about age three.

TEOTI ANDERSON, CPDT-KA, Pawsitive
Results, LLC, Lexington, SC

Puppies should not have adult dog privileges—they need to earn them as they age. Puppies are puppies and will do puppy things. Be successful by training, building a positive relationship, exercising, and monitoring your puppy.

NANCY TANNER, CPDT-KA, Paws &
People, LLC, Bozeman, MT

Use a 10-foot (3-m) indoor dragline on your puppy for all supervised waking hours to prevent problems and to be able to catch him if you need to redirect him.

BECKY SCHULTZ, BA, CPDT-KA,
Becky Schultz Dog Training and
Behavior, Golden Valley, MN

Puppies do the darndest things—they go potty on the floor, chew up our shoes, and eat poop out of the kitty litter box, just to name a few. These behaviors all stem from innate canine instincts and therefore can be difficult to eradicate. Fortunately, there is one way to prevent all of these behaviors: Supervise your puppy! A great way to maintain constant supervision is to tether him right to you—you can use a key clip or just loop the leash through your belt loop so that he is always by your side. Not only will this allow you to see little behaviors that mean "I have to pee now," you will have a dog who develops a habit of watching your movements and is aware of where you are, which will help in later training, especially with leash manners.

ꙮMARNI EDELHART, CPDT-KA, Pioneer Pets LLC, Easthampton, MA

As a trainer, one of the most common questions I hear from my clients was how to control the interactions between their puppies and strangers. They found it difficult because usually a puppy is already being petted before the owners have a chance to explain what is okay (e.g., no petting if jumping). As a result, I have made dog jackets with "I'm Learning" written on the side. Strangers, accustomed to respecting the space of a working dog wearing a jacket, will generally ask first for permission before petting. This allows the puppy's owner to explain some guidelines first. Some states or provinces may have laws prohibiting the words "In Training" so that the puppy isn't confused with a true working dog in training, but "I'm Learning" has always brought respect and smiles from strangers.

ꙮMICHELLE SEVIGNY, BA, DOGSAFE Canine First Aid, North Vancouver, BC, Canada

The most useful tip I give to owners or puppies and young dogs is what I call "pup on a string." The basic premise is to keep a short, lightweight leash on your dog whenever he is out of the crate. If he is on leash, he knows he can't play keep-away because you can easily and quickly put an end to that game. He is also less likely to have housetraining accidents because you can tether the leash to your chair and keep him close. If your pup gives potty signs, you see it right away and can quickly get him outside.

ꙮTONIA WHILDEN, Houston Dog Ranch, Houston, TX

Lower your expectations! I hear from clients all the time that they have had their new puppy for "two whole weeks" and he is still peeing in the house. Remember that you are living with a new baby. Regardless of whether the new baby in the house is human or canine, we must

> **Puppies have 28 "milk teeth," which erupt between the third and sixth week of age.**

understand that he will go through tough times and must be taught what acceptable behavior is and what is not. Everyone is always in such a hurry to allow their new puppy free run of the house and then become disappointed and angry when at five months of age, he spends the day destroying their house—the owners have unrealistic expectations. Young dogs need time to learn not only a new language but also an entirely different culture, which is not something that is accomplished in two weeks or during the course of a puppy class. Give your new dog the time he needs to learn what is right and what is not so acceptable in our human world, and take the time to teach him what you need him to learn to stay in his new home.

✑SILVIA GOLZ, CPDT-KA, "Best Friend" – Companion Dog Training, Appleton, WI

PUPPY KINDERGARTEN

Puppy preschool classes are geared specifically to a puppy's developing physical and social needs. Like humans, canines have biologically prepared critical periods for social development commonly called socialization windows. These

windows of opportunity start to close by the time a puppy reaches 16 weeks of age.

✑MARGARET JOHNSON, CPDT-KA, The Humaner Trainer, Inc., Austin, TX

Puppies who learn good doggy social skills look to their guardians for guidance, and those who think training is a lot of fun become adult dogs who are a pleasure to live with. As the saying goes, you never get a second chance to make a first impression, and the life of a puppy is just one first impression after another! Puppy kindergarten classes offer guardians a safe place to socialize their puppies, with the added benefit of professional guidance in puppy raising.

✑LAUREL SCARIONI, CPDT-KA, Pawsitive Results Critter Academy, Santa Rosa, CA

When selecting a puppy kindergarten, ask three questions: 1) Does it use treats? 2) Does it let the puppies play together off leash most of the time during class? 3) Does it "pass the puppies" around to other dog owners to handle and meet? If the answer to all of these questions is yes, then that class is a good bet. If the answer to *any* of the questions is no, keep looking for another class!

✑DEB WALKER, K9-Behavior Company, Lake Oswego, OR

Look for a puppy class instructor who uses reward-based training methods, monitors play closely to ensure that everyone is having fun, and interrupts play frequently with exercises that refocus the puppies on their guardians.

✑LAUREL SCARIONI, CPDT-KA, Pawsitive Results Critter Academy, Santa Rosa, CA

QUIET

Teach your dog the *quiet* command. Train him in the circumstances that trigger his barking. For instance, if the doorbell is the trigger, enlist a friend to ring it while you wait behind the closed door with your dog. Allow one or two barks, then while holding a treat to your dog's nose say "Quiet," count to five, and then treat him. Holding the treat to his nose will prevent the barking, and counting to five will ensure that you are reinforcing your dog for being quiet rather than barking. As you continue to practice, you can begin to increase the time from five seconds to six and so on, until your dog is able to maintain the *quiet* command and treats are no longer necessary.

&CHRISTINA SHUSTERICH, BA, CBC, NY Clever K9, Inc., Queens, NY

You can teach your dog to "speak," but you'll also want to teach him to be "quiet" so that the barking is under control. Get the behavior first. Usually a word is sufficient to interrupt barking. Initially reward him for being quiet after only two to three seconds. Gradually build up the time he needs to be quiet before getting a reward.

&ANN ALLUMS, CPDT-KA, Best Friends Animal Society, Kanab, UT

RALLY

Here's a backing-up trick for rally. Have the dog stand and push a yummy treat from nose level at his standing height slightly back and just a little down into his chest. Reward him for any tiny foot shuffle back. A fun cue can be a high-pitched "beep beep" sound that imitates a vehicle in reverse.

&P.J. LACETTE, the original Best Paw Forward, Osteen, FL

> **Rally (also known as Rally-o) is a competitive sport that combines agility and obedience.**

REACTIVE DOGS

For a reactive dog in an outdoor class, I ask the owner to move back to put more distance between her and her dog and the rest of the class. Once the dog relaxes with enough distance between him and a perceived threat, I have the owner proceed to follow the directions of the first lesson, which will develop focus and attention. This is merely the food lure work that allows the dog to focus on his owner and work for rewards. For a mildly reactive dog, by the second week the owner will be able to work closer to the rest of the class. Sometimes the focus is so good that the team is integrated into the class. For a dog who is more reactive, with a very nervous handler, the process may take several weeks, with gradual reduction of the distance as the team relaxes.

ᐤJOAN B. GUERTIN, Common Sense Dog Training and Behavior Solutions, East Texas

When working with any reactive dogs in public, I have them wear dog jackets with "I'm Learning" written on the side. These jackets help people around them understand that the owner is working on an issue and won't be negatively judged. This reduces an owner's anxiety, which is an important step in helping the dog.

ᐤMICHELLE SEVIGNY, BA, DOGSAFE Canine First Aid, North Vancouver, BC, Canada

For reactive dogs in an indoor location, where dogs are working in close proximity to each other, I have found that by blocking the view of the rest of the class with a barrier (such as two chairs or an x-pen draped with a sheet or blanket), you can effectively prevent the dogs from making eye contact. Then the owner can effectively begin getting the focus and attention from her dog, which will allow him to successfully ignore the other dogs. We are generally able to eliminate the barrier within a week or two. Remember to use only positive reinforcement and absolutely *no* correction or admonishment.

ᐤJOAN B. GUERTIN, Common Sense Dog Training and Behavior Solutions, East Texas

REINFORCEMENT

[handwritten: copy in light green on paper]

Positive reinforcement works on anything with a brain stem, provided that you can determine the right reinforcers (motivating to the animal), that your timing's good (reinforcing the right things), and that you set up enough successful trials to establish the desired behavior and "proof" it in a variety of circumstances (building reliability).

ᐤANN DUPUIS, CPDT-KA, Your Dream Dog, Randolph, MA

Use mild reinforcers like praise and pets for good responses, and reserve treats for better than average responses. Give just enough reinforcement to keep your dog's interest in training but not so much that he isn't guessing, "What am I getting next?"

ᐤJACQUELYN ENGLAND, A Dog's Life, Sunnyvale, CA

Reinforcement doesn't always have to be a treat; if a dog is outside, it may be more reinforcing to get his favorite toy or for you to throw a stick. So use what will be reinforcing at that moment.

ᐤSTEPHANIE LARSON, AKC CGC Evaluator, Gentle Paws, Lexington, NE

R

Use a "schedule of reinforcement" for rewards, as follows:

1. Continuous: Initially, every time command is performed, the dog is treated (first week after command is taught).
2. Intermittent: Every other time command is performed, the dog is treated (second week after command is learned).
3. Random: Dog is treated randomly after command performed (e.g., 1 out of 1, 1 out of 3 up to 5) (third week after command learned).
4. Life reward: Treats are phased out and life reward used (fourth week after command is learned).

&CHRISTINA SHUSTERICH, BA, CBC, NY
Clever K9, Inc., Queens, NY

Use an intermittent reinforcement schedule. Whenever you are teaching a new behavior, reward your dog every time he performs the desired behavior. Once he is fairly consistent in responding, give him the treat sometimes but not others. This is the best way to maintain reliable behavior.

&PATRICIA BENTZ, CPDT-KA, CDBC,
K-9 Training & Behavioral Therapy,
Philadelphia, PA

While performing any behavior, a dog is receiving internal reinforcement. For example, while eating out of the trash, he is getting food rewards for making a mess. Therefore, when trying to train him to *not* engage in unacceptable behaviors, a trainer must try to reward the new behavior with something

that is more valuable to the dog than the internal reinforcement he receives for doing the behavior. For example, when training a dog to "leave it," the reinforcement must be better than the object that the dog is about to pick up. To your dog, is that piece of kibble better than picking up that frog? You may need a small piece of cheese instead.

&COLLEEN B. HURLEY, Orlando, FL,
and Gainesville, FL

Remember, it's the feedback that gets the results, not the cue/command! One of the most common troubles a novice trainer has is not giving enough positive, well-timed feedback to her dog. Novice trainers tend to rely on commands more than the reinforcement, or they give attention to incorrect behavior and ignore good behavior. Experienced trainers give feedback six to ten times per minute, while novice trainers do so only about two to three times per minute. The feedback makes it clear to the dog: "Yes! That's it!"

&ELIZABETH L. STROTER,
TDI Evaluator, AKC CGC
Evaluator, House Calls
Dog Training,
Highland, NY

R

RELEASE

Your dog should learn that he must stay in a position until you give him the *release* command. The *release* command is a word, such as "okay!", that signals to your dog that he may now move out of position. For example, use the *release* command when teaching your dog to sit and stay or to wait before going out doors. If you neglect to use a release command, your dog will develop his own cue system. The key to your dog staying in position is to release him!

&LUCINDA LUDWIG, Canine Connection LLC, Dubuque, IA

Because I do not always use clicker training when teaching clients, I make certain that they use a release word when working with their dogs. My procedure is as follows: Get the dog's attention, ask for the behavior wanted, and once the behavior has been given, use your release word to let the dog know that the request has ended. For example: "Fluffy" (dog makes eye contact), "sit" (dog sits), "stay" (dog stays), "all done" (dog is released). I find that the release word is easy for the owners to comprehend and puts them in control of their dog's behavior from the beginning of the exercise until the end.

&AMY WEEKS, MA, CPDT-KA, Tampa, FL

Choose a release word other than "okay" when you signal your dog to end a behavior. "Okay" comes up too much in everyday conversation, and he can pick that sound out from what you are saying.

&CARYL WOLFF, CPDT-KA, CDBC, Doggie Manners, Los Angeles, CA

The *release* cue is a positive way to end a mistake. Rather than follow an error with a re-cue, I can say "Okay!" and leave the dogs wishing they'd taken advantage of the cue when they had their chance.

&JENNY RUTH YASI, Head Trainer, Whole Dog Camp, Peaks Island, ME

RESOURCE GUARDING

If your dog has begun resource guarding (e.g., growling at a family member who tries to take a chew), you must consult with a qualified professional for a complete evaluation and guidance. While in most cases resource guarding is a highly treatable problem, if not done correctly, it can be very dangerous. Because every dog and every situation is unique, there is no "quick fix" or "recipe" for treatment. To successfully modify a dog's behavior and make sure that everyone stays safe during the process, you need the guidance of a professional who will thoroughly investigate his behavior and outline a specific plan for you to follow.

&LISA PATRONA, Dip. DTBC, CPDT-KA, PDT, CBC, Trainers Academy, LLC, President, Troy, MI

R

REWARDS

Rewards are something the dog wants. Just because you think those expensive new treats are a great reward doesn't mean that they are. If your dog turns his nose up at them, they're not much of a reward in his mind. A reward can be petting, verbal praise, a throw of the ball, a quick game with a favorite toy, sniffing grass, saying hello to another dog, etc. The sky's the limit. Consider what your dog finds rewarding, and use it!

—JAMIE DAMATO, CPDT-KA, Animalsense Canine Training and Behavior, Inc., Chicago, IL

You need to have some nonfood options as rewards for your dog. There may be times when you want to reinforce your dog's behavior, and food is not available or appropriate. Do something that you know your dog enjoys, like a gentle scratching of the chin or hindquarters, with a reinforcing affirmation like "Good boy."

—PAT HENNESSY, CAP2, CPDT-KA, N2paws, Leawood, KS

Each dog has a reward hierarchy, meaning that some rewards are more important than others to a dog. Examples of rewards are food (hot dog, chicken, kibble), objects (balls, chew toys), and activities (attention, walks, playing, tug games). Rewards are specific to each dog, as they depend on the individual dog's preferences. So figure out all the things your dog likes, including food, objects, and activities, and use those things as rewards.

—ANN ALLUMS, CPDT-KA, Best Friends Animal Society, Kanab, UT

Use real-life rewards as often as possible, and integrate training into your pup's everyday life to teach him the relevance of your cues. "Oh, I can only go play if I sit? Well, I'd better sit!"

—JACQUELYN ENGLAND, A Dog's Life, Sunnyvale, CA

It's important to be a slot machine, not a soda machine—slot machines pay off intermittently and with variable degrees of rewards, keeping people interested enough to keep dropping in money. With a soda machine, you don't keep dropping in money when no soda is forthcoming!

—JACQUELYN ENGLAND, A Dog's Life, Sunnyvale, CA

Because canines are predators and opportunistic scavengers, it makes sense to use food and/or toys as a reward during training.

—NANCY TANNER, CPDT-KA, Paws & People, LLC, Bozeman, MT

When using reward removal to stop an unwanted behavior, the thought process goes like this: What reward is my dog getting out of this obnoxious behavior, and how can I prevent him from getting that reward? What will I be rewarding instead? For example, use reward removal as a loose-leash walking technique—don't allow forward motion when your dog is pulling; only allow forward motion when the leash is loose.

—JACQUELYN ENGLAND, A Dog's Life, Sunnyvale, CA

Train yourself to notice when your dog is being good. Here are some things to look for: sitting or lying down; looking at you with "soft" eyes; standing and looking relaxed; being quiet in the crate; keeping "four on the floor" when likely to jump up (on someone or to counter surf). When you notice your dog being good, try the following: Say "Good dog!" in a friendly, happy voice (but not too loud or high-pitched if your dog gets too excited); give him a treat; play fetch (a minute or two is all it takes); or give him attention, including petting.

   ANN DUPUIS, CPDT-KA, Your Dream Dog, Randolph, MA

Always have a picture in your mind of the behavior you want from your dog. So many times we know the things we don't want them to do, but we must counteract that with a behavior we like. So remember to praise and reward your dog for all the things you like. It's easy to ignore a good dog, but that's the time to pay attention to him!

   DAYNA VILLA, IACP, Taking the Lead Dog Training, PA

Be sure to reward only the act you intend.

   EMILY BURLINGAME, A Dog's Life, Sunnyvale, CA

Reward your good dog and ignore your bad dog. Dogs learn very quickly how to get attention from humans, usually by barking, whining, pawing, jumping up, or some other equally annoying but attention-getting behavior. Your dog doesn't typically command your attention, however, when he's quietly chewing on a nice bone. Start noticing and rewarding him when he's

TOP TIDBIT

A bribe is given in advance to get your dog to do something; a reward is given after the dog has performed the task correctly.

doing all the right stuff, and ignore him or leave him alone completely when he's being a demanding pest.

   JACQUELYN ENGLAND, A Dog's Life, Sunnyvale, CA

REWARDS, LIFE —

Using rewards or reinforcers to teach and maintain behaviors is part of the science of behavior modification. While treats are very effective in training new commands, they should not be used as a way to maintain obedience once the commands have been learned; rather, life rewards should be used. Life rewards consist of rewards embedded in your dog's daily life, such as being fed, being walked, being greeted, being played with, and others. Once commands are learned, your dog should perform a command to get the life reward. A common example is your dog needs to sit in order to be fed.

   CHRISTINA SHUSTERICH, BA, CBC, President, NY Clever K9, Inc., Queens, NY

Use "life rewards" to train. For example, if your dog likes to go outside, he must sit before going out. Or before coming out of his crate, he must make eye contact with you.

   LYNETTE TATAY, Nashville, MI

Rewarding your dog for good behavior is a vital part of training, and in many situations, you can use "life rewards." This means that your dog earns something valuable by following a cue from you. Make a list of daily interactions that you have with your dog, with an eye toward turning them into training opportunities. Ask for a *sit* before you put the dinner dish down. Ask for a *sit* when you're putting his leash on or taking it off. Is he a fetch fanatic? Ask for a *sit* before you throw the ball or the flying disc. Well-mannered canines shouldn't rush past you through an open door. Ask for a *sit* before you open the door. If you use your daily interactions with your dog as mini training sessions—a few minutes around dinnertime, a few minutes practicing *recalls*, etc.–you'll be amazed at what you and your canine pal can accomplish!

MARY LEATHERBERRY, CPDT-KA, Good Dog! Santa Fe, Santa Fe, NM

RULES

Dogs need clear and consistent rules and boundaries. Dog owners need to communicate their expectations to their dogs and be consistent. Changing the rules can be confusing and lead to behavioral issues.

CINDY STEINKE, CPDT-KA, TDI, CGC, PetTech, K-9 Elementary LLC, Mosinee, WI

SCHUTZHUND

My German Shepherd Dog, Britta, recently refused to track during her trial to earn the Schutzhund III title. I had been using food on a variable reinforcement (VR) 12 schedule during training. Britta had figured out after only two trials that no food on the "scent pad" (an area that the tracklayer stomps and scuffs on the ground at the track's beginning) meant no food on the track. She then shut down and stopped after the first leg of the track. The next three tracks I alternated food/no food on the track and scent pad to remove the predictive value of "no food."

DAVE PORT, The Way Of The Dog, Union City, CA

SENIOR DOGS

Senior dogs still love to learn and play. The only difference with training is that you must take into consideration any physical limitations they may have. Older dogs still have the willingness to do things but don't always have the physical capability (like when arthritis flares up). On days like that, take your senior for car rides instead of walks so that he can get out of the house. Do light work like a *leave it* with a cookie on his paw. Try *stays* with distraction work using cookies on the floor. If your senior is struggling with a weight issue, use low-calorie treats like carrots, toasted oat cereal, etc., for training. Remember that just because a dog gets older doesn't mean that he has stopped wanting to learn. Senior dogs deserve the best from us, and that includes giving them the respect for their brains as well as the pampering of their bodies.

&CRYSTAL FRANKLIN, CPDT-KA,
Bethesda, MD

Can you teach an old dog new tricks? Absolutely! It's never too late to start training your dog. Just as we continue to learn things as we age, so can a dog. It's true that your dog may have a more difficult time overcoming bad habits because he will have had more time to practice them. But your older dog has a great advantage over a young puppy— attention span! An older dog has a greater attention span than an easily distracted puppy, so your training time can be longer.

&TEOTI ANDERSON, CPDT-KA, Pawsitive
Results, LLC,
Lexington, SC

For senior dogs, check with a vet on a good age to start cutting down on vaccinations.

&LYNETTE TATAY,
Nashville, MI

Be patient with your senior dog. Realize that he may not feel 100 percent every day, and his hearing and eyesight may diminish. Take

him to the vet more often for checkups because problems tend to progress quickly as dogs get older. Take advantage of resources like special beds, supportive harnesses, and ramps. Be sensitive to changes in behavior, and provide the best care and pampering possible.

&KATE GORMAN, CPDT-KA, Gentle Spirit
Pet Training, Basking Ridge, NJ

If you are training a senior dog, be mindful of any health issues that could affect your training. For example, a dog with hip arthritis is going to find it hard to hold the *sit* position for a length of time. Don't ask a dog to perform something that will be painful for him. If you have any concerns about your dog's health, consult your veterinarian.

&TEOTI ANDERSON, CPDT-KA, Pawsitive
Results, LLC, Lexington, SC

Much like humans, our dogs' bones and muscles get weaker as they get older, and it is harder to move efficiently. Swimming is very easy on the bones and muscles, so your senior dog can achieve a much better workout. I've seen older and injured dogs come back to life through swimming. Swimming is natural to dogs— and humans, for that matter. So get in the pool with your senior dog and get you and your dog in shape! It's never too late.

&MARY DISNEY,
Marina del Rey, CA

Encourage owners to train an older dog they may have at home. I use my own dogs as an example to clients: Dancer, who became a therapy dog at age 12 and served for five and a half years; and my adopted Yorkie, Fergie, who was successfully trained at age 15. If clients have concrete examples rather than just a blanket statement, I think it gives them more incentive and hope to address behavior issues with their older dogs. It also helps the resident older dog not be shunted aside in favor of the newer and possibly more obedient dog.

     ✐ANNE SPRINGER, BS, AKC Evaluator, Therapy Dogs, Inc., Tester, Paws for Praise, Danvers, MA

Always make sure that your senior dog is in good health before engaging in a new activity. A veterinary checkup is a good idea, letting the veterinarian know what type of activity you are planning to do with your dog to ensure that his structure is sound and he doesn't have a heart murmur or some other underlying issue. Our dogs can have problems for a long time before ever showing any signs. You may want to do agility to keep your dog active, but if he has a bit of movement in the knee, then you may want to consider rally or tracking so as not to exacerbate the problem. No matter which activity you choose, monitor your dog, looking for any change in his gait, breathing, or behavior. Stop any activity at the first sign of a problem—better yet, be proactive in preventing any injuries.

     ✐PAT HENNESSY, CAP2, CPDT-KA, N2paws, Leawood, KS

Look for good-quality, low-protein dog chow for seniors. And if they are having

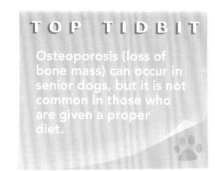

TOP TIDBIT

Osteoporosis (loss of bone mass) can occur in senior dogs, but it is not common in those who are given a proper diet.

trouble getting to their food, raise food and water dishes.

     ✐LYNETTE TATAY, Nashville, MI

When engaging in physical activity, you can help your senior dog by doing some gentle massage, TTouch™ (a light touch method for enhancing wellness), and some monitored swimming.

     ✐PAT HENNESSY, CAP2, CPDT-KA, N2paws, Leawood, KS

For your senior dog's achy joints, try supplementing with glucosamine/chondroitin/MSM.

     ✐LYNETTE TATAY, Nashville, MI

When your senior's hearing starts to go, use body language to continue communication. If his sight starts to go, don't move the furniture, and guide him around the house with his leash.

     ✐LYNETTE TATAY, Nashville, MI

SENIORS

For seniors who are homebound and have a dog loaded with energy, trick training can give the dog mental stimulation and physical work and is loads of fun for both

S

the person and the dog. Rolling over and shaking are just the beginning!

✎NANCY TANNER, CPDT-KA, Paws & People, LLC, Bozeman, MT

SEPARATION PROBLEMS

Dog hates his crate? Is it really a crate problem, or does your dog have a separation-related problem? If he does the same thing if you leave him in the bedroom, follows you from room to room, or is destructive around doors or windows when left alone, you should have him evaluated for separation problems.

✎BECKY SCHULTZ, BA, CPDT-KA, Becky Schultz Dog Training and Behavior, Golden Valley, MN

Separation anxiety is a learned behavior, usually resulting from an emotional dependency between the unsuspecting owner and the dog. It is important for dog owners to understand the importance of establishing an appropriate leadership role with their dog. The owner, being in charge, will give the dog a sense of security and calmness. His environment needs to be controlled by setting up the necessary structure, with both physical and emotional boundaries, regardless of if the owners are home or not. An example of this would be for the dog to spend some time "alone" and "ignored," such as in a crate, when the owners *are* home, so that when they are gone, it is no big deal.

✎DIANA FOSTER, Assertive K-9 Training Kennels, Corona, CA

Providing a variety of toys, stuffed chews, plenty of exercise, and a safe, comfortable place and bed area can help your dog be comfortable and secure in your absence.

✎CHRISTINA SHUSTERICH, BA, CBC, NY Clever K9, Inc., Queens, NY

Be sure to make your entrances and exits as neutral as possible to help prevent separation problems. Although it may go against your emotional inclinations, it is best not to say goodbye to your dog but rather to simply leave. On your return home, have him wait at least five to ten minutes until you greet him, and while your greetings may be affectionate, try to also keep them fairly matter of fact and as a matter of course.

✎CHRISTINA SHUSTERICH, BA, CBC, NY Clever K9, Inc., Queens, NY

Puppies instinctively fear being alone because they are not equipped to take care of themselves. But being alone for brief periods each day will be a fact of life for most puppies living in a human household. You can help your puppy learn to be alone by introducing the concept gradually, starting from the day he comes home. Rather than spend every waking moment with the puppy, put him in a puppy-proofed room or x-pen with an extra-special treat and leave the room for a few minutes at a time, building up alone time as he comes to accept it. Or as the puppy is falling asleep, quietly place him in the crate to nap, leaving the crate door open so that he can emerge upon awakening.

✎ANN ALLUMS, CPDT-KA, Best Friends Animal Society, Kanab, UT

NYLABONE

To prevent separation problems, it is best to gradually accustom your dog to your absence.

*CHRISTINA SHUSTERICH, BA, CBC, NY Clever K9, Inc., Queens, NY

Teaching your dog to be alone should begin the first day you bring him home. Don't spend every second showering him with attention because he's novel and fascinating or because you want to make him feel at home and secure. Your dog will be so let down when normal life begins. Immediately place him on a schedule that includes alone time. Leave for short periods, and avoid making elaborate exits and entrances. Place your dog in his designated space 15 minutes before you depart with something good to chew on, and leave him in this place 15 minutes after you come home. Do not remove your dog from his space if he is still overly excited about you arriving home. You must teach him that coming and going is no big deal—it is a normal, everyday part of living in your home.

*CRYSTAL COLL, All Ways Pawsitive Pet Behavior and Training, Queen Creek, AZ

SHAKE

To teach "shake," simply say "Shake" while gently lifting your dog's paw; once the paw is horizontal, treat him and then let go. As he learns, you will be able to pick up his paw with less and less force as he starts to raise it. You can then progress to tapping the back of his front paw to signal him to lift it, to finally using a hand signal of placing your hand palm up in front of him while saying "Shake," at which point he will place his paw in your hand.

*CHRISTINA SHUSTERICH, BA, CBC, President, NY Clever K9, Inc., Queens, NY

The simplest way to teach your dog to shake is by first putting him in a *sit* position. Take his paw in your hand as you say "Shake," and then follow with praise. Once your dog has the idea, you can ask him to shake on command!

*LUCINDA LUDWIG, Canine Connection LLC, Dubuque, IA

SHOWING (CONFORMATION)

Rather than teaching the dog to stand perfectly all at once, train the perfect stack in pieces. At first, just reinforce standing. Once he is easily standing, begin perfecting the *stand* by reinforcing just proper front foot placement. Once the front feet are easily placed, teach the dog to back up to fix his rear foot placement.

ℰVICKI RONCHETTE, CPDT-KA, CAP2,
Braveheart Dog Training, San Leandro, CA

Always start teaching new show puppies to stack as early as possible. Hold a piece of string cheese right in front of the puppy's mouth while you use your other hand to reposition his legs.

ℰVICKI RONCHETTE, CPDT-KA, CAP2,
Braveheart Dog Training, San Leandro, CA

If you have a dog who slips on the concrete building floors at dog shows, put a little cola on his feet. It will dry just sticky enough to give him some traction.

ℰVICKI RONCHETTE, CPDT-KA, CAP2,
Braveheart Dog Training, San Leandro, CA

SHYNESS

If a shy dog acts fearfully toward you (e.g., cowers, turns head, lip licks, leaks urine, exposes belly in a submissive manner), immediately ignore him. Do not reinforce the fear or submissive gesture with attention. Look away or turn your side to the dog, thereby making yourself less threatening. If you approach a dog who is cowering in submission, he will be reinforced for the submission and will think that this behavior resulted in a safe experience with you. But it's better for the

dog to overcome his fear and learn that people will not hurt him.

ℰANN ALLUMS, CPDT-KA, Best Friends
Animal Society, Kanab, UT

Targeting is a great behavior to teach a shy dog because the skill can help raise his confidence by teaching him how to interact in his environment to get good things from people. Targeting can also help a dog overcome fear of new objects by training him to target new objects for a reward.

ℰANN ALLUMS, CPDT-KA, Best Friends
Animal Society, Kanab, UT

I use the "Hansel & Gretel method" for distracting a shy, nervous, or fearful dog. When working with shelter dogs and other dogs who are hesitant to do something like cross thresholds, walk on a leash, etc., rather than trying to force the dog to move, I find it useful to divert his attention to something he is familiar with and enjoys. I toss a small treat in the direction I want to take the dog but still close to him. I continue to toss treats, and by the time the dog is moving in the direction I want, he often forgets what worried him.

ℰCAROL A. SIEGRIST, CPDT-KA, SIEGRIST
LLC, Dog Training & Behavior Consultation,
Philadelphia, PA

For a shy dog, try some very gentle circular touches and light stroking down his body for calming and focus. Expose him to a low level of stimulus (person in room at a distance). Provide a treat reward for confident behavior when exposed to the stimulus. Slowly increase his exposure to the stimulus (distance and duration), along with providing gentle touch and a treat reward. Highly reward the dog when his choice is to be more confident around the stimulus.

PAT HENNESSY, CAP2, CPDT-KA,
N2paws, Leawood, KS

Apply a small amount of pure lanolin to your hands to get a shy dog more at ease and interested in approaching you to take a treat.

DARLENE PINO, Clever Canines Dog
Training, Albany, GA

Sometimes when I go to a client's home for an in-house private lesson, the dog may be so shy or fearful that he will not come anywhere near me. To earn his trust quickly, I need to separate him from the security he feels being close to his owner. So I ask the owner to put the leash on the dog (be sure that it is secure, as some dogs will try to escape), and I walk him outside the house. The parent can watch from the window inside the home. Getting a shy or fearful dog away from the security of his owner forces the dog to quickly look to me for guidance. I'll reward the dog for any good behavior he shows me while walking in front of the house, including just the simple act of walking with me. In most cases, I'm able to gain his confidence within five minutes and can then continue with the lesson in the house with the owner and a dog who is not fearful of me.

JANICE DEMADONA, Dog Training With
Janice, Orlando, FL

SIT

When teaching and practicing the *sit*, it may help to put a leash on your dog to limit his options. Stand on the end of the leash so that you can't pull on it. In this way, the dog only has a few feet (m) of space in which to get distracted. When you have rewarded the *sit* behavior numerous times, you can start to allow your dog more room during training because he will be more likely to respond to your request even in the face of distractions.

ANN ALLUMS, CPDT-KA, Best Friends
Animal Society, Kanab, UT

When you are trying to lure a dog into a *sit* and he keeps backing up all over the room, try putting his backside up against a wall. (For a small dog, you can sit on the floor with your legs in a "V" with your feet on the wall.) Lure the *sit*. This will keep the dog from backing up too far since he'll either hit the wall or your leg. Even if he half-sits on your leg, click and treat. That is the start of your *sit*. Then progress to a couple of *sits* on the leg, then move your leg and you'll have a *sit* on the floor.

DEBBIE REVELL, RN, Dip.CABT,
CDBC, Pets Behave LLC, Niceville, FL

S

When asking your dog to sit, do not bend over toward or lean over him, which is a threatening act to a dog. Threatening or forcing him to obey is not a positive or even a reliable way to ensure compliance. If taught using rewards, your dog will enthusiastically want to respond to your cue to sit (as well as any cue), not just in hopes of a reward but because he has a positive relationship with you.

～ANN ALLUMS, CPDT-KA, Best Friends Animal Society, Kanab, UT

When teaching a pup to sit for an upraised cookie, be careful to bring the treat directly up rather than back over his head. Keeping the cookie directly vertical will get you a tuck *sit* from a pup who sits close enough to hold onto, rather than a dog who backs up to sit and ends up out of hand range. A closer puppy is a safer pup, and it just happens to get you better front positions for obedience competitions too.

～P.J. LACETTE, the original Best Paw Forward, Osteen, FL

Teaching your dog to sit in distracting situations is not nearly as tough as you might think. The secret is to stop using a verbal command and start teaching your dog to *offer* the *sit* to get what he wants. Start by putting a treat in your hand and holding it over your dog's head. Wait silently and ignore any antics such as jumping. When he finally sits, say "Yes!" and then toss him the treat. Each time you do this, the *sit* will happen faster. Try this with your dog's toys, chews, and meals too. At doors, put your hand on the knob and quietly wait for him to offer a *sit*. When he does, say "Yes!" and then open the door for him. The more you practice this, the more often *sits* will happen without you even asking!

～LAUREL SCARIONI, CPDT-KA, Pawsitive Results Critter Academy, Santa Rosa, CA

Does your pup pop up out of a *sit* as soon as you give him his treat? Try the "SPOT" method–Sit Pet Offer Treat. This teaches your puppy to politely sit while being greeted and petted by simply petting him before giving him a treat. The most difficult part is retraining you, as most people seem to naturally want to pet their pup after giving him a treat. If your pup jumps up at your petting hand or shies away from it, begin with just a brief touch under his cheek or chin. And if you use a lure to teach the *sit*, it is easy to distract your pup with your luring hand while you pet with your other hand. Continue SPOT and soon your pup will remain sitting while you pet him with both hands. SPOT also teaches your pup to like petting more!

～CERENA ZUTIS, San Mateo, CA

S

SLEEP

Many dogs (like most people) do not like to be jolted awake while sleeping. Oftentimes they grow up learning that growling or even snapping at someone when disturbed like this makes the offender "go away." Unless a dog has been taught from puppyhood that sudden disturbances during sleep are nonthreatening (a very good idea!), he is likely to see this type of thing as frightening and probably a bit frustrating too. When in doubt, it is always safest to just leave him be. Do not touch him—instead, waken him verbally with an upbeat "Doggy, let's go!" before attempting to move or otherwise interact with him. Once he "comes to," he should be alright and look forward to being touched.

ᏋᏝLISA PATRONA, Dip. DTBC, CPDT-KA, PDT, CBC, Trainers Academy, LLC, President, Troy, MI

SMALL DOGS

Always check with your vet to be sure that you know the appropriate amount and type of exercise for your small dog. Tiny Chihuahuas have different capabilities from little Yorkshire Terriers! And flexible young pups have different exercise needs from achy older dogs.

ᏋᏝDIANE PODOLSKY, CPDT-KA, CTC, The Cultured Canine, LLC, White Plains, NY

One big mistake that owners of little dogs make is thinking bad behavior is cute. A toy dog who growls over his toys or when you go to brush him is not funny—he's aggressive. True, he can't do as much damage as a larger dog, but what if a child is involved? If it wouldn't be cute in a Great Dane, then it's not adorable in a Maltese. If you're having issues with growling, snapping, or biting behavior, don't chuckle. Call a professional reward-based trainer or certified applied animal behaviorist for assistance today.

ᏋᏝTEOTI ANDERSON, CPDT-KA, Pawsitive Results, LLC, Lexington, SC

All dogs need physical exercise and mental stimulation, even the tiniest ones. But often tiny dogs can't go outside when the weather is too hot or too cold. What's a dog lover to do? Play a game like "sit, stay, come!" Teach your dog to sit and stay. Once this is well learned, ask him to sit and stay while you walk a short distance away with a supply of kibble or treats in your pocket. Release and call your dog to you, cheerleading him as he runs toward you. When he arrives, give him a generous amount of food. Then ask him to sit and stay again while you move a bit farther away this time. After a few repetitions of this exercise, your dog will be using energy and brain power sitting, staying, and rocketing toward you when you release and call him.

ᏋᏝDIANE PODOLSKY, CPDT-KA, CTC, The Cultured Canine, LLC, White Plains, NY

> **"Small dogs tend to live significantly longer than larger dogs."**

Many owners of small dogs complain that their dogs won't come when called. However, many do respond, only to stop a few feet (m) away, just out of arms' reach. The reason? Often when a small dog responds to the *come* command, the dog is swooped down upon and lifted into the owner's arms; that overhead swoop is frightening to the dog. Owners can fix the behavior by taking a different approach to lifting their dog—stoop, don't swoop! Crouch down, turn your body sideways, then pet your dog. After a moment, gently pick the dog up. Alternately, ask him to jump up onto a cushion or couch, and lift from there.

> ✑NICOLE WILDE, CPDT-KA, Gentle Guidance Dog Training, Santa Clarita, CA

Don't reward jumping—unless you like it! This is particularly noticeable with smaller dogs who jump up to take a treat from your hand. If you don't want your small dog to jump on humans, then make sure that you bring your hand toward your dog's face

in a low and horizontal manner, as opposed to vertically.

> ✑PATRICIA BENTZ, CPDT-KA, CDBC, K-9 Training & Behavioral Therapy, Philadelphia, PA

A fun indoor game for a small dog is "doggy step agility." Purchase a few sets of doggy steps. (Many different models are available commercially.) Teach your dog to use the steps—the lure and reward method works very well. Once he is comfortable going up and down the steps and onto the sofa or an armchair, start naming the locations. Say "Sofa" and direct your dog (most dogs will follow an exaggerated arm gesture) to the sofa for a treat. Say "Chair" and direct your dog to the armchair for a treat. Before you know it, you'll be able to send him to various locations in the living room (and who knows—maybe other rooms too!), running up and down the doggy stairs in pursuit of treats and belly rubs.

> ✑DIANE PODOLSKY, CPDT-KA, CTC, The Cultured Canine, LLC, White Plains, NY

SMALL DOGS, TRAINING

Small dogs can learn just as well as their larger canine cousins. A common mistake people make when training their little ones is treating toy breeds like fragile objects. If your toy never touches the ground, how can he learn to walk on four paws? Fussing and worrying over a toy breed will only make him insecure and could cause shyness or aggression. Have confidence! Little dogs are perfectly capable of all sorts of activities, including dog sports.

> ✑TEOTI ANDERSON, CPDT-KA, Pawsitive Results, LLC, Lexington, SC

S

Small dogs carry with them natural vulnerabilities that are associated with being prey as well as predator. Wild rabbits weigh more than many tiny dogs! In addition to a sense of personal territory that all dogs possess, tiny dogs are especially sensitive to interactions that resemble hovering, swooping, and grabbing. Training tables greatly reduce perceptions of hovering, and target sticks can reduce perceptions of hovering and swooping. Squatting down to allow a tiny dog to jump into your lap, then standing up with him in your arms, can reduce perceptions of swooping and grabbing when picking him up.

&KRIS BUTLER, American Dog Obedience Center, LLC, Norman, OK

One of the top issues I hear about with small dogs is that they are difficult to housetrain. As the owner of two rescue dogs who were given up because of house soiling issues, I know this is a major issue. I believe it is due to the fact that people think that because small dogs are cute, they somehow come trained. The owners don't bother to offer guidance or training—only punishment for normal dog behavior. For dogs, if it's not a bed, it's a toilet! Small dogs need supervision and training, just like big dogs.

&DEENA MCIVER, K-9 Kind, Portland, OR

The idea that little dogs are difficult or impossible to housetrain is just a myth. Physiologically, small dogs function the same as large dogs, and they are just as capable of becoming housetrained as their larger counterparts. The principles of behavioral learning theory and science apply to a Maltese or Toy Poodle, just as they do to a Great Dane! A commonly reported problem is that small dogs react more to inclement weather, which is understandable. There are some things that we can do to help: Buy a doggy coat for extra comfort when it is cold or chilly outside; build a small sheltered area right outside the door and train him to use it for elimination; and teach your dog to do his "business" quickly. His reward will be not only relief but a quick return to the comfort of your cozy house.

&LISA PATRONA, Dip. DTBC, CPDT-KA, PDT, CBC, Trainers Academy, LLC, President, Troy, MI

When training small dogs, get on the floor! A lot of small dogs jump up on you just because they are small, and to reach a reward/treat, they'll jump up to you. Get down on their level and things will go a lot smoother.

&ROBERT JORDAN, CPDT-KA, Pavlov's Dogs Pet Training, Mechanicsville, VA

dog is enthusiastic about hand-feeding, unstuffing puzzles, and playing "go find it," you're ready to use your everyday food as reinforcers when training.

    ℯ◞DIANE PODOLSKY, CPDT-KA, CTC, The Cultured Canine, LLC, White Plains, NY

If you're having trouble luring your small dog into a *down*, start by luring the behavior, but when you reach the floor, move the treat toward the rear of the dog. Move your hand very slowly and along his side. Your dog will try to turn his head with you, and sometimes this will cause him to go into a *down*.

    ℯ◞NATALIA ROZAS DE O'LAUGHLIN, CDPT, Houston Pet Help, Houston, TX

A great way to teach the *down* to small dogs is to sit on the floor with your legs bent. Your knees should just be tall enough so that your dog has to bend down to get under them. Give the cue "Down." Use a friendly voice! With a treat in one hand, lure your dog under your legs. The second his belly touches the floor, mark the behavior with your marker word, "Yes!" Give him the treat and praise him. Give the *release* cue, "Okay," and encourage him to get up. Repeat a few times, but keep your training session short so that he doesn't get bored. When he's lying down reliably, sit on the floor with your legs crossed. If you go straight to standing upright, it may confuse him. Use your same hand motion as if you were luring him down under your knees—this has become your hand signal. When he lies down, mark "Yes!" and give him a treat. Repeat. Gradually work to standing upright with your dog lying down.

    ℯ◞TEOTI ANDERSON, CPDT-KA, Pawsitive Results, LLC, Lexington, SC

As a trainer who specializes in working with toy-breed dogs, I often hear the complaint, "…but my dog doesn't like food." Unless the dog is ill or very underweight, this usually means that he has free access to food or receives more food than he can or wants to consume at each mealtime. (Always check with your vet so that you know how much food your dog should consume each day for good health.) Assuming that your little dog is in good general health, try the following to increase his enjoyment of food (and thereby make it a more powerful motivator): Hand-feed your dog; be sure that food is only available when you'd like it to be; build your dog's confidence by feeding via puzzle toys and hollow chews; and teach him to scavenge for food by playing "go find it!" Once your

S

To lure a small dog into a *down*, start by luring the command, but when you reach the floor, move the treat toward his chest (as if you were going to put your hand below him). Some dogs will go into a *down* trying to follow the treat; other dogs will just walk backward, so if this happens, try something different.

꙳NATALIA ROZAS DE O'LAUGHLIN, CDPT, Houston Pet Help, Houston, TX

When I encounter a small dog who refuses to go into a *down* on cue using a food lure/clicks, I try to encourage the behavior by placing him on a soft mat (a bath towel) folded and placed covering the floor. I've found good results with this extra-cuddly spot enticing him to down.

꙳LEIGH SANSONE, JD, CPDT-KA, PMCT, Ruff Customers Dog Training, New York, NY

Small dogs can sometimes be difficult to teach to lie down. Try putting the dog on a table and luring him holding the treat below the edge of the table. Most will lie down pretty quickly.

꙳JACKIE LOESER, CPDT-KA, Riverbend Agility Dogs, Stevensville, MT

When working with small dogs who are already so close to the ground, I have been asked, "What is the point of having him lie down? He's already so close to the ground!"

The *down* is a great cue to use to either let your dog know to relax or that you will be in this position a while (think sitting at a café or a park bench).

꙳LISA COLÓN TUDOR, CPDT-KA, KissAble Canine, LLC, Arlington, VA

For a small dog who's not going into the *down* position, start by luring the command, but when you reach the floor, move the treat toward you (and away from your dog). He will try to follow and crouch down while trying to walk. Some dogs go into a *down* here; others just walk forward without going into a *down*, so if this is your case, try something different.

꙳NATALIA ROZAS DE O'LAUGHLIN, CDPT, Houston Pet Help, Houston, TX

When training a small dog for position (*sit*, *down*, *stay*, *stand*, etc.), place him a few steps up on stairs. It's easier on your back, it "confines" him somewhat, and it imposes some structure. A single stair is easier to learn the *stand-stay* on, as he doesn't have much room to spin, lie down, turn around, or roll over!

꙳TERRY PRIDE, Missing Link Pet Services, Virginia Beach, VA

Some little dogs do not like to sit or down on a cold floor. (After all, many of them are used to being held.) Ask the pet parent to bring a mat, towel, or bed to class.

꙳DARLENE KOZA, Scooter's School of Sit & Stay, Rochester, NY

When training a small dog, it is sometimes easier to start teaching stationary behaviors with the dog up on a sturdy table. By elevating him, you can more easily help him be successful in learning to sit, stand, or down. Be sure that the table is not wobbly or slick. Once the dog can perform the desired behavior on the table, put him on the floor and begin working the behavior down there. Your dog and your back will thank you!

&DAWN ANTONIAK-MITCHELL, Esq., CPDT-KA, BonaFide Dog Academy LLC, Omaha, NE

I use a bamboo back scratcher to teach targeting and heeling to small dogs. Put cream cheese or baby food meat on the end of the back scratcher, and reward the dog for touching the end of the scratcher. When he's comfortable with that, walk with him in the *heel* position with the back scratcher held in your left hand and the end of it at the dog's nose level. When he stays beside you, allow him to lick off the cream cheese; if he is not beside you, allow him to see the scratcher but not get the cream cheese. Make sure that the food is something he really likes.

&REENA S. WALTON, Pups-R-Us Dog Training, Redwood City, CA

If you are delivering a treat using a fly swatter or kitchen spatula, make sure that you're not using it to lure your small dog. Keep the targeting tool down at your side.

&MONICA JOY, Happy Tails Pet Resort, Hubbard Lake, MI

Having difficulty getting through to owners of small dogs to teach their pups to keep their feet on the floor instead of scampering up people's legs? Have the owners attend class wearing shorts.

&JOANN KOVACICH, Grateful Dog Pet Care, Inc., Penfield, NY

The physical size of your canine students can directly influence both your sales and the effectiveness of your training. Offering "Petite Pooch" courses for dogs under 20 pounds (9 kg) can dramatically add to your sales. Many pet parents are concerned that their dogs will not do well when attending classes with larger dogs. Petite Pooch classes can help these individuals feel more comfortable enrolling in your course. Without the fear of larger dogs, many of these smaller dogs will become much more relaxed. This creates fewer management problems for you and allows full concentration on your course materials. A Petite Pooch course, designed around your basic adult course, is win-win for everyone.

&WAYNE SHAFFER, ABCDT, Pawsitive Methods, Kelseyville, CA

Training small dogs may be difficult, depending on the flexibility of the guardian. Teaching a solid targeting cue (nose to a stick or spatula) can be very helpful. You can then use this to teach other behaviors, like *heel*, which can be taught by holding a long target stick at your side and having the dog follow the stick. You can also use the target stick to teach a *spin* or *down* or any behavior that requires you to bend down over the dog.

&HEATHER MOHAN-GIBBONS, MS, RVT, CPDT-KA, ACAAB, Collected Wisdom Animal Behavior, LLC, Milwaukee, WI

SOCIALIZATION

One of the most important aspects of having a puppy is socialization. The puppy has a socialization window—the time when he is more open to accepting novel things than at any other time during his life—from age 3 weeks to 16 weeks. During this time, the more proper socialization (positive experiences) owners can provide their puppy, the better adjusted he will be when encountering new things later in life.

&ANN ALLUMS, CPDT-KA, Best Friends Animal Society, Kanab, UT

It's extremely important to socialize your puppy, especially up to the age of five months. Socialization should be positive. Expose your puppy to as many different people, puppies, and experiences as possible.

&DARLENE KOZA, Scooter's School of Sit & Stay, Rochester, NY

Proper socialization is the key to preventing many future behavior problems, but it's important that you take the right approach. All experiences must be positive ones, especially for a young puppy. For example, if you take your puppy to a dog park and all the other dogs gang up around him to smell him and this frightens him, he may learn that other dogs are scary. If you take your puppy to a friend's and there are loud, boisterous children who frighten him, he may learn that children should be avoided. These kinds of experiences may cause your puppy to grow up to be a dog who growls, snaps, or even bites children and other dogs. To prevent this, control the experiences he has. Only let him meet and play with safe, gentle dogs. Start with one dog at a time, then gradually work up to multiple canine friends. Only let your puppy meet friendly, gentle people of all ages. Set up all your puppy's experiences so that they are positive ones. He will learn that the world is a friendly, safe place, which will make him less likely to develop fear or aggression problems later.

&TEOTI ANDERSON, CPDT-KA, Pawsitive Results, LLC, Lexington, SC

Socialization is a key to a good relationship with your dog for the rest of his life. Proper socialization should begin as soon as you get your puppy. If he's younger than ten weeks of age and you're socializing him to another animal, begin with the puppy at a distance away from that animal. Dogs exposed to your pup should be gentle, with a good temperament. Never expose your puppy to a dog who has a poor temperament or any inkling of aggression. Also avoid any dogs who are ill.

&STACY L. BRUSSEAU, CBC, Positive Pet Training, Rochester, NY

Puppies are like sponges—they want and need to absorb as much as they can! It is important to expose your puppy to as many positive experiences as possible during his formative weeks and months. Let him explore different textures under his feet, like sand, rocks, tile floors, or grass. Set up an obstacle course in your own living room or backyard, and use baby gates to walk across, branches from a tree to crawl through and over, and paper and plastic trash bags to provide exposure to unique sounds and textures. Then let the games begin!

&KAREN VASS-DEEDS, Canine Connection, Ft. Worth, TX

Make all interactions with your dog short and positive, including greeting new people wearing hats and uniforms and attending new places and new surfaces (sand, gravel, concrete, and grass). Do the same with household appliances, including vacuum cleaners and lawn mowers. Let your dog sniff the device and give treats when turning it on and off so that he gets used to it.

&BONNIE KRUPA, Happy, Clean and Smart, Muncie, IN

The best gifts you can give to your new puppy are positive experiences and exposure to as many people, places, things, events, and other appropriate dogs as possible.

&NANCY TANNER, CPDT-KA, Paws & People, LLC, Bozeman, MT

If your dog is afraid of new people, help him learn that strangers are safe. Forget about forcing him to accept petting from a stranger, which will only serve to increase his fear and feeling of hopelessness around strangers. Instead, arm yourself with tasty treats for your dog. When he becomes aware of a stranger, *you* (not the stranger) should begin feeding your dog. Do not ask the stranger to give your dog a treat until your dog is comfortable approaching the person. Otherwise, he may take the treat but do so fearfully. By initially feeding the dog yourself, you are showing him that good things happen when strangers are in sight.

&ANN ALLUMS, CPDT-KA, Best Friends Animal Society, Kanab, UT

S

Don't push your dog to be social with dogs (or people) beyond his comfort zone. If he is already in a strange place, his tolerance threshold will be reduced. Most people will understand if you ask them to back off from your dog.

ꙮDEVENE GODAU, CPDT-KA, Trainers Academy, LLC, Royal Oak, MI

Before becoming a dog trainer, when it came to socializing my dogs, I always thought "Make the dog endure it if he's scared–he'll learn." But now that I know learning theory, I like to tell my clients this story: Suppose you were adopted by aliens and those aliens are friendly with polar bears–yikes! The aliens take you to a room where eight polar bears are staring at you and wiggling their claws and growling (which happens to be their way of laughing). Imagine how stressful that would be! Conversely, imagine if those eight polar bears were not looking at you and were not interested in you and in fact were on the other side of the room. Would that make you feel better? Each day or week you'd become more curious about those polar bears, and eventually you'd be playing soccer with them! The point is to not force a shy or fearful dog into a stressful situation beyond his threshold. Slow and steady wins the socialization race.

ꙮDONNA SAVOIE, CPDT-KA, Pack of Paws Dog Training, Charlton, MA

Regarding socialization, gender-specific socialization should not be overlooked. Recently, one of my single male clients met the woman of his dreams, but the sound of her hair dryer each morning was *not* the sound included in the dog's dreams! Because the male dog owner never used a

blow-dryer, this sound was completely new to the dog and he was incredibly fearful of it. I was called to help desensitize and countercondition the dog to the sound of the blow-dryer. Before the behavioral work, the dog cowered at the other end of the home. After desensitization and counterconditioning, he would eagerly sit and wait for treats outside the door to the bathroom when the new girlfriend blow-dried her hair! If you are single at the moment, think of things that your dog might need to be introduced to and socialized to in regard to a significant other who may come into you and your dog's life. These things may include the smell of strong perfumes or colognes, scented deodorants, male- or female-scented clothing items, hair dryers and blowers, electric razors, and more!

ꙮMADELINE ARONSON-FRIEDMAN, Innovative Reality Dog Training & Dog Behaviour Consulting, Staten Island, NY

I love sending my new puppy clients to hang out in front of a big home improvement store. The puppies meet a variety of people and they get to hear and see strange things to them, such as large trucks with beeping sounds as they back up, large carts with wobbling wheels, and lots of men wearing hats. Take a pocketful of treats and make it a fun time for the puppies.

♒TERRI ERICKSON, CPDT-KA, Pawlite Pups, LLC, Glendora, CA

Afraid to get your puppy out there for proper socialization? Try one of the new pet strollers. They're not just for cats, small dogs, or rabbits! You can now safely stroll your puppy through local stores, parks, and your neighborhood. When he has finished his vaccinations, you can sell your stroller to another new puppy owner.

♒TRACEY SCHOWALTER, Puppy Adept, Inc., Gainesville, GA

Want to get your new puppy used to all kinds of people? Take him to your local city hall or municipal building, bring lots of good treats, and gently introduce him to everyone coming and going. He'll meet people in uniform, business types, families, and people of different races. And it will be all positive if you encourage him with a treat when he does well.

♒PAULA KELMAN, CPDT-KA, Eagle Ridge Kennels, Buffalo, NY

Train and socialize your puppy outside of supermarkets. Take him for a short visit to a shopping center, and bring lots of delicious treats. Position yourself near the entrance. Have your puppy sit, and reward him every time someone passes by to go in or out of the supermarket. If anyone wants to pet your pup, have him sit and then allow the person to pet him. Ask the person to give him a treat. Your puppy will practice sitting for lots of people, will learn

that meeting new people is fun, and will be exposed to lots of new sights and noises. Keep the trip short and happy so that he has a good experience.

♒BARBARA LONG, CPDT-KA, Paw in Hand Dog Training, Chapel Hill, NC

SPEAK

The first step in teaching any behavior is to get the behavior. Dogs aren't born knowing English, so telling your dog to do something like "speak" is irrelevant until it is associated with a behavior that he offers. To get the behavior, do something that elicits a bark. Some examples include getting him excited with a toy, teasing him with a treat (showing it to him but not giving it to him), or jumping around yourself acting excited, all the while waiting for any type of vocalization he makes. He may offer only a slight noise at first, which you should reward immediately because it is the first step in barking. (Rewards should be a small but luscious treat.) As your dog learns that you want him to make noise, hold out for a louder noise until you finally get a bark. After he is reliably offering the bark, introduce the verbal cue ("Speak") followed by your original enticement to get the bark so that he connects the verbal cue with the behavior.

♒ANN ALLUMS, CPDT-KA, Best Friends Animal Society, Kanab, UT

SPITE

When a dog does something wrong, some owners believe he is being "spiteful" or "stubborn." In truth, dogs do not think or learn like humans. They neither process nor assign moral values to their behaviors. This statement is not based on opinion; it's based on cognitive and behavioral science. Rest assured that conclusive research has already invalidated any possibility of the existence of moral codes directing canine behaviors.

When words like "spiteful" and "stubborn" are used to describe a dog's behavior, we need to move our thinking to reflect the real problem—the dog has not been trained properly or effectively.

    ᐤDEVENE GODAU, CPDT-KA, Trainers
Academy, LLC, Royal Oak, MI

SPORTS

It has been my experience that it is far more effective and fun to let a dog find his favorite sports and talents than to choose a dog because *you* want to do a particular sport. Try taking your herding purebred or mix for a herding lesson, or take your tennis ball-loving dog to try flyball. And if you have a mixed breed for whom it is hard to pin down any single breed, try the "universal"

sports: swimming, dock diving, tracking, agility, skijoring, mountain bikejoring, flying disc, or canicross (jogging/running with your dog cabled to your waist as if you were a dogsled). Every dog needs an outlet, and every relationship is strengthened when an owner and dog find joy in doing something fun together.

    ᐤSUE STERNBERG, Animals for Adoption
and Great Dog Productions,
Accord, NY, and Moab, UT

When practicing dog sports or other competitive events, keep your mood and tone upbeat. If you make a mistake and frown or sigh, your dog may misinterpret that look as a mistake on his part, and you may find yourself with a disheartened dog who no longer wishes to work. At an agility practice session, I witnessed this when an owner got lost on the course. She stopped, frowned, and shook her head, and her dog immediately wandered off, sniffing the ground. She had a difficult time getting his attention back until she forced a smile and a happy tone to reassure him that all was well.

    ᐤM. CECILIA STERNZON,
CPDT-KA, Canine Higher
Learning, San Jose, CA

Right before the next obedience, rally, or agility trial comes up, load up on extra treats for a week or two during every training session. The dog's increased excitement and attention should

> **Some companies now make sports drinks and bottled water specifically for dogs.**

last through an extinction burst of great attention and responsiveness in the ring. Of course, be careful that this is a time for rewards, not lures—don't show your dog the cookie first. The time to wean off frequent treats is before you sent your entries, not right before the event, so that you have a longer pattern of good behavior before delivering a primary reward, toys, or play.

✏️P.J. LACETTE, the original Best Paw Forward, Osteen, FL

STAIRS

Practice safety when it comes to stairs. Teach your dog to sit, down, or stand-stay at the top or bottom of stairs so that you won't get bombarded or even fall. Position yourself in the middle of the steps while still holding the railing. If there is a railing, most dogs will choose to go up or down on the outside of the stairs next to the railing rather than the middle. Have your dog sit-stay in the center at the top or bottom of the stairs. Dogs tend to choose a straight path, and by you going up or down in the middle of the stairs, you'll take up more space; this will temporarily block your dog's path and/or vision.

✏️BEVERLEY HAGUE KEZAR, Canada

Some dogs are afraid of using spiral stairs because they tend to be both smaller and steeper than regular stairs. Begin by showing your dog the stairs; stand by the landing and treat him. After he is comfortable with being on the landing, take a few steps down the stairs and call him. Mark and reward any step toward the stairs' edge—praise your dog's exploration. If he takes any steps onto the stairs—jackpot! Reward as many steps as he will take. Move slowly, and *do not* pull your dog down the stairs. Next, place high-value treats on each step, and encourage him to take steps down. When he backs up, end the session. Encourage your dog at the end of successive sessions both with your presence farther down the stairs (or all the way down the stairs) and with more treats and praise. Progress as slowly as your dog needs, and wildly encourage and mark with treats every step, or even with every slight exploration downward, until he progresses all the way down the stairs. Over a period (which depends on the fear level of the dog), after he gets down the stairs the first time, it's party time with liver treats or cheese!

✏️LEIGH SANSONE, JD, CPDT-KA, PMCT, Ruff Customers Dog Training, New York, NY

STAND

I like to teach all puppies and dogs in my class how to stand. Your vet and groomer will highly appreciate it if your dog knows how to do this (even better if he will stand and stay still). This command comes in useful when you are bathing or brushing your dog at home. And I really like it when it is rainy out and my yard is muddy, and I can bring my dogs in the back door, tell them to stand, and they accept me wiping off their muddy paws!

Start with your dog sitting, and show him a treat right in front of his nose. Slowly bring the treat forward, level with his nose, just enough to get him into the *stand* position. Tell him "Good stand," give him a treat, and release him. Each week, do more of a progression until you can get your dog to stand still for up to the amount of time it would take to groom, brush him, or give him a bath. It's an excellent command for your dog to learn!

—SHIRLEY RICHARDS, CPDT-KA, Coulee Region Humane Society, Onalaska, WI

STAY

The first step in teaching a *sit-stay* is to start in the most boring, quietest room in the house, with the most exciting treats in your dog's world (e.g., roast beef, chicken, cheese.) Without saying a word, lure your dog into a *sit*. As soon as his bottom hits the floor, begin feeding him tiny pieces of treats, one at a time, in rapid succession so that he sees that his bottom on the floor is a good thing. Say a release word (e.g., "release," "go play," "okay"), at which point he is free to do what he wants to do, but he does not get treats after the release. Repeat, gradually increasing the time in between treats, during which your dog is still maintaining the *sit*. By feeding him multiple treats when he is in the position you want, you are building a rewardable behavior, showing him that as long as he maintains the *sit*, he gets treats. By incorporating the release word, he will learn to hold the behavior in hopes of getting another treat until he is released.

—ANN ALLUMS, CPDT-KA, Best Friends Animal Society, Kanab, UT

When teaching the *stay*, it's important to choose and use a consistent word to release your dog from the command. Many people use "okay," but because that word is used so commonly in regular conversation, you might instead choose a word like "free" or "release" to signal the end of a *stay* to your dog.

—ERICA PYTLOVANY, CPDT-KA, WOOFS! Dog Training Center, Arlington, VA

For the *stay* command, I always say: "The best way to get success is to get success—and be able to reward it!" In other words, keep the *stays* just easy enough for the dog to succeed and be rewarded and released, rather than pushing him to the point of breaking the *stay* and then correcting it. This will give you much faster results.

&M. CECILIA STERNZON, CPDT-KA, Canine Higher Learning, San Jose, CA.

It's easier than you think to teach your dog to stay when you incorporate it into your regular daily routine. If you can spare 30 seconds a few times a day, you have the time it takes to teach your dog the basics of a *stay*. For example, ask him to sit and stay when you put his food bowl on the floor. Or every time he goes out the front or back door, you have another place in your daily routine that you can integrate a *stay*. Our house has a "magic door" that only opens if there are doggy butts on the ground. Try to find other places in your own daily routine where you can spend 30 seconds to practice a *stay*; other examples could include getting out of the car or getting to go sniff a favorite hydrant while out on a walk.

&ERICA PYTLOVANY, CPDT-KA, WOOFS! Dog Training Center, Arlington, VA

Until your dog is proficient at a *stay*, don't make it any harder by adding duration (how long he has to sit), distance (how far away you are from your dog), or distractions. If he is not successfully doing a *sit-stay* when you ask, it is your job to make it easier (e.g., less distractions) so that he does succeed.

&ANN ALLUMS, CPDT-KA, Best Friends Animal Society, Kanab, UT

I've found that a great place to practice the *stay* for duration is in the bathroom. It's a small, quiet environment that limits distractions and helps keep the pup focused on you.

&LEIGH SANSONE, JD, CPDT-KA, PMCT, Ruff Customers Dog Training, New York, NY

Training a dog to stay before doors and follow you through rather than pull you through is a very useful command. It not only makes taking your dog out more convenient, but also once learned, it utilizes obedience as a part of life for life rewards (going out) and eliminates treats. It is a critical command for apartment dwellers and those with dog-aggressive or people-aggressive dogs, as both people and dogs can be near your front door, the elevator door, or the lobby door.

&CHRISTINA SHUSTERICH, BA, CBC, NY Clever K9, Inc., Queens, NY

Train *stays* when your dog is tired, like before bedtime, after a hard run, after eating, etc.

&LYNETTE TATAY, Nashville, MI

STEALING

If you want your dog to stop running off with things, try this: When he grabs something, surprise him by saying "Yes! Good dog," and toss a handful of small, really yummy treats at him. Unless the item is dangerous for him to have, don't worry about reclaiming it. Every time he picks something up, repeat this. Soon you will find that when your dog picks up something, he will no longer start to destroy it but will look at you in expectation of a treat. It won't be long until he'll bring things to you to trade. You've just successfully trained a retrieve and solved your stealing problem!

     ᴇ✐TERRY LONG, CPDT-KA, DogPACT Training and Behavior Services, Long Beach, CA

Some dogs take things they shouldn't because they love the attention of the chase you give them after they "steal." To help discourage the behavior, consider giving your dog his "reward" when he has something he *should* have. For example, whenever he picks up a doggy toy, chase him around like you would if he had your best dress shoe. Don't act angry—talk to him happily as you pursue him in a lovely game of chase. Teaching him that your attention is given when he nabs a dog toy will soon have him choosing toys over shoes!

     ᴇ✐CJ BENTLEY, CPDT-KA, Michigan Humane Society, Detroit, MI

Got a tissue or napkin stealer? I did. She would steal them and then I would find little paper pieces all over the room, or worse, would find only a few pieces. The obvious fix is to keep napkins out of your dog's reach. But if you're not so good at this (like me!), you may want to try what I did. To change my dog's behavior, I started paying her for whole napkins. In other words, if I caught her with the whole napkin in her mouth (or even a large piece at first), I would ask if she wanted to trade it for a yummy treat that I would hold up to her mouth. After several of these opportunities, she started searching me out with the whole napkin in her mouth hoping to trade for something better. The downside? Sometimes she brings me other things too. The upside? She could have chosen to chew up those other things too.

     ᴇ✐TRACEY SCHOWALTER, Puppy Adept, Inc., Gainesville, GA

SUBMISSIVE URINATION

Some dogs urinate out of excitement or as a signal of submission. If your dog greets you vigorously, then rolls over or squats and pees, you need to keep your greetings very calm. It helps to ignore your dog for a few minutes after you arrive home and to teach him relaxation exercises like a long *sit* or *down-stay*.

     ᴇ✐JIM BARRY, CDBC, CPDT-KA, Reston Dog Training, Reston, VA

If you have a dog who submissively urinates, ask arriving visitors not to look at or talk to him and to ignore him momentarily. After a few minutes, the guest can stand or sit–still not looking directly at the dog–and using slow motions, give treats or pet him when he approaches.

ℰ BONNIE KRUPA, CPDT-KA, Happy, Clean and Smart, Muncie, IN

SWIMMING

If you're swimming for the first time with your dog, start in shallow water and coax him in by calling his name. Encourage him with toys or treats. Or let him follow another experienced dog with whom he is friendly.

ℰ JAMIE DAMATO, CPDT-KA, Animalsense Canine Training and Behavior, Inc., Chicago, IL

SWIMMING POOLS

Pool safety is an important thing to consider if you have a dog and a pool. Not only is it important to teach your children the importance of pool safety, but it is also something you need to teach your dog.

Many people have come home to find that their beloved family dog has drowned in the pool. You may think that your dog can swim if he has to or that he won't try to go in the pool, but he can accidentally fall into it. If he has not been taught how to exit the pool, he may not know how to find the way out. Everyone who has a pool in their yard should take the time to teach their dog how to find the stairs and exit the pool safely should he fall in.

ℰ JAMIE LURTZ, Solutions! Pet Services, Anaheim, CA

Try this when your swimming pool's temperature is about 70°F (21°C). Attach a long leash or rope to your dog's collar/harness. Put him in the pool at various entry points. Guide him gently but quickly with tension on the leash (to prevent tangling), using a high-toned "Come" to the stairs or area that he will associate with safe exiting. Praise lavishly! Repeat as often as necessary.

ℰ LISA NEYER, Advanced Master Bark Busters Behavioral Trainer and Therapist, IACP Professional Member, San Clemente, CA

S

Even dogs who know how to swim can drown in the family's swimming pool because they cannot find the stairs and scratch endlessly and futilely at the walls to get out. To prevent this, teach your dog the following: Select a large target for him, such as an urn, large houseplant, or any other landscaping object at least 6 inches (15 cm) high that you will be comfortable having by your pool steps. Place a fabulous treat in the selected container and tell your dog "Go get it." Start with the container very close to him. Slowly bring him farther and farther away until he is running happily from a distance that is at least as long as your pool. Now place the container by the pool steps, put on your bathing suit, and put the dog on a leash and harness if he's never swum before. Bring him into the pool on the top step facing the container. Tell him "Go get it" and let him go. Bring him down to the second step and repeat. Slowly bring him farther and farther into the pool, always facing the container. Once his legs no longer reach the bottom, be sure to swim with him. Practice putting him in the pool in all areas and having him swim to the container. Eventually, a dog who swims a lot will know where the stairs are and not need the container anymore; dogs who hate to swim will need you to keep the container there in case of an accidental submerging.

✑RACHEL LACHOW, CPDT-KA, Positively Obedient, Reisterstown, MD

TEETHING ⊢ Green

A teething puppy's mouth hurts—his gums are sore. To relieve their stress, puppies

like to chew. It's not just their favorite pastime—puppies *need* to chew! But more often than not, they choose things we don't want them to have. Provide your puppy with appropriate chew toys to help with teething.

✑HELEN HOLLANDER, CPDT-KA, The Educated Pup, LLC, Long Island, NY

For teething puppies, try wetting some old socks, braiding, and then freezing them.

✑LUCINDA LUDWIG, Canine Connection, Dubuque, IA

What can you give a puppy to relieve his aching gums, satisfy his need to chew, keep him engaged, and help him stay safe? Frozen bagels! They are 100 percent edible, they dissolve in the mouth, and they provide a chewing challenge for the youngest puppy (and adult dogs love them too). And best of all, you don't have to

supervise the way you would with a fuzzy chew toy. When your puppy gnaws on the bagel, soft bread shavings are created. They dissolve quickly, so he can't choke. By the time the bagel thaws out, it is rather soft and easily consumed.

Take an ordinary bagel and cut in half or in quarters, or leave it whole, depending on your puppy's size. (Halve or quarter the whole bagel—do not slice as if to butter it.) Soak it in some warm water and then freeze it overnight. Give it to your puppy in his crate or on his mat to keep him busy and out of trouble. His gums will be relieved, his hunger will be satisfied, and you will have one content, happy puppy.

☙HELEN HOLLANDER, CPDT-KA, The Educated Pup, LLC, Long Island, NY

TERRIERS

When it comes to puppy training and bite inhibition, some tweaking is often needed for terrier puppies. Because their job usually included ridding the farm of vermin, it would have been inefficient to breed dogs who let go when you squeal like a captured rodent. A softer cry and a moment or two of shunning are often more effective if the classic Ian Dunbar-style "Ow!" is not working fast enough for you.

☙P.J. LACETTE, the original Best Paw Forward, Osteen, FL

If I am introducing my American Staffordshire Terrier to new people, kids, or tentative dogs, I will put a light coat on him to soften the look of his muscular body. People warm up to the dog easily with a coat on, and it hides muscularity and body lines to which uncertain dogs may react. Take it off after everyone is smiling.

☙SARAH CONNAUGHTON, CPDT-KA, Second Chance Pet Obedience, East Aurora, NY

Terriers, even tiny terrier pups, love big toys!

☙P.J. LACETTE, the original Best Paw Forward, Osteen, FL

TETHERING

Tethering your dog enables you to include him in activities while still controlling his behavior. Using a comfortable harness and a short leash, tether him to something sturdy. Intended for short, supervised periods, tethering is useful for family dinnertime, gatherings in the family room, and teaching skills like "go to your bed."

☙KATE GORMAN, CPDT-KA, Gentle Spirit Pet Training, Basking Ridge, NJ

If you need to use a tether line on your dog, he should always be supervised.

☙KATHY FARDY, MA, Dog's Time, It's Their Time!, Billerica, MA

NYLABONE

and I do therapy work, we must ask each patient to put antibacterial gel on her hands prior to petting Zack. I have trained him to wait until the person is finished rubbing her hands together before he can interact with her. He knew his *say hello* command already, so I just paired the two cues together.

SUSAN M. MILLER, CVT, CPDT-KA, CDBC, The Canine Counselor, Northampton, MA

THERAPY

Getting involved in therapy work is a great way to promote responsible dog ownership and handling, and you have the chance to light up someone's life as well. What's involved in getting your dog certified as a therapy dog? You will need to do basic obedience training, plus socialize him to the environments you will be encountering as a therapy dog handler. This usually calls for getting your dog around people in wheelchairs, walkers, crutches; learning to behave going up and down steps; and learning how to lie still for extended periods. Your best option is to seek out a qualified dog trainer who is also a certified therapy dog handler and evaluator. When you sign up for classes, you will be able to get the obedience training you need, and the trainer will be able to mentor you through the therapy portion of the training too.

JASON MANN, ABCDT, Top Dog K9 Training Solutions, Lexington, KY

Therapy dogs can be trained for a cue that means to "say hello" to a person. In the facility where Zack, my Border Collie,

THUNDERSTORM PHOBIA

Fear of thunderstorms is a common problem in dogs. Unfortunately, storm phobias are very difficult (if not impossible) to treat using desensitization. To successfully treat a fear-related behavior, you must identify and desensitize all of the triggers that elicit the behavioral response. Even if the dog is initially only afraid of the loud sound of thunder, eventually other factors that "cue" him to the impending thunder will create the same response— before the storm even hits. Think of it this way: When a storm is approaching, there are atmospheric factors like changes in barometric pressure that dogs sense long before we do that "cue" him that the thunder is coming. Obviously, barometric changes cannot be actively desensitized; therefore, neither can the response. Before you get discouraged, there is hope for your storm-phobic dog! The use of melatonin (a nonpharmaceutical hormone supplement) has been helpful in treating storm phobias.

LISA PATRONA, Dip. DTBC, CPDT-KA, PDT, CBC, Trainers Academy, LLC, President, Troy, MI

Many dogs are very fearful of storms, and the fear can range from mild anxiety to full-blown panic. Although systematic desensitization can greatly help in treating noise phobias, thunderstorms are often not treated as successfully due to the fact that atmospheric changes take place. Dogs will frequently run into bathrooms and tubs during thunderstorms because they are insulated against the static electricity in the air caused by storms. Therefore, do not try to coax your dog out; rather, make the bathroom as safe a haven as possible. Bring in some toys, a stuffed chew, and his bed to help him "ride out the storm" in as much comfort as possible.

CHRISTINA SHUSTERICH, BA, CBC, NY Clever K9, Inc., Queens, NY

TIME-OUTS

Time-outs are a great method for dealing with a dog's undesirable behavior because a time-out is a way to control the consequences of his behavior. They also remove the dog from the situation so that he cannot continue practicing the undesirable behavior.

ANN ALLUMS, CPDT-KA, Best Friends Animal Society, Kanab, UT

Anger has no place in a time-out because you do not want to be in confrontation with the dog or add more tension to the situation. (Aggression begets aggression!)

ANN ALLUMS, CPDT-KA, Best Friends Animal Society, Kanab, UT

TOYS

Always supervise your dog with any new toy to ensure that he can't rip through it and ingest any pieces before leaving him alone with it.

DANA COOPER, CPDT-KA, Woofers Canine Companion Training, Round Rock, TX

A favorite outside toy is a very hard plastic ball (that comes in different sizes) that the dog is unable to "possess" because it is too big for his mouth. When the dog goes after the ball, it rolls, bringing out his prey drive/instinct to chase. This is great cardiovascular exercise and a terrific "job" for herding breeds.

JOANN BLUTH, CDPT, A Canine Academy Int'l, Phoenix, AZ

Even a dog who has a ton of toys will grow bored with them. Try rotating teams of toys. Set one group out and hide the others. In a week or two, switch them. Your dog will find them fresh and new!

TEOTI ANDERSON, CPDT-KA, Pawsitive Results, LLC, Lexington, SC

T

Chew toys come in all shapes and sizes. They can be hard or soft, and they can fly through the air or bounce on the floor. They can be fuzzy or smooth, with or without squeakers, and all are cleverly designed to keep puppy busy and happy. But just because they have been manufactured for dogs does not make them chew proof and 100 percent safe. With any toy, close supervision is needed to gauge the wear and tear for your puppy's safety.

HELEN HOLLANDER, CPDT-KA, The Educated Pup, LLC, Long Island, NY

Make sure that your dog's toys are the proper size. For example, Golden Retrievers should not play with golf balls—they are too small and could easily be swallowed. Use tennis balls instead. If your dog can fit an entire chew bone in his mouth, it's time to throw it away. Small bones can be swallowed and get stuck, or sharp edges could poke through an esophagus, stomach, or intestine. If you have any questions about appropriate toys for your dog, consult a professional dog trainer or your veterinarian.

TEOTI ANDERSON, CPDT-KA, Pawsitive Results, LLC, Lexington, SC

Puppies are sure to chew through toys quickly. Wholesale clubs are great places to stock up on stuffed toys, and for a longer life, when the stuffing comes out, you can place it back in and re-sew it. Once rubber squeaky toys are destroyed, you can save the squeaker and place it in a sock—but only if your puppy does not chew on or have access to regular socks!

CHRISTINA SHUSTERICH, BA, CBC, NY Clever K9, Inc., Queens, NY

Select durable rubber toys that your dog can't choke on. You can also try durable chew bones purchased in the store and soak them in chicken or beef broth to make them more palatable.

LUCINDA LUDWIG, Canine Connection LLC, Dubuque, IA

If your dog gets bored with his toys after just a few play sessions, try keeping them in a toy box, available for play when you offer them. Offering toys at special times can help keep your dog interested. For plush toys, try storing them in your laundry hamper (dog proof, of course). Saturating the toys with your scent can make them infinitely more interesting to your dog.

DIANE PODOLSKY, CPDT-KA, CTC, The Cultured Canine, LLC, White Plains, NY

Be careful what items you teach your dog to chew. If you tie a knot in an old sock and give it to your puppy to play with, you're teaching him that socks are fair game. He will not know the difference between his socks and the ones on your feet! The same goes with old shoes or any other household item. Before you give it to your dog to play with, ask yourself "Is it okay if my dog chews on all of these items in my house?" If the answer is no, then choose another toy for your dog. Take stuffed animals, for instance. There are stuffed animals especially made for dogs. If you purchase these for your dog and he enjoys chewing them, then you're teaching him it's okay to chew on stuffed animals. But if you have children in your home who also have stuffed animals, you could have a problem. Your dog will not understand that he can only chew on the stuffed animals that came from the pet supply store. To him, a stuffed toy is a stuffed toy. So if you have children in your life, it may be best to choose another toy for your dog.

&TEOTI ANDERSON, CPDT-KA, Pawsitive Results, LLC, Lexington, SC

TOYS, INTERACTIVE

Interactive toys will keep your dog mentally stimulated and challenged during the day. A mentally stimulated dog burns physical energy, therefore finding less destructive things to do in the house while left alone.

&NICOLE CORSON, CTC, CPDT-KA, Wag This Way™, Salt Lake City, UT

Enrichment is vital to the well-being of your dog. Try making your own interactive

toys. Cereal boxes put inside of each other with treats or kibble between the layers is a great way to entertain your dog. Tubes from paper towel rolls can be filled with kibble and the ends folded over. If your dog is not excited about kibble, you can always toss a few stinky treats into these devices to increase his motivation to get the food out.

&HEATHER MOHAN-GIBBONS, MS, RVT, CPDT-KA, ACAAB, Collected Wisdom Animal Behavior, LLC, Milwaukee, WI

Does your dog need something to keep him busy and there are no more funds for expensive and elaborate dog toys? Get a rope toy. Take a knot in each hand, and counter-twist to loosen the strands between the knots. Place some treats (like cheese or jerky) in the loose strands and then twist the rope back into place. The work your dog does to get at the treats will help mentally wear him out and send him to nap time!

&DANA COOPER, CPDT-KA, Woofers Canine Companion Training, Round Rock, TX

T

Buy a toy that you can stuff food in, and feed your dog out of the toy instead of his bowl. This will give him something fun to do without adding a lot of extra calories.

ᘓKRISTINA N. GAGE, CPDT-KA, SmartDog Dog Training, Saratoga Springs, NY

Keep a dog busy and cool in the summer heat by putting peanut butter inside an interactive stuffable toy and freezing it overnight.

ᘓJOYCELYN SCHEDLER, CCTS, Tail Town Training, Bastrop, TX

Add something new to your dog's environment each day to provoke thought and interaction with new stimuli. Things that may be interesting to dogs include cardboard boxes with toys and treats in them; old socks tied in knots and stuffed with treats; the core of paper towels with a little paper left on them; oatmeal boxes with holes punched in them with treats and toys inside and the top put back on; or an empty plastic bottle with your dog's whole meal in it (throw away the top), to name just a few. Supervise all of these, of course!

ᘓNAN ARTHUR, CDBC, CPDT-KA, KPACTP, Whole Dog Training, Lakeside, CA

TRACKING

Engaging your dog in an activity where he can use his nose, such as tracking or canine scent work, not only uses his natural abilities but is so fun and rewarding. This is one activity where your dog is in charge and you just get to go along for the ride. To get started, some trainers will use food (laying it on the track) to "motivate" the dog to follow the track. Other trainers will have the track layer stay at the end of the

track and let the dog find the person. If you are using the person method, you may still use food to reward your dog when he finds articles on the track to teach him to indicate an article. Be mindful that you use one cue to encourage him to "track" and another cue when he "finds" an article. Just like other types of training, use a fun and enthusiastic voice when encouraging him on the track, and if you use food for an article reward, use a really high-value treat (e.g., hot dog, meatballs, chicken). Provide motivation with your voice by saying "Track" to get him going, and once he gets on the scent, by saying "Good boy." Both methods, the human-only scent (with a person at the end) or laying food drops on the track, have proven success.

ᘓPAT HENNESSY, CAP2, CPDT-KA, N2paws, Leawood, KS

TRAINER, CHOOSING

I encourage people to find a trainer who uses a holistic approach, which means taking into consideration all of the elements of the dog's environment. A trainer or behavior consultant who considers the dog's history, health, personality, physical abilities, and family dynamics will be better able to create a program that will help the dog achieve his fullest potential.

ᴥ KATE GORMAN, CPDT-KA, Gentle Spirit Pet Training, Basking Ridge, NJ

Ask around to find a good trainer! Ask friends, family, or people you see on the street with a well-trained dog. Also check out training facility websites. Call trainers and don't be afraid to ask questions. Ask for references, and if the trainer offers a group class, definitely go and watch. See how she trains and if you agree with her methods. Most importantly, ask yourself if you would feel comfortable using these methods on your own dog.

ᴥ CAROLYN STROMER, CPDT-KA, Baltimore, MD

When finding a trainer, talk to your vet, groomer, or your friends or neighbors for referrals. You can also use the Association of Pet Dog Trainers' (APDT) website to research trainers in your area. If you find a trainer you are interested in, call her and find out if she has the type of training style you are looking for. Go observe one of the classes, and see how the owners and dogs interact with the trainer.

ᴥ PATTI REICHEL, Glen Ellyn, IL

When seeking a good puppy/dog trainer, I would absolutely look for someone who is certified. Anyone can call herself a dog trainer, but certified trainers go through rigorous testing and training. They also have hands-on training with a variety of dogs.

ᴥ ALICE PISZCZEK, CPDT-KA, BIG PAWS/ little jaws, Naperville, IL

I recommend that people research a trainer, seek references, and also ask the trainer about both her experience and education. A personal reference library, the range and diversity of the texts she has studied, and who she has apprenticed under all make a huge difference in the criteria from which to choose.

ᴥ CYNTHIA KURTZ, The Pet Geek, West Linn/Sandy, OR

If you have trouble finding a trainer who teaches primarily with positive reinforcement (giving the dog something he will work for) in your area, you're better off "going it alone." Read articles and books, watch videos, and join clicker training discussions online. Or find a positive reinforcement trainer who can advise you from a distance using e-mail, phone, and video. Mixing aversive and correction-based methods with positive reinforcement methods tends to slow learning and can confuse the dog.

ᴥ ANN DUPUIS, CPDT-KA, Your Dream Dog, Randolph, MA

Finding a trainer is no different than looking for a babysitter for your child, so hold an interview with the trainer. You have the right to know her philosophy, methods, and temperament before paying a dime or committing to a class.

Here are a few questions to ask of your dog's potential trainer: Can I come by and see your facility and watch a class? What method of training do you use? How long is each of the classes and for how many weeks? What happens if my dog doesn't pass? What happens if my dog is aggressive? Do you accept all breeds? You may have many other questions, but this will get you off to a great start. Most importantly, follow your instincts; if you meet a trainer and there's just something about her that you aren't fully comfortable with, don't work with her.

ꝏDONNA FOURNIER, CPDT-KA, Animal Talk Training, Garden City, MI

I highly recommend that people pick a trainer like they would a doctor. You should feel like, for that one hour, your dog is as important to the trainer as he is to you.

ꝏPHYLLIS MAZZARISI, No Bones About It Dog Training, St. Petersburg, FL

When trying to determine which trainer to use, make sure that you are permitted to observe her in action if you are thinking about enrolling in a class. Never use a trainer whose methods make you uncomfortable. You are the final say. Your dog trusts you to take care of him. Be his voice.

ꝏDEBBY MCMULLEN, CDBC, Pawsitive Reactions, LLC, Pittsburgh, PA

Board-and-train programs present specific challenges unlike home or group training classes. Make sure that these issues are addressed humanely, effectively, and legally. Ask the following questions:

- Is this facility licensed to legally house the dogs in training *plus* the trainer's own dogs? Ask to see a license.
- Is this a full-time job for the trainer? If training is part-time, should your dog be there full-time?
- Can the trainer demonstrate a plan for you to achieve results at home?
- Is the training area safe and secure?
- *Exactly* where will your dog stay? Will he be kept in a crate or in a kennel? Where will that crate or kennel be located?
- Who is the trainer's veterinarian? Call the veterinarian to verify that a good relationship exists.

ꝏKRIS BUTLER, American Dog Obedience Center, LLC, Norman, OK

Be honest with yourself and your trainer. You know your limits and you know your dog. Never do anything that you are uncomfortable doing. Training should be enjoyable for both of you. If it's not, read a different book or talk to a different trainer. There is no one training method or technique that works for all dogs and all owners. You can only be successful if you both are happy.

ꙅTONIA WHILDEN, Houston Dog Ranch, Houston, TX

TRAINING

Your dog has unlimited learning potential. Training helps shape his behavior and is a proactive way to be involved in what he does learn because he's learning all the time anyway! You could start training by simply catching your dog in the act of doing something cute or desirable and rewarding those behaviors. He will start repeating those behaviors more often in the hope of receiving rewards.

ꙅANN ALLUMS, CPDT-KA, Best Friends Animal Society, Kanab, UT

Training is a way to communicate with your dog, and it must be done with the idea to enhance your relationship with him.

ꙅDAWN NARGI-FERREN, CPDT-KA, Metropolitan Pets, New York City, NY

A haphazard approach to training will give you haphazard results. If you want a well-trained dog, follow a solid training plan that builds on success.

ꙅCYNTHIA EDGERLY, Bingo! Dog Training, Watsonville, CA

Beware the latest dog training fad. Every few years a new celebrity-inspired method comes along, like compulsion in the 1960s, corrections in the 1970s, alpha dominance in the 1980s, operant conditioning in the 1990s, and dog "psychology" today. Favored equipment has run the gamut from rope to choke chains to prong collars to shock devices. Whether a hit TV series, a best-selling book, or a slick new tool, what the media purports as popular may not be right for either you or your dog. Clicker training, a very humane, dog-friendly teaching method, might prove too cumbersome for a novice dog owner juggling a clicker in one hand and treats and a leash in the other. Trainers rave about head halters to better control dogs who pull, but many dogs either merely tolerate the device or totally revolt against it, sometimes to the point of injury. For them, a body harness offers more comfortable handling. If a training technique or tool feels at all inappropriate for you or your dog, look for a kinder, albeit less popular way.

ꙅAUDREY SCHWARTZ RIVERS, MS, PetShare: Pets and People for Positive Change, Argos' Memories Blog, Houston, TX

When you first get a dog, start training immediately. Make it fun, use treats, and start with something easy. Your dog will start to feel like part of the family in no time.

ᥱᕙSHANNON COYNER, RVT, CPDT-KA, Ventura, CA

I tell my clients that the best time to train is when their dog is about to hit the "puppy spaz" hour—that time of day when he races around the house or yard for no apparent reason. I find that it is usually around the same time every day. This is the perfect time to do some training.

ᥱᕙMELANIE WALKER, Surprise, AZ

Behavior that is rewarded is more likely to recur. This powerful principle is a key component of reward-based training. Dogs do what works. If your dog receives praise and a treat for sitting, he is more likely to sit the next time you ask. If he knows that jumping on you will earn your attention, he will keep jumping because attention is rewarding to him.

ᥱᕙJAMIE DAMATO, CPDT-KA, Animalsense Canine Training and Behavior, Inc., Chicago, IL

The three most important things to keep in mind while training are: 1. Have fun! 2. Be patient! 3. Be consistent!

ᥱᕙDARLENE KOZA, Scooter's School of Sit & Stay, Rochester, NY

Training can help with behavior issues. Whether your dog is fearful, confused, or has set up his own set of rules about how to function with humans, basic obedience training can lay a good foundation and begin to clarify the leadership role in your home.

ᥱᕙANN ALLUMS, CPDT-KA, Best Friends Animal Society, Kanab, UT

Take the time to teach your dog what it is you need him to know instead of waiting for him to fail and then correcting him.

ᥱᕙNANCY TANNER, CPDT-KA, Paws & People, LLC, Bozeman, MT

Set your dog up for success! Working in small baby steps will give him a better chance at getting it right and will keep him interested in learning. If you notice that your dog isn't getting it right very often, you are probably working above his skill level, and he will quickly lose interest in training. When your dog loses interest, don't get frustrated. Instead, take a break, reassess your standards, and make it a little easier for him. Practice makes perfect, and you'd much rather have your dog practice good habits than bad ones!

ᥱᕙJACQUELYN ENGLAND, A Dog's Life, Sunnyvale, CA

Practice "seize the moment" dog training. Dogs are learning all the time. Whether you know it or not, you are training your dog every time you interact with him. Depending on what you do, you're either training him to do things you like or you don't like. So consistency is key—always (noticing!) praising and rewarding good behavior. In that way, think of training as not just little sessions you set aside for practicing; it should occur when you interact with your dog throughout the day, when the opportunity arises.

ℰELIZABETH L. STROTER, TDI Evaluator, AKC CGC Evaluator, House Calls Dog Training, Highland, NY

All training should start with a great relationship. Teaching your dog that he has choices is a good first step toward enriching your bond of trust.

ℰCHRISTINE BEVILLARD, CPDT-KA, Member IAABC, ABMA, Great Canines (GR–K9S, LLC), Mount Airy, MD

Start training early! Find a well-educated, positive trainer and enroll in her training program. Not only is a well-trained dog easier to live with, but training will improve your relationship with him and make it easier to bring him with you for a variety of activities.

ℰKRISTINA N. GAGE, CPDT-KA, SmartDog Dog Training, Saratoga Springs, NY

Your dog is always learning. Make sure that he's learning what you want him to learn!

ℰANN DUPUIS, CPDT-KA, Your Dream Dog, Randolph, MA

Owners need to remember that dogs are not computers. You cannot load information and expect to retrieve it three months later. Training needs to become a way of life.

ℰCINDY STEINKE, CPDT-KA, TDI, CGC, PetTech K-9 Elementary LLC, Mosinee, WI

I always tell my clients that the two most important words to keep in mind when training are repetition and consistency (with lots of patience thrown in as well). There are no magic wands out there!

ℰTRICIA MOORE, BA, Best Behavior, Newtown, PA

The three secrets to dog training are patience, repetition, and consistency. You need to have patience when you are training your dog—you want to be upbeat and in a good mood. For him to become reliable and understand the cues you are training, you need to practice, so this means a lot of repetition. And finally, be consistent with your dog. Everyone in the family should use the same cues when working with him.

ℰJAMIE LURTZ, Solutions! Pet Services, Anaheim, CA

Don't wait for your dog to ask you for a training session—it's up to you to plan the training sessions every day. Be proactive, be prepared, and have fun!

ℰNANCY TANNER, CPDT-KA, Paws & People, LLC, Bozeman, MT

Believing that your dog is stubborn or defiant will keep you from training him properly.

ℰCYNTHIA EDGERLY, Bingo! Dog Training, Watsonville, CA

Keep a few clickers and treat bowls scattered around the house to make everyday training easier. Dry treats and a clicker can easily be hidden in a covered dish or in a desk drawer (just be sure that the treats are in a place not readily accessible to your dog) to make training easier.

ᏋᎧDAWN ANTONIAK-MITCHELL, Esq. CPDT-KA, BonaFide Dog Academy LLC, Omaha, NE

Training is not only about teaching your dog behaviors, it is also about learning about him. Pay attention to what he likes. What will he work for? (Toys, treats, game of tug or fetch, a gentle rubdown, or pats on the back?) Be creative in what you train your dog to do, and use his natural tendencies to help determine what you are going to train next. If he doesn't want people holding onto his paws but you want to train him to "shake," you can work on training him to accept gentle restraint of his paws first to eventually train this trick. Or you can train your dog to do a "high five" instead—no holding the paws required. Or if everyone else in class is training their dog to turn on a touch lamp with a paw but your dog likes to touch it with his nose, I say train him to turn it on with his nose!

ᏋᎧCOLLEEN B. HURLEY, Orlando, FL, and Gainesville, FL

Determine what behaviors you are going to work on during the training session before you begin. Have an idea of how far along in the training process you want to get by the end of the session. Attempt to follow what you have set out to accomplish, but remember to be flexible and willing to change your goals.

ᏋᎧCOLLEEN B. HURLEY, Orlando, FL, and Gainesville, FL

Most people begin basic obedience with the *sit*. But for a very energetic dog, sitting calmly beside you might be a difficult skill for him to master. Don't give up—your dog is perfectly trainable! Try putting some other actions on cue first. For example, teach him to do a 360-degree turn or to jump up and touch his nose to your hand. The goal is to find some action that is easy for him to do that you can connect with a cue and reward him for accomplishing. Once you have set up that relationship, calmer skills like *sit* and *down* will be easier to teach.

ᏋᎧELLEN MAHURIN, MA, Clever Critters, Knoxville, TN

When training your dog, it's important to break everything down into small parts. It's also essential to keep him engaged and encouraged, so he needs to succeed in almost every attempt at a training technique. For example, when teaching a dog to down, it's best to reward every tiny movement downward. Do not reserve the reward for the end. Give a little reward when he goes down 2 inches (5 cm), then another 2 inches (5 cm), etc. This will keep your dog motivated and also communicate to him that he is going in the right direction.

    ✍DAYNA VILLA, IACP, Taking the Lead Dog Training, PA

Have patience; Lassie wasn't trained in a day.

    ✍EMILY BURLINGAME, San Jose, CA

When training your dog, wear pants or shorts with pockets (cargo-type pants). This way, you'll have a place to hold your treats, clicker, leash, or anything else you may need while training, and it leaves your hands free for the dog.

    ✍AILIGH VANDERBUSH, Dip. CABT, Animalia, Inc., Indianapolis, IN

The biggest gift you can give your dog is to try to see the world through his eyes. We view the world very differently from our dogs. Imagine being on a planet filled with another species that speaks a different language than you, yet it is demanding that you do all sorts of behaviors. You would quickly become confused and frustrated, and you'd want to escape. Be patient when training your dog, make sure that what you are asking is fair and clear, and have a plan about how to train the behavior before starting the session with your dog. You will be amazed with the results.

    ✍HEATHER MOHAN-GIBBONS, MS, RVT, CPDT-KA, ACAAB, Collected Wisdom Animal Behavior, LLC, Milwaukee, WI

There are four variables that influence how easy (or difficult) it will be for your dog to learn. Trainers call these the "Four Ds": Distance (how far you are from your dog), Duration (how long you ask your dog to work), Delivery (how quickly, frequently, and intensely you reinforce the behavior), and Distractions (well, you know!). Balancing these variables affects how quickly and how well your dog learns.

    ✍MARGARET JOHNSON, CPDT-KA, The Humaner Trainer, Inc., Austin, TX

Always end each training session on a happy note. If you're having a frustrating session teaching *down*, for example, end that session with *sit* or some other behavior your dog knows. He will look forward to his next training session, and so will you!

    ✍JERRY D. PATILLO, CPDT-KA, Happy Human Happy Dog, Richardson, TX

The keys to reliability are understanding (help your dog learn), reinforcement (be generous), and practice!

    ✍ANN DUPUIS, CPDT-KA, Your Dream Dog, Randolph, MA

End training on a positive note. If your dog does not understand what you are trying to train, then make sure that you throw in a behavior he knows well so that he can feel confident.

    ✍DEBBY MCMULLEN, CDBC, Pawsitive Reactions, LLC, Pittsburgh, PA

When starting a training session, begin with a desired result in mind. If training a complicated behavior, set acceptable criteria in your mind. When the dog gets to a point where you say "Yes, I am happy with that!" end the training session then. End on a happy note for both you and the dog. You'll get so much more in the long run by doing this than by trying to get the dog to repeat that perfect behavior.

ᴇ∕JENNIFER SKELDING, Fryeburg, ME

There are several helpful ways to assure your client's focus during training. Train initially in a controlled environment, and then make the skills more versatile in different formats. Ask your client to be well rested before training. Find what motivates the dog and also which method the client is receptive to using (treats, praise, petting, toys, walks, drives).

ᴇ∕CYNTHIA KURTZ, The Pet Geek, West Linn/Sandy, OR

Once you have been through a training class, don't call it "good to go" for the duration of your dog's life. Go to the maintenance level. Every day, give him the gift of a "behavior vitamin." Practice your behaviors and learn a new trick together, but do this on a daily basis for the health of you and your dog.

ᴇ∕NANCY TANNER, CPDT-KA, Paws & People, LLC, Bozeman, MT

Once a new behavior has been learned, incorporate it into your daily routine.

ᴇ∕JAMIE DAMATO, CPDT-KA, Animalsense Canine Training and Behavior, Inc., Chicago, IL

Obedience is a way of life; once learned, the goal of obedience training is to make

TOP TIDBIT

Treat bags are belted pouches worn like fanny packs that store treats and keep your hands free.

that training become part of your dog's life, without having to set aside specific training sessions.

ᴇ∕CHRISTINA SHUSTERICH, BA, CBC, President, NY Clever K9, Inc., Queens, NY

Getting a dog trained is a lot like going to the gym. When you are practicing with your dog, think of each session as a workout. Over time, he will become behaviorally fit, just as a body will become physically fit by working out. Remember that the very best sit-up still needs to be performed thousands of times for rock-hard abs. Your dog needs to practice again and again if you want to achieve your behavior goals. Don't give up!

ᴇ∕ADRIENNE CARSON, Harmony, NJ

No matter how frustrated you get during training, never use a harsh voice. It will only cause your dog to *not* want to participate. If you do get frustrated, take a break from training. Throw a ball for him, or softly stroke or pet him. Gently petting your dog will make you both feel better.

ᴇ∕PAT HENNESSY, CAP2, CPDT-KA, N2paws, Leawood, KS

TRAINING, DURATION

"How many minutes should I train my dog?" is a common question I receive from students. People want a magical number that applies to every dog, but the truth is that a lot of factors come into play: age of dog, breed, personality, owner's schedule, and current level of training are but a few. Ideally, a beginning-level dog should have at least one formal session each day in which one or more of the basic exercises are reinforced. For most dogs and owners, 20 minutes is manageable and effective, but even a 5-minute training session can be very successful. A short session might concentrate on a heeling segment with quick and straight *sits* or be limited to a *sit-* and/or *down-stay* of varying times and distances. A longer session might encompass all or more of the basic elements, depending on the dog's training level. Involving play to both reward and break up the elements will make the sessions more fun for both the owner and dog.

ℰMARIAN POTT, Miramar Dog Training: Obedience, Herding, Behavior, Half Moon Bay, CA

Training should only last for as long as you both are having fun. Short and upbeat are the keys to success. It is better to go for a 3-minute walk with excellent results than a 15-minute walk with pulling. It is important that you both feel successful and happy with your efforts.

ℰTONIA WHILDEN, Houston Dog Ranch, Houston, TX

Training sessions don't have to be hour-long sessions. They can be multiple 10- to 15-minute sessions, and you'll both excel at the training together.

ℰJEFF BAME, CPDT-KA, Paws for Adventure, Paulden, AZ

Keep your training sessions short and fun! Have three or four training sessions each day, and keep them short—less than 15 minutes each session. If you find yourself getting frustrated, stop. Training should be fun for you and your dog.

ℰJACQUELYN ENGLAND, A Dog's Life, Sunnyvale, CA

When you begin training with your dog, keep the sessions short. If you know that his normal attention span is only about five minutes, begin by training for three minutes and then quit. Always quit training before your dog loses focus. Training in several short sessions throughout the day will be much more effective than one long training session once a day. This will also help your dog understand that training is a part of his everyday routine, not just a special time of the day.

ℰSUE BROWN, CDBC, CPDT-KA, Love My Dog Training, Littleton, CO

Train in short sessions to keep you and the dog interested and to prevent frustration. How short? Grab ten treats. Now train ten repetitions of one behavior (*down*, for example). When the treats are gone, that session is over. If you and the dog are still having fun, grab ten more treats. Now train ten repetitions of another behavior.

&ELAINE COUPÉ, For Pet's Sake (& Memphis Agility), Oakland, TN

Keep training sessions short. I like to tell my students to practice for five to ten minutes several times throughout the day. Practice a few minutes in the morning before work, then after you get home, and maybe again before bed. Training doesn't have to be a chore, and you don't need to designate a whole hour at a time. Do short, manageable training sessions, and work training into real-life situations.

&JAMIE LURTZ, Solutions! Pet Services, Anaheim, CA

I have advised students in my classes to remove their watches when they begin a training session at home with their puppy or dog, which enables them to concentrate on their pet. It also helps end the training session when they are actually finished, rather than when the clock says it's been 32 minutes or whatever. This allows for total concentration on the dog and a very relaxed trainer. One session may be 40 minutes, another may be 13—it's all okay.

&ROSIE STEEL, Rosie Steel Dog Training, Mahaska, KS

You will give your dog better information with shorter, more frequent training sessions. Five minutes of training four times a day is far more productive than one long 25-minute session.

&NANCY TANNER, CPDT-KA, Paws & People, LLC, Bozeman, MT

Don't drill—asking for the same behavior over and over again quickly gets boring. Instead, run your dog through several behaviors he knows really well. Keep practice sessions short (two to five minutes), but do many throughout the day. You can get ten or more "touches" (hand targeting) into a minute-long session! Other behaviors may take longer to perform (especially *stays* or behaviors with any duration), but you can still build reliability by practicing the behavior a couple times a day.

&ANN DUPUIS, CPDT-KA, Your Dream Dog, Randolph, MA

TRAINING, FINDING TIME

If you are a busy person like most people, you have mastered the art of multitasking. If your time is limited but you still need to train your dog, the best way to do this is to incorporate training into your regular daily routine. This approach will make training seem less time consuming and more practical.

꿏TONIA WHILDEN, Houston Dog Ranch, Houston, TX

Don't have time to train your dog? Train during your favorite TV show! Because dogs learn in quick bursts, it's better to keep the sessions short and fun. TV commercials are the perfect opportunity for busy dog owners to train their dog. You can start with easy behaviors like *sit* and *down*. As your dog advances, practice longer behaviors like the *down-stay* during the actual program portion of your favorite show. You and your dog will both be entertained!

꿏LORI MELHUISH, The Smiling Dog, Yorktown, VA

Too busy to train your dog? Do it while watching television! Many people watch at least 30 minutes of television every day, so it's a wonderful opportunity for training. During one advertisement, work on *sit*. During the next commercial, work on *down*. During the ad after that, work on *come* or some other behavior. Several short, two-minute training sessions every evening will accomplish a lot more than one long 20- or 30-minute session. This will be good for your dog's short attention span (and perhaps your short patience span).

꿏JERRY D. PATILLO, CPDT-KA, Happy Human Happy Dog, Richardson, TX

Whenever you have ten seconds to spare, you have time to train your dog. While your bagel toasts, reward five *sits* or *downs*. Call your dog from across the house, have him heel around the room, or have him stay while you put down his food bowl. Toss him his meal a few pieces at a time for lying quietly on his bed while you eat dinner. Reward a *stay* while you tie your shoes, or practice heeling as you carry the laundry to the washing machine. Ask your dog to sit before you open the door, throw his toy, or pet him. Keep a few containers of treats stashed around the house so that you are always ready to reward good behavior. Take advantage of ten-second training opportunities, and you'll be rewarded with a well-mannered dog for life!

꿏LAUREL SCARIONI, CPDT-KA, Pawsitive Results Critter Academy, Santa Rosa, CA

A few short training repetitions can easily be snuck in before meals, at potty breaks, and other times throughout the day. It is easier for busy people to find a few minutes throughout the day to intentionally train than to find a big block of time daily.

꿏DAWN ANTONIAK-MITCHELL, Esq. CPDT-KA, BonaFide Dog Academy LLC, Omaha, NE

I encourage my students to keep training short and relevant by working sessions into everyday life: heel to the mailbox or to get the paper, eye contact while waiting for coffee to brew, long *downs* during meal preps or dinner, puppy push-ups while microwaving leftovers, etc. Because everyone has little bits of downtime throughout the day, it's easier to get training in this way.

✎JILL MILLER, CPDT-KA, Mad City Dog Training, Madison, WI

To train throughout the day without having to set aside 15 minutes or more to do a formal training session, fill decorative wall sconces and bowls with dry treats and put them around your house in strategic locations. Putting them in places like the hallway (for working on door manners), in the bathroom, on the dresser in the bedroom, on the living room shelves, on top of the mantel or TV, and on the kitchen counter, etc., will remind you to ask your dog to perform a behavior. It will be in a real-life situation and will allow you to train your dog without taking time out of your normal routine.

✎SUSAN SMITH, CPDT-KA, CDBC, CTC, Raising Canine, LLC, Austin, TX

When training your dog, forget about setting aside training times during the day. They never happen, or something always seems to come up. Instead, I tell my students to try to find three or four real-life situations that happen regularly and train at that time. For example, instead of just putting your dog's dinner down, have him do a *sit* and *down* and a *wait*. Let him eat when he is released. For breakfast, feed him something dry and call him from the yard to come in and get his treat. Then release him to go play, which is a great way to reinforce *come*. When playing, practice *leave it* or *give*. Or when you are out for a walk, you can practice any number of behaviors.

✎ANITA ZIEBE, RN, MS, CPDT-KA, Napa, CA

TRAINING, FOOD REWARDS

Trainers use food rewards for initial training procedures because food is high on the reward scale for dogs (dogs need food to live), and food can be handled and delivered easily by the trainer in small portions.

✎ANN ALLUMS, CPDT-KA, Best Friends Animal Society, Kanab, UT

Regarding hesitant owners on the use of treats: I look at using treats like paying my dog a salary. How long would you work for your boss without a salary? Now that you have given your dog a job, pay him for it.

✎KAT BERGER, New York, NY

I often hear clients say that they prefer not to use treats when training their dog. Their reasons range from "I don't want my dog to get fat" to "I'm afraid he won't listen to me if I don't have a treat in my hand." While these concerns are valid, they should not prevent you from appropriately using high-quality treats to reward and motivate your dog. Although some dogs are motivated by soft verbal praise, chest rubs, butt scratches, walks outside, and/or playing games, many are *only* motivated by food. If you are lucky enough to have a dog who is responsive to two or more of these, then don't limit yourself to only rewarding good behavior with treats—mix it up!

e⁄PATRICIA BENTZ, CPDT-KA, CDBC,
K-9 Training & Behavioral Therapy,
Philadelphia, PA

I like to think of food rewards as a pay scale. Some treats are like $1 (dry biscuits), and some are like $100 (liver or real meat). If your pooch gets $100 for something simple, it decreases the value of that item to him, so pay him according to how hard the job is, not just because you only have liver in your pocket.

e⁄DEENA MCIVER, K-9 Kind, Portland, OR

Have food rewards readily available. The last thing you want to do is interrupt your dog's concentration by fussing with the treat packaging. Many dogs will stop what they are doing and immediately focus on nothing but the treat. Instead, have the treats either in your pocket or sitting on a shelf nearby.

e⁄PATRICIA BENTZ, CPDT-KA, CDBC,
K-9 Training & Behavioral Therapy,
Philadelphia, PA

A food lure is an excellent way to get a behavior started, so don't be afraid to use it. But be aware that food lures must be removed as soon as possible (within a couple training sessions) because you do not want "food in hand" to become the signal to start.

A training sequence is signal–behavior–consequence. Be sure that you move the food as quickly as possible from "signal" to "consequence." If not, you'll teach the dog to wait until he sees the signal "food in hand" to begin.

e⁄PAM SHEEHAN, 4 Paws Training, LLC,
Broken Arrow, OK

Do not show the dog the treat to get him to do something because treats should not be used as a bribe. The food should appear as a reward for the dog responding to you. By rewarding frequently, you build up a reward history so that he does not need to see the reward ahead of time to respond to your cues.

e⁄ANN ALLUMS, CPDT-KA, Best Friends
Animal Society, Kanab, UT

Don't use treats as a bribe! There is no harm in using a treat to lure your dog into performing a new behavior. However, it is critical that you phase out the lure as soon as possible. After he offers you the behavior several times using the lure, get him to offer the behavior without showing him a treat beforehand. Once he complies, praise him and then offer him the treat. You want your dog to trust that good things will happen if he responds to your request.

℘PATRICIA BENTZ, CPDT-KA, CDBC, K-9 Training & Behavioral Therapy, Philadelphia, PA

Be unpredictable! Dogs are pretty good at figuring out when you have treats and when you don't. To be unpredictable, have treats when you don't look like you do. Don't always use a bait bag and/or use things like sealed jars of baby food hidden in your pocket.

℘JACQUELYN ENGLAND, A Dog's Life, Sunnyvale, CA

"When can I stop using food?" is a frequent question, and the answer is "when the behavior is intrinsically reinforcing." To make a behavior intrinsically rewarding, build up a very long, rich reinforcement history for that behavior. Start out with favorite foods to build a strong foundation

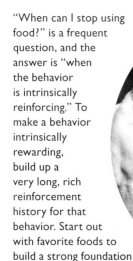

of reinforcement for any given behavior. Start off easy and increase difficulty slowly. Then mix nonfood rewards into your training. Toys and play, the chance to sniff, and your attention can all be rewarding to your dog. Finally, reinforce the behavior intermittently (not every time he complies).

℘ANN DUPUIS, CPDT-KA, Your Dream Dog, Randolph, MA

Food rewards should be pea sized so that the dog does not get full, which will decrease his motivation to train and may cause digestive upset. This will also allow you to reward and continue training without waiting for him to finish chewing a large treat.

℘ANN ALLUMS, CPDT-KA, Best Friends Animal Society, Kanab, UT

Look for training treats that are either small in size or soft enough to be broken into smaller pieces. You can cut them up in advance, or if they are moist, break them into smaller pieces with your fingernail.

℘PATRICIA BENTZ, CPDT-KA, CDBC, K-9 Training & Behavioral Therapy, Philadelphia, PA

When I do basic training, I prefer to use sliced, cooked hot dogs as opposed to dog cookies. First off, dogs love them, but most important, it takes no time for them to chew/eat them, so I can get right back to training.

🐾BARRY ZIONS, Alpha Dog Training, Spring Hill, FL

When training, I think that dogs are more interested in how many treats they get as a reinforcer as opposed to how big a treat they get. I believe that the food simply going into the dog's mouth is reinforcing, even if the treat is very small.

🐾PAULA ZUKOFF, Coordinator of Behavior and Training, Animal Humane Society, Golden Valley, MN

Hard treats (like baked bones) take way too long for your dog to finish eating, and you'll lose valuable training time. Soft treats (like cheese) work better because your dog won't take too long to chew them.

🐾JACQUELYN ENGLAND, A Dog's Life, Sunnyvale, CA

When using hot dogs as rewards, microwave the pieces first because it takes away the sliminess. For a healthier treat, put the microwaved hot dog pieces in a baggie with toasted oat cereal—the cereal will absorb the flavor and smell of the hot dogs and are a lot healthier for your dog!

🐾ROBERT JORDAN, CPDT-KA, Pavlov's Dogs
Pet Dog Training, Mechanicsville, VA

Make your treats last longer by giving only one treat at a time rather than several pieces because usually the dog will just gulp it down whether it's one or five pea-sized treats.

🐾ANN ALLUMS, CPDT-KA, Best Friends Animal Society, Kanab, UT

For your everyday training in the house, it's good to use pieces of your dog's daily ration of kibble as rewards. Bring out the big guns (better training treats) for training in higher-distraction environments like group class, out on walks, or at the park.

🐾JACQUELYN ENGLAND, A Dog's Life, Sunnyvale, CA

Use training treats strategically. For behavior that your dog already knows (e.g., *sit*), use lower-value treats, like pieces of his kibble. When you want to encourage him to learn a new behavior, use higher-value treats. The reward should be commensurate with the difficulty of the task.

🐾PATRICIA BENTZ, CPDT-KA, CDBC, K-9 Training & Behavioral Therapy, Philadelphia, PA

It is a good idea to use a variety of high-value treats when training, and they should be something that is different from your dog's daily diet. The next time you can't finish all the food on your plate, cut up that steak and make a training session out of it for your dog.

🐾PAT HENNESSY, CAP2, CPDT-KA, N2paws, Leawood, KS

Keep in mind that training treats should compose no more than about 10 percent of your dog's daily food intake.

     ℰ◌PATRICIA BENTZ, CPDT-KA, CDBC,
K-9 Training & Behavioral Therapy,
Philadelphia, PA

Whether you make your own training treats or purchase them, choose high-quality, low-calorie options. Make sure that meat treats are made from "real" meat. Foods to avoid include chocolate, pork, onions, salt, processed sugar, soy, and rich or spicy prepared foods. Grapes and raisins in large quantities should also be avoided because they can lead to vomiting, diarrhea, and kidney failure. Many dogs cannot digest corn, so it is best to avoid products that contain it.

     ℰ◌PATRICIA BENTZ, CPDT-KA, CDBC,
K-9 Training & Behavioral Therapy,
Philadelphia, PA

For unmotivated dogs, I mix a different of type kibble than their own, dried liver, or other extra-special treats into a jar of baby food that's half full. I let those treats soak up the baby food overnight and I then have a concoction that even the toughest dog can't resist!

     ℰ◌CHRISTINE KELLY, CTC, CPDT-KA,
TDI evaluator, AKC CGC evaluator, K9to5,
Colorado Springs, CO

When working with new distractions, carry at least two different types of food rewards.

     ℰ◌JACQUELYN ENGLAND, A Dog's Life,
Sunnyvale, CA

Many of my clients with puppies going through housetraining need fast, easy reinforcement available. I recommend that they buy peanut butter in a squeeze tube (it looks like an upright toothpaste tube) and keep it by the back door. (Another option is peanut butter in a baby food jar.) Peanut butter requires no refrigeration, and it can be squeezed directly into your puppy's mouth or he can lick right from the jar. Perfect, easy reinforcement!

     ℰ◌AMY FLANIGAN, BA, Civil Obedience Dog
Training, Columbus, OH

If your dog is overweight, choose healthy treats for training, such as carrots, green beans, sweet potatoes, oat cereal (place in a small plastic bag the night before and shake with a pinch of garlic powder), or low-fat string cheese (pinch off small bites).

     ℰ◌TEOTI ANDERSON, CPDT-KA, Pawsitive
Results, LLC, Lexington, SC

To fade treats, use the 100 percent, 75 percent, and 25 percent model. When you're training a new behavior, use a 100-percent reinforcement schedule. Once your dog knows the behavior, start using a 75-percent reinforcement schedule, meaning that you reinforce three out of four trials. To avoid having to keep track and form patterns, just reinforce everything but the absolute worst behaviors. Do this for a couple of training sessions, then move to a 50-percent reinforcement schedule. Now reinforce anything that you consider average or better. Then move to a 25-percent reinforcement schedule—only reinforce the good responses, not mediocre or poor behaviors. Remember, because you're reinforcing only good behavior, your dog will start offering better behavior overall. Once you're at 25 percent, start thinking of ways to give him life rewards for his good behavior; don't stop reinforcing altogether, but don't rely on food either. Now use things like dinner, going for a walk, a quick play session, or a back scratch, etc., as a reward for a job well done.

SUSAN SMITH, CPDT-KA, CDBC, CTC, Raising Canine, LLC, TX

Treats are one of the most popular motivators used in dog training.

As the owner of a dog with food allergies and another with irritable bowel syndrome (IBS), finding appropriate training treats was difficult until I discovered these helpful tips: Prescription canned food that comes out of the can in a loaf can be cut into slices and baked at 350°F (176°C) for 30 minutes to create a much less messy reinforcer. Or dry food can be ground up in a blender, then mixed with water to a doughy consistency, and then shaped/flattened into cookies and baked as above. Oregano can be added to enhance the flavor if your dog's stomach can tolerate it. The treats will last for a week if kept refrigerated and will help create a little variety for your diet-restricted pooch.

JILL LYDIC, Asheville, NC

Does your dog stare at your hands when training, expecting a food treat? If so, wait for eye contact before actually delivering the treat.

ANN DUPUIS, CPDT-KA, Your Dream Dog, Randolph, MA

Using food treats (even tiny pieces) for training can sometimes be problematic for dogs with food allergies or weight issues. To create tasty but low-calorie training tidbits, chop a carrot into tiny pieces and put them in a plastic bag. Place a piece of hot dog in the bag, and seal and store it in the refrigerator overnight. Remove the hot dog and use the hot dog-scented carrot pieces as low-calorie, tasty training tidbits!

ᕦDAWN ANTONIAK-MITCHELL, Esq., CPDT-KA, BonaFide Dog Academy LLC, Omaha, NE

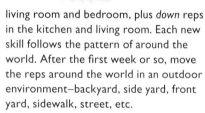

TRAINING, LOCATION

Dogs benefit from being trained in a variety of locations. They certainly need to be trained in their home environment, not just in a group class. By working on *sit-stays* and *down-stays* in the family room, for instance, the dog will be better behaved during preparation and eating of human meals.

ᕦMARIAN POTT, Miramar Dog Training, Obedience, Herding, Behavior, Half Moon Bay, CA

To help with generalization for foundation clicker class skills (*sit/down/release/stay*), I recommend that my students "train around the world" from day one. For example, on day one, practice a series of *sit* repetitions in the kitchen (easy!). On day two, practice one set in the kitchen and one set in the living room, and also do a series of *down* reps in the kitchen. On day three, do *sit* reps in the kitchen,

living room and bedroom, plus *down* reps in the kitchen and living room. Each new skill follows the pattern of around the world. After the first week or so, move the reps around the world in an outdoor environment—backyard, side yard, front yard, sidewalk, street, etc.

ᕦMIRA LEIBSTEIN, CBC, CPDT-KA, Click-n-Train, Oceanside, NY

Take any behavior you wish to train (*attention*, *sit*, *down*, etc.) Begin in a nondistracting environment inside your house. Choose one room, and when your dog is doing well there, go to another room and begin the training process again. Utilize every room in your house, including the bathroom and laundry room. Next, expand your training horizons to include porches, doorways, and staircases. Once he's doing well in all of those areas, begin outdoor training in a yard or courtyard with minimal distractions, slowly increasing to walks and more stimulating situations.

When your dog is doing well, increase the areas to parking lots, pet stores (where dogs are allowed), and your veterinary office waiting room (ask permission first!).

&WENDY DECARLO-YOUNG, CPDT-KA, Dog Obedience Group, Chicago, IL

Want to raise the bar a little above the usual training sessions around the house? Something other than in your neighborhood with all of its distracting smells, critters in the grass, and other dogs out and about? Train just around the corner at the strip shopping center during off-peak hours. The glass windows will allow you to see what you or your dog is doing, and the conditions may be better too!

&REBECCA ENGLE, MA, CPDT-KA, First Steps and Beyond K-9 Obedience, Plano, TX

Dogs are not humans, so they can't have the same learning expectations as human children do. Far too many people think that just because they have told their dog to sit, he should know how to do it in all places and circumstances. Dogs need to be coached through the behavior in a variety of places—not just at home.

&DEENA MCIVER, K-9 Kind, Portland, OR

Make a list of places in your home where you want your pup to do something, and incorporate this into your training. Plan a walking course in the house to determine where you want him to perform certain behaviors. Help him learn that appropriate behaviors are for

different places—not always in front of you. If *sit* is always trained with your puppy in front of you, then he may decide that this is the *only* place to perform the behavior. Variety is the spice of life for both you and your pet.

&GLORIA J. WHITE, CPDT-KA, Pawsitive Waggers Training, Cincinnati, OH

A common mistake in training is teaching our dogs a behavior in one location and then expecting them to do it everywhere. Dogs need help with baby steps to learn behaviors well. Break a behavior down by teaching *stay* in different rooms in your house, then when someone walks through the room, then when a toy is dropped on the floor, then when you leave the room, then outside. Try to remember the first time you learned how to play a sport. First you learned the rules, then you practiced the moves, and then you played on a new field.

&HEATHER MOHAN-GIBBONS, MS, RVT, CPDT-KA, ACAAB, Collected Wisdom Animal Behavior, LLC, Milwaukee, WI

I encourage people to work with their dogs outside of post offices and in front of storefronts. This helps with a dog's socialization skills, as well as attention. Dogs can practice the *sit* for introductions, the *leave it*, and *watch me* commands, and *stay* and *heel* exercises.

&MARIAN POTT, Miramar Dog Training, Obedience, Herding, Behavior, Half Moon Bay, CA

Where to train? In as many different places as you can think of! Start out at home in a nondistracting environment. As your dog learns a behavior, such as *come*, train it in the backyard, in the front yard (on leash), on walks, at the pet store, at your friend's house, etc. This will teach him that *come* is *come*—no matter where or when he hears it!

ELAINE COUPÉ, For Pet's Sake & Memphis Agility, Oakland, TN

Dogs do not generalize well. This means that if they learn something in one context or situation, they will not easily transfer that behavior to another situation. For example, if you do most of your training at home, your dog will probably not respond well on a walk or at the vet. Practice training in all the places where you want him to respond to you. In a new or distracting situation, don't ask as much of your dog as you would at home. He will improve with practice

KRISTINA N. GAGE, CPDT-KA, SmartDog Dog Training, Saratoga Springs, NY

Training sessions should begin in a familiar, distraction-free environment. As your dog becomes more reliable with the behaviors you are working on, change the training location. You may begin to add in mild distractions if he maintains correct responses to your commands. New locations and distractions may cause your dog's behavior to change—be ready to communicate clearly to him when he is correct, and reward him for it!

NOELLE NASCA, Positive Puppy Southtown's Dog Training Club, Hamburg, NY

TRAINING LOG

Keep notes! Keep notes of training sessions to determine your dog's compliance level and thus your approach to training. If during ten attempts to get your dog to follow your cue he is only successful seven times, you may want to make it a little easier for him by using hand signals, lures, or just by removing distractions. If your dog is successful ten out of every ten tries, you may want to make it a little harder for him—only reward the best responses and/or add distractions. Keeping track helps you set your criteria appropriately!

JACQUELYN ENGLAND, A Dog's Life, Sunnyvale, CA

T

When I am working with clients and want them to keep track of their daily progress in a training session, they often have a hard time keeping a log. So I have them put a colored star up on the calendar for each session. Gold means that the session occurred with only the behaviors that we wanted to keep (walking nicely on leash). Silver means that it was okay but could have been better. Blue means that the client saw the behaviors that we were trying to eliminate (aggression, etc). At a glance, you can see how the training is progressing, and over time, the number of blue stars is replaced by gold stars.

— HEATHER MOHAN-GIBBONS, MS, RVT, CPDT-KA, ACAAB, Collected Wisdom Animal Behavior, LLC, Milwaukee, WI

TRAINING, POSITIVE

Traditional training uses aversives like force and pain. It says to the dog, "Do this or else something bad will happen to you!" Modern training (positive training) uses rewards like treats, toys, play, and attention. It says to the dog, "Do this and something good will happen to you!" There are many advantages to positive training, and one is reflected in the old adage "You can catch more flies with honey than with vinegar." Similarly, you can teach your dog better with carrots than with sticks. Positive training is proven to be more effective than traditional training. Your dog learns that training is fun, and so do you. This will make him eager to work with you and quick to learn—just like a fun, encouraging schoolteacher makes students eager to cooperate and learn.

— CARMEN BUITRAGO, MS, CAAB, CPDT-KA, Cascade Pet Camp, Hood River, OR

To raise an emotionally sound pet, we, the teachers, must be aware of our power to teach and the examples we share by our actions as well as our words. A positive attitude and facial expression or a quiet voice and praise will get the results we want much quicker than negative responses. And in the beginning, be aware of the power of that reward—a yummy treat, a smile and praise, or a fond pat on the chest or shoulder.

— JOAN B. GUERTIN, Common Sense Dog Training & Behavior Solutions, Mabank, TX

Positive training opens a mutually enjoyable window of communication between two species that can't talk to each other. It's a joy! We don't have to resort to pushing, yelling, yanking on necks, or bullying. As the more intelligent species, we can use our brains, not brawn!

— CARMEN BUITRAGO, MS, CAAB, CPDT-KA, Cascade Pet Camp, Hood River, OR

Most average dog owners who end up in my class have no idea there's a choice in how to train their dog (positive versus negative or anything in between). They may have already tried different techniques they stumbled across in an outdated book or from another source and are proud to mention it. People cannot make an educated decision if they don't know there is a choice or difference in the first place. Now I make a point to explain the differences in training techniques on the first day of class. I explain why I choose to train the way I do—using positive reinforcement. I mention that my mentors are crossover trainers and explain that when they first began dog training, there were no options, but now there are many. I talk about dogs I know who have been trained in different ways and my personal observations, and hope they educate their friends. I'm even thinking of using a "plug" at the end of class: "We know you have choices when it comes to training your dog. Thank you for choosing positive reinforcement."

ℰMONICA J. OESTERLING, CPDT-KA, Galaxy Dog Training, Reno, NV

TRAINING, POSITIVE ATTITUDE

When training your dog, remember to relax and enjoy it because he can sense your emotions and will react to them. If you are nervous, then your dog will be nervous and may not catch on to what you are trying to get him to do.

ℰJEFF BAME, CPDT-KA, Paws for Adventure, Paulden, AZ

Only train when you are in a positive mood. If you're not happy, your session will likely be unproductive, and more importantly, your dog will know that you aren't enjoying it. As a result, neither will he.

ℰTONIA WHILDEN, Houston Dog Ranch, Houston, TX

When training for the first time, it is good to keep the following in mind: "Calm will get you everything, pushy gets you nothing."

ℰNANCY TANNER, CPDT-KA, Paws & People, LLC, Bozeman, MT

If you or your dog gets stressed during training, stop training and pick up again later.

ℰCYNTHIA EDGERLY, Bingo! Dog Training, Watsonville, CA

When training any animal, you want to remember to train when you are in

a good mood and not in a rush. Everything that you are feeling goes straight down the leash and into your dog. If you train when you are frustrated, he will most likely perform many incorrect behaviors, resulting in few treats and causing him frustration as well. Work on something that your dog is having difficulty with when you have time to devote to working on it and when you are in a creative mood. The creative and relaxed atmosphere you create with your mood will travel into your dog, therefore helping him learn more readily and easily.

COLLEEN B. HURLEY, Orlando, FL, and Gainesville, FL

Keep an upbeat attitude when training. Don't train when you're cranky.

JAMIE DAMATO, CPDT-KA, Animalsense Canine Training and Behavior, Inc., Chicago, IL

Teachers who are calm, patient, and encouraging usually have more success getting through to their students and earning their respect. Teachers who are demanding, out of control, and unfair are usually not successful in establishing trust and respect from their students, and they make them feel hesitant and self-conscious. Be a good teacher/leader to your dog, and understand that he will make mistakes.

Help him learn from his mistakes and be successful.

ANGIE KOBER, BS, Canine Solutions, Neenah, WI

Sometimes we as trainers forget how overwhelming training information can be to our clients. Remember to have fun during the training process, which makes it so much more pleasant for the dog and owner. Keep a happy tone, and try not to get bogged down with the process. Teach the owner that having a good time with her dog during training is just as important as enjoying her dog's company in everyday life. This can make a huge difference in how much work actually gets done by the owner and how well the dog receives the information.

NORA ANDERSON, ABC Certified, Anderson Canine Training LLC, Skillman, NJ

The more you enjoy training your dog, the more fun he will have learning. Why do most dogs learn tricks so quickly, while their obedience leaves little to be desired? Because the trainer/owner is laughing, yelping in excitement, and thoroughly enjoying the training process for tricks but is often somber and strict during obedience sessions. Make obedience fun, and your dog will enjoy a *sit-stay* as much as jumping through a hoop.

COLLEEN B. HURLEY, Orlando, FL, and Gainesville, FL

TRAINING, PUPPY

A puppy's brain is fully formed by seven weeks of age, so training can be started at that time. There are many benefits to early training. Training is mental exercise for the puppy (i.e., the more he learns, the better he gets at learning). The more acceptable behaviors a puppy learns, the less room there is for undesirable behaviors. Therefore, early training should increase the odds that he will stay in the family for his lifetime rather than be given up due to behavior issues.

&ANN ALLUMS, CPDT-KA, Best Friends
Animal Society, Kanab, UT

Keeping your puppy interested in training depends on several factors, including the pace of the training session and how reinforcing it is. To maintain your pup's interest, keep your training sessions upbeat by asking for behavior after behavior after behavior, with little downtime in between. Also, be sure to make the training easy enough for your pup to win treats more often than not. Winning lots of reinforcements makes training more fun than exploring the house or chewing on his favorite toy.

&JACQUELYN
ENGLAND,
A Dog's Life,
Sunnyvale, CA

A long-lasting benefit of training your puppy is that it strengthens the bond between the two of you through improved communication.

&ANN ALLUMS, CPDT-KA, Best Friends
Animal Society, Kanab, UT

The younger the puppy, the shorter the attention span—young puppies can pay attention for just a few minutes at a time. So you don't have to have a "formal" training session with your puppy. You can sit down, watch TV, and train during the commercials.

&DARLENE KOZA, Scooter's School of Sit &
Stay, Rochester, NY

Even though it may seem that puppyhood lasts forever in terms of chewed-up rugs and potty accidents, it's really just a brief time in your dog's life. Train him to have good family manners now so that you can enjoy his company for a long lifetime.

&TEOTI ANDERSON, CPDT-KA, Pawsitive
Results, LLC, Lexington, SC

Training helps a puppy develop confidence that he has some control over his environment; that is, he can make good things happen depending on his behavior. In addition, training provides structure that helps a puppy feel secure. Training teaches your puppy that it is rewarding to respond to you, which could potentially save his life if he gets in a dangerous situation

&ANN ALLUMS, CPDT-
KA, Best Friends Animal
Society, Kanab, UT

Don't allow or reinforce behavior in your puppy that you would not want him to exhibit when he is fully grown. These behaviors include jumping up on people and barking for attention—behaviors that may be cute or unproblematic in a puppy but that may become a nuisance from an adult dog. More importantly, focus on what your puppy is allowed to do, as simply stopping him from doing something undesirable creates a behavior void that he will somehow fill. Make a point of generously reinforcing many behaviors that your puppy does naturally or easily and that would be appropriate behaviors for an adult dog.

ANN ALLUMS, CPDT-KA, Best Friends Animal Society, Kanab, UT

As a trainer and once-in-a-while breeder of Golden Retrievers, I want my puppies to easily adjust to their new homes and to not have behavior problems. When I breed a litter, I condition the puppies to offer calm behavior from the start. To accomplish this, I teach the entire litter that the clicker means feeding time as soon as I start to supplement the mother's food. I begin by clicking right before I put the food down, and after only a few meals, the pups associate the click with dinner. Next, instead of clicking, I prepare a meal with the litter contained in a puppy pen placed where they can see what is happening. They will get excited and jump on the sides of the pen. Once the food is ready, I hold the bowl and patiently wait, clicker in hand. It helps to step out of sight and peek around a corner. I wait until one or two of the pups put their feet on the floor. As soon as that happens, I click and immediately feed. I do this every meal, and eventually more and more pups settle until the entire litter is sitting calmly while I prepare their food. This works great with young puppies because they tire quickly, so waiting for them to settle takes less time. When each puppy goes home, I demonstrate to the new owner how to wait until the puppy sits prior to feeding, and so the new owner will continue to reinforce calm behavior.

MARTHA WINDISCH, CPDT-KA, Personalized Dog Training, LLC, Chatsworth, NJ

TRAINING, TIMING —

Timing is critical to effective dog training. Using appropriate verbal markers can help you tell your dog *exactly* what you like and don't like. The sooner your reward follows his display of a desirable behavior, the more quickly he will learn. When teaching your dog a new behavior, reward him within half a second of completing the behavior.

JACQUELYN ENGLAND, A Dog's Life, Sunnyvale, CA

Dogs (like people) have their own timing. Some are slower, some are faster. For example, if you give the *sit* command to a hound, he will sit down slowly; a Border Collie will sit down quickly. Learn your dog's timing and adjust your training to his timing, which will help teach him to think. Give the command and wait a few seconds while he tries to figure out what you want. If you watch closely, you will see him try different things, such as a paw lift or turning his head, stepping back a little or forward a little. If he isn't figuring it out, help him by showing him. If teaching *sit*, lift a treat over his nose toward his back end.

  ✍DAINA BECKMAN, Happy Tails Dog Behavior & Training, Hornell, NY

Timing is everything; rewards should be swift.

  ✍EMILY BURLINGAME, San Jose, CA

TRAINING, TROUBLESHOOTING

Is your dog not cooperative during training? In the case of dogs who have little or no training, the problem may simply be that you and the dog have a communication problem. You aren't making yourself clear as to what you want. Patience in guiding him in the direction you want should help clarify your wishes. A reward should stimulate his eagerness to continue pleasing you.

  ✍JOAN B. GUERTIN, Common Sense Dog Training & Behavior Solutions, East Texas

Never let your dog practice it wrong—because he'll get very good at it!

  ✍BECKY SCHULTZ, BA, CPDT-KA, Becky Schultz Dog Training and Behavior, Golden Valley, MN

Every dog is an individual. They learn at different paces and have different motivators, fears, and talents. If your dog has trouble learning a new behavior, remember to work in a quiet environment, be patient, and don't be afraid to get creative or try a new approach.

  ✍CYNTHIA EDGERLY, Bingo! Dog Training, Watsonville, CA

Often we get so enthusiastic about our training that we overdo it or overwork the dog, and he ends up tired and confused. In this case, back up, ask the dog to do something he knows how to do and likes doing, and when he complies, end the session and have some playtime.

  ✍JOAN B. GUERTIN, Common Sense Dog Training & Behavior Solutions, East Texas

If your dog doesn't do what you ask, there's a reason. Possibilities include: 1. Your dog doesn't understand what you are asking—you may think "He knows this!" but he really doesn't. 2. What you're asking is too hard in the given situation—this could be due to distractions, anxiety, pain, tiredness, etc. 3. Your dog doesn't see anything in it for him that makes it worth the energy expenditure (mental or physical).

It's your job as a trainer to make sure that your dog understands what you're asking, is able to do it under those specific circumstances, and knows he'll get something worthwhile out of it.

ANN DUPUIS, CPDT-KA, Your Dream Dog, Randolph, MA

When you hit a training snag, rather than intensifying the training, it sometimes pays to completely back off and work on something new. In trying to learn a new behavior, quite frequently a dog will try offering an older, more familiar behavior instead because it's "easier" than coping with the stress of learning something new. The new behavior becomes the "difficult" one. Now the dog isn't as stressed over that first behavior and it's no longer perceived as difficult. If you intensify the training, both you and the dog may become overly stressed and make little or no progress.

MELINDA MURPHY, Goldog, Blue Springs, MO

If your dog is normally very cooperative but for some reason just isn't connecting, it may be a deeper issue. Ask yourself: How does he feel? Is he acting normally? If not, when was the last time he saw the vet? Has his behavior changed, such as being unusually quiet, sulking, or lacking interest in food, treats, or play? If your dog's temperature is normal, he may just need some downtime. If it's elevated, go to the vet—it may be the early stages of a physical problem or the result of extreme activity, like a strained muscle. Never assume that your friend will want to work all the time. Like us, there may be a legitimate reason for his lack of interest in you and your wishes.

JOAN B. GUERTIN, Common Sense Dog Training & Behavior Solutions, East Texas

Work in baby steps and set your dog up for success. Increase distance, distractions, and duration as his performance permits. If your dog fails to respond correctly to a cue three times in a row, stop asking and go back to working at the level where he was last successful.

CYNTHIA EDGERLY, Bingo! Dog Training, Watsonville, CA

TRAVEL

Train and prepare your dog for traveling with you—for instance, teach him to be quiet on command because barking is the number-one public nuisance when it comes to dogs. Life is just better with dogs than without! Dogs who spend lots of quality time with their owners are happier dogs. People who spend more quality time with their well-trained dogs are happier people!

SUE STERNBERG, Animals for Adoption and Great Dog Productions, Accord, NY, and Moab, UT

To make traveling with your dog easier, compile a checklist of essentials. This may include basics such as food, leash, pills, bed, training gear, tug toys, and crates. Essentials should also include a copy of his rabies certificate and other vaccinations, as well as some "clean up" materials such as an enzymatic cleaner and paper towels. If staying in a hotel, a nice thing to include is an old sheet to cover the bed. Also, making a checklist for yourself (with such essentials as rain shoes and rain gear for walking the dog) will ensure that you and your dog can travel in safety and comfort.

ELAINE COUPÉ, For Pet's Sake & Memphis Agility, Oakland, TN

Make a travel-only dog tag that lists your cell phone number or local telephone contact while you're traveling.

SUE STERNBERG, Animals for Adoption and Great Dog Productions, Accord, NY, and Moab, UT

Save yourself from embarrassment! Include on your travel checklist a generous supply of poop bags. You should have two to three per day per dog. Poop bags can be tucked into your trunk or a door pocket to keep them handy. And tie one or two around each leash handle so they are there when you need them while walking your dog.

ELAINE COUPÉ, For Pet's Sake & Memphis Agility, Oakland, TN

Before traveling by car, freeze a few gallons (liters) of your dog's regular water in plastic gallon (liter) bottles with screw-on caps. Use the ice to chill your cooler, and as it melts, your dog will be able to drink his regular water for your trip.

LAURA DORFMAN, CPDT-KA, kona's touch, inc., Glencoe, IL

Before taking a car trip with your dog, bring him to the back of grocery stores and malls to get him familiar with the sounds and size of big trucks. At rest areas it can be stressful with so much activity going on, so the more you plan in

> **In 1908, the first dog biscuit appeared in the United States—it was called "Malatoid."**

advance, the safer and calmer you and your dog will be. The dog area is almost always where the trucks pull out. Just give him yummy treats during "rehearsals" and he will learn to love those big trucks.

LAURA DORFMAN, CPDT-KA, kona's touch, inc., Glencoe, IL

Be prepared for emergencies when traveling with your dog by car. On a large index card, write "Traveling with pets! In case of emergency, please look in the glove compartment for instructions." When you travel with your dog, post this index card in your car window. Then create an index card for each of your pets that might be traveling with you. Include their names, ages, species, breed or mix information, any health conditions, necessary medications, veterinarian contact information, and emergency contact information in case you are injured. Give directions for temporary care of your pets. For example, "Please take my dog to the nearest veterinary hospital. All costs will be reimbursed by me or my emergency contacts." (Be sure to make arrangements with your emergency contacts ahead of time.) Keep these index cards in your glove compartment so that accident responders can access them if necessary.

TEOTI ANDERSON, CPDT-KA, Pawsitive Results, LLC, Lexington, SC

Make sure that your dog is a welcome guest by keeping him on leash in public areas of the hotel. Check with hotel staff about areas that are off-limits to dogs—like the pool area, kids' play areas, gardens, etc. Don't let him socialize with other guests or staff members unless invited. For potty breaks, take him to an out-of-the way spot, like a corner of the parking lot, and be sure to pick up after him. Unless he's confined in a crate, don't leave your dog alone in the hotel room. Even with the "do not disturb" sign on the door, hotel staff may enter your room. If your dog is loose, he can bolt out the door or frighten staff members.

MARY LEATHERBERRY, CPDT-KA, Good Dog! Santa Fe, Santa Fe, NM

Don't plan a road trip or stay overnight in a motel or hotel until your dog can be quiet through the night and not alert you and all the other guests to everything that goes bump in the night.

SUE STERNBERG, Animals for Adoption and Great Dog Productions, Accord, NY, and Moab, UT

TREATS

Too many people equate treating their dogs with "spoiling" them. The best way to show dogs that we care is to keep them fit and healthy. If the day does not allow much time for exercise, don't be afraid to scale back your pooch's evening meal and then sit down for some quiet clicker shaping with bits of apple or carrot for an after-dinner snack.

DANIELLE JOHANNEMANN, Garden City, SC

For summertime fun, pour chicken or beef broth in ice cube containers and have an ice cube frenzy in the backyard to help cool off your dog during the hot summer months.

᳁BONNIE KRUPA, CPDT-KA, Happy, Clean and Smart, Muncie, IN

When working with your dog in class or someplace distracting, try making a puppy popsicle by filling an old yogurt container with beef or chicken broth and then freezing it. When you need your pup to settle down, take off the lid and let him lick on the "pupsicle."

᳁VICKI RONCHETTE, CPDT-KA, CAP2, Braveheart Dog Training, San Leandro, CA

As a trainer, I often use baked treats in my classes and give out baked goods as prizes for games played during class. I recently learned that I need to label my goods for people or dogs. One of my clients took some cupcakes home for her dog and put them in the refrigerator. Her husband, craving a midnight snack, ate one that night. He learned the next morning they were actually for the dog–he had a good laugh after brushing his teeth twice that morning!

᳁BONNIE KRUPA, CPDT-KA, Happy, Clean and Smart, Muncie, IN

VACUUM CLEANERS

Many dogs become reactive around vacuum cleaners, barking and attacking them. To create peace while vacuuming, start by having a silent, unmoving vacuum cleaner in the same room as the dog. If he is calm at this point (and he probably will be because there is nothing exciting about a quiet vacuum cleaner), move the vacuum to another room away from him. If he shows fear or excitement for the quiet vacuum, give him a treat every time he acts calmly near the vacuum until he can be in the room and ignore it. Then move on to the exercise of turning on the vacuum, which will take two people to perform correctly. Before you turn it on, have some tasty treats ready to give your dog, preferably tiny, chewy, and full of flavor, like hot dog, cheese, chicken, etc. Move the vacuum far away from him into another room. One person should be with the machine, while the other should be with the dog, armed with treats. Turn on the vacuum, and while it is running, give him treats when he ignores it. Move the vacuum to a closer room, but still keep it out of sight of the dog. Again turn it on and have the person reward him for not reacting to the sound. If he tries to run into the room with the vacuum, move it farther away until he ignores it and keep giving him treats for good behavior. Slowly move the vacuum from being out of the dog's sight to having it in sight of him, all the while rewarding him for being relaxed and not trying to get at the vacuum. Any time he starts to react, back the vacuum up to where he remained calm and start again from that point. This may take some time, but eventually the dog will be calm around the vacuum.

🖉JANE BRYDON, M.S.Ed., M.Ed., CPDT-KA, Jane Brydon, Dog Training Coach, LLC, Clifton Heights, PA

VETERINARIAN, CHOOSING

Choose a veterinarian *before* you get your puppy. Visit the veterinary offices in your area, and look for friendly staff, clean offices, and convenient business hours. Ask for references from each veterinarian you like to further narrow down your decision. Many vets offer a "new puppy package" that includes the vaccinations and a socialization class.

🖉ANN ALLUMS, CPDT-KA, Best Friends Animal Society, Kanab, UT

When looking for a veterinarian, feel free to ask her questions. Does she have the same ideals as you? Does she feel comfortable referring you to a specialist if needed? If she doesn't refer, you may want to question her—she can't be an expert at everything. Just like human doctors, if a problem is serious, a vet will refer to a specialist.

🖉SHANNON COYNER, RVT, CPDT-KA, Ventura, CA

VETERINARY VISITS

From a socialization standpoint, a puppy's initial visit to the vet should be a positive experience, such as a meeting with the vet, a physical exam, or just a visit to the waiting room for some treats. Then make another appointment in which to have any shots or other possibly painful procedure administered.

🖉ANN ALLUMS, CPDT-KA, Best Friends Animal Society, Kanab, UT

When taking your dog to the vet, exercise him thoroughly before going and let him finish completely all outdoor business.

🖉MELANIE MCKEEHAN, Assistant Director of Operations, Red Dog Pet Resort and Spa, Cincinnati, OH

When a person brings a puppy or new dog home, one extremely important factor should be his first vet visit. I am a firm believer in making a couple of fun mock trips to the vet with a lot of treats from the vet staff. Spend a few minutes with the staff and vet and then leave. After these fun visits, the initial first visit will be a piece of cake. First impressions are huge for dogs, and making the first vet trip fun will be helpful throughout his life.

&TONY VILLARREAL, Humane Society Calumet Area, Munster, IN

To help prepare your dog/puppy for vet examinations, gently, slowly, and calmly touch him all over his body (including his rear area and back paws) while he is both lying down and standing, pairing each gentle touch with a favorite treat and plenty of praise. Teaching him to stand on command will make it easier for both your dog and the vet. Walk or drive (whichever you normally use), taking the exact same route to the vet office and using the exact same procedures (like putting him in a carrier), but go to the park instead. Do this more frequently than the vet trips (eight or nine out of ten trips). If driving, occasionally stop the car and walk past the vet office, then return to the car and continue to the park. As soon as you enter the vet office for an appointment, give your dog extra-special treats and a favorite or new toy before the exam (try to play the entire time if you have to wait, or keep giving treats) and immediately after the exam.

&CHRISTINA SHUSTERICH, BA, CBC, NY Clever K9, Inc, Queens, NY

VOICE

Remember to fluctuate your tone of voice when giving verbal commands to your dog. High-pitched, happy voice commands will elicit more action. Low-pitched, stern voice commands will elicit caution and slow or stop action. Keeping your voice tone neutral on commands like *sit* and *down* can keep your dog focused.

&MERIT DAY, Top Dog Training, Broken Arrow, OK

TOP TIDBIT

Rabies vaccines are mandatory by law in the United States, and a few states require revaccination every year.

Your voice is one of the most effective tools you have. Dogs respond very well to tone of voice. A high-pitched voice is great for praise. The sillier you can be, the more your dog will like it! A voice command should not be a question—it should be a statement. Don't say "Sit?" in a questioning way; rather, say "Sit" in a stern (but not a punishing) tone. A deeper voice is good for commands.

ᕛDARLENE KOZA, Scooter's School of Sit & Stay, Rochester, NY

WAIT — Rink

The *wait* command can be taught in five steps, each one making the next step easier. Master the command at each level before proceeding to the next. At each successive step, a reliable *wait* is more critical for your dog's safety but easier to teach because of past learning. The steps are:

1. waiting for a release word to approach a bowl of food after it has been placed on the ground
2. waiting for a release word before coming out of a crate door
3. waiting for a release word before going out an open house door (teach at every door in your house)
4. waiting for a release word before going out a gate (teach at all your gates)
5. waiting to have a leash clipped on and for a release word before exiting a vehicle

ᕛMARTY SWINDELL, BS, CPDT-KA, LickSkillet Dog Training, Lee's Summit, MO

A practical habit to teach your dog is to wait at doorways. This will prevent door dashing, ensure safety among all (including other dogs) at the limited opening, and teach him self-control.

ᕛANN ALLUMS, CPDT-KA; Best Friends Animal Society, Kanab, UT

WAKING YOU UP —

Does your dog wake you up in the morning by whining, pawing, or barking at you? The all-time best method for getting rid of this behavior is to take away the reward for it by ignoring him. Ignoring means don't talk to him, don't look at him, and don't let him know you're awake. Take all attention away from that behavior. At first your dog will escalate his efforts, possibly whining louder and pawing at you. This is normal because he is trying harder with what worked in the past. But if you consistently ignore him, he will eventually give up. But you must be consistent. If you reward him with any kind of attention (because you are tired of his persistence), he'll only try harder next time because he learned that his attempts eventually paid off!

ᕛANN ALLUMS, CPDT-KA, Best Friends Animal Society, Kanab, UT

WALK NICELY

"Loose lead walking" means whatever you can tolerate from your dog. If you don't mind him walking at the end of the leash but not pulling, that is fine. If you want your dog to walk next to you, that is fine too. Work to what you can tolerate.

ℰ TRISH O'CONNOR, Denver, CO

continue on my walk. Here is the important part—if he is walking nicely by my side, I surprise him with a small but quick hidden treat. That way, he knows he is making the right choice by walking nicely by my side. In no time at all, my dog decides that I am still his favorite thing in the world!

ℰ CHRISTINE CRUZ, Eustis, FL

To get your dog to walk on a loose leash, you really don't need to be a seasoned trainer. Simply let the leash do the work. Take your dog outside on a 6-foot (2-m) leash and walk a few steps forward. If he starts to pull ahead, simply stop and wait. The leash will tighten, so you'll stop moving. When the dog turns around and the leash isn't tight anymore, praise and continue moving. By simply being consistent and not moving when the leash is tight, your dog will soon understand that nothing fun happens unless the leash is loose.

ℰ DAYNA VILLA, IACP, Taking the Lead Dog Training, PA

Walking a dog should be great exercise and lots of fun! Once I put a leash on my dog, I start the no-pull game. If he makes the leash go tight, I stop walking. As soon as the leash is loose, I praise him, toss a small treat on the ground beside me, and

Your body language is much more effective in guiding your dog's actions during training than using the leash/collar to direct him. To prevent a dog from pulling too much, start off by using body language exclusively with your puppy. Keep the leash very loose by moving with him when he moves. Redirect him only when he is looking at you.

ℰ MERIT DAY, Top Dog Training, Broken Arrow, OK

Your pup wants to smell a tree on your walk? Use the leash to keep him out of range of the tree. After pulling, barking, and sitting have failed and your dog looks at you to see what is going on, capture that moment of eye contact with calm praise; then reward him with slack on the leash so that sniffing can begin.

ℰ JAMIE DAMATO, CPDT-KA, Animalsense Canine Training and Behavior, Inc., Chicago, IL

During walks, alternate between letting your dog be carefree and keeping his attention on you. Practice in baby steps—work on one criterion at a time for a few days in a row, then work on a different single criterion. When your dog's skill is up to par, start combining two criteria together. For example, for three days, work on position and reward when your dog is close to you. Then for the next three days, work on attention and reward when your dog's head is up and/or facing you. When he has proven proficient at both, reward only when his head is up *and* he's in position.

&JACQUELYN ENGLAND, A Dog's Life, Sunnyvale, CA

People seem to have a difficult time clicking and treating frequently enough while training loose leash walking. In small classes (six people or less), I have everyone count out 20 treats and start walking. Whoever clicks and treats the most is the first to sit down. I tell them to continue the idea by feeding the dog his meals during walks. The dog is hand-fed, has to earn the good stuff in his life, and he's getting frequently reinforced for polite walking.

&JILL MILLER, CPDT-KA, Mad City Dog Training, Madison, WI

When teaching a puppy to walk on a leash, don't be in a hurry to get from place to place. Allow him to explore the area, but stand still every time he pulls to the end of the leash. Eventually, the leash will become loose again when the puppy moves close to you. Together you can begin walking just a bit more, ready to stop again when the leash becomes tight. You will be doing more standing than walking in the beginning, but eventually your dog will learn to walk greater distances without pulling. Go slowly. It takes time for a young dog to figure out the message you are sending.

&ADRIENNE CARSON, Harmony, NJ

One common mistake owners make is giving their dog too much leash. You should give your dog 12 to 1– inches (30 to 46 cm) or just enough leash for your arm to hang comfortably at your side. This way, your dog can't build momentum by getting out in front.

&TONIA WHILDEN, Houston Dog Ranch, Houston, TX

When walking your dog on leash, do not allow him to cross behind you. Doing so can result in him pulling you off your feet as he bolts after a squirrel.

&JOANN KOVACICH, Grateful Dog Pet Care, Inc., Penfield, NY

To have your dog practice walking at your side, he also needs to learn to get fed at your side, not just in front of you. You can practice side feeding when your dog does a *sit* in front of you. When he's sitting, hold the treat in front of his nose but do not let him have it—he can just lick your fingers in trying to get it. While he is doing this, turn your body so that you are next to him, then say "Yes" (or click and treat) and release the treat. As your dog gets better at longer *sits*, you will not have to hold the treat as close—just move your body, and then click and treat when you are at his side.

—KATHY FARDY, MA, Dog's Time, It's Their Time!, Billerica, MA

I had a client whose dog was wonderful on a leash until he would see a squirrel. We tried teaching a solid *leave it* command, habituating him to walking around the small animals, lots of off-lead exercise prior to walks, etc., but nothing helped. Then I decided to use a body block after saying "Leave it" by stepping between the dog and the squirrel. The sudden appearance of my leg did the trick, and from there we worked on phasing out the body block slowly to just putting one foot forward. From there we faded it out so that we only had to give the verbal *leave it* command.

—CARI MESSICK, CPDT-KA, FitHound Puppy + Dog Training, Frederick, MD

WATCH ME

When you're looking for attention from your dog, friendly eye contact can be extremely useful. The *watch* command tells him to look you in the eyes during moments of distraction. To teach this, hold a small treat between your eyes as you say "Watch." Hold your gaze forward, and reward when your dog makes eye contact with you. After a few repetitions, you may feel that he's looking more at the food than at your eyes. At this point, place the food, pinched between your thumb and forefinger, between your eyes, then slowly move it, parallel to the ground, about 6 to 12 inches (15 to 30 cm) to the left or right of your face. Most likely, your dog's eyes will follow the treat and stare at it when you stop. He may continue to stare for several seconds or even longer, trying to will the treat to his mouth through osmosis. It's okay—just continue to hold your gaze forward and wait your dog out. At some point, he will stop and suddenly look you straight in the eye, as if to say "Dude! Are you going to give it to me or what?!" At that moment, you've gotten the eye contact you were waiting for, so reward your dog and try it again.

ℰ◌SHAYNA STANIS, Canine Manager/ East Bay SPCA, Oakland, CA

One of the best times to teach your dog to watch you is in a training class. While your instructor is talking, simply watch your dog out of the corner of your eye. Every time he looks at you, give him a treat immediately. Then when he is looking at you expectantly, wait one or two seconds before delivering the next treat. Very gradually, over the course of the class, increase the time your dog has to watch you to receive his treat. He will learn to watch you like a hawk whether or not he has received a command in a distracting environment.

ℰ◌KAREN OWENS, M.Ed, CPDT-KA, Clever Canine Dog Training, Concord, NC

I use the *watch me* to manage leash frustration issues. On walks, when I see a dog approaching (and this requires my vigilance, so it's before the dog I'm walking reacts to the advancing dog), I ask my dog to sit and then watch me. I get ten seconds or more of the *watch me* before I mark and reward. I repeat the *watch me* until the dog passes.

ℰ◌LEIGH SANSONE, JD, CPDT-KA, PMCT, Ruff Customers Dog Training, New York, NY

ABBREVIATIONS

Associations

AABP – Association of Animal Behavior Professionals

ABC – Animal Behavior College

ABMA – Animal Behavior Management Alliance

ABS – Animal Behavior Society

AKC – American Kennel Club

APBC – Association of Pet Behavior Counsellors

APDT – Association of Pet Dog Trainers

CASI – Companion Animal Sciences Institute

CCPDT – Certification Council for Professional Dog Trainers

CGC – Canine Good Citizen

COAPE – Centre of Applied Pet Ethology (COAPE)

IAABC – International Association of Animal Behavior Consultants

IACP – International Association of Canine Professionals

TDI – Therapy Dogs International

Certifications

ABCDT – Animal Behavior College Certified Dog Trainer (through the ABC)

ACAAB – Associate Certified Applied Animal Behaviorist (through the ABS)

CAAB – Certified Applied Animal Behaviorist (through the ABS)

CABC – Certified Animal Behavioral Consultant (through the IAABC)

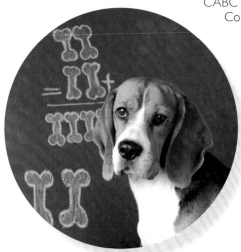

CAP – Certified Clicker Competency Assessment Program

CAP2 – Certified Clicker Competency Assessment Program, Level 2

CBC – Canine Behavior Consultant

CCTS – Certified Canine Training Specialist

CDBC – Certified Dog Behavior Consultant (through the IAABC)

CPDT-KA – Certified Professional Dog Trainer - Knowledge Assessed (through the CCPDT)

CTC – Certificate in Training and Counseling (through the San Francisco SPCA)

CVT – Certified Veterinary Technician

Dip. CABT – Diploma in Practical Aspects of Companion Animal Behaviour and Training (through the COAPE)

Dip. DTBC – Diploma of Dog Training and Behavior Consulting (through the CASI)

KPACTP – Karen Pryor Academy Certified Training Partner

PABC – Professional Animal Behavior Consultant (through the AABP)

PDT – Professional Dog Trainer (through the AABP)

PMCT – Pat Miller Certified Trainer

RVT – Registered Veterinary Technician

Education

BA – Bachelor of Arts

BS – Bachelor of Science

JD – Juris Doctor

MA – Master of Arts

MEd – Master of Education

MS – Master of Science

MSc – Master of Science

MSEd – Master of Science in Education

RN – Registered Nurse

TRAINER DIRECTORY

UNITED STATES

Alabama

LEAH GANGELHOFF
Flint Hill K-9 Training LLC
Greater Birmingham, AL
Phone: 205-267-7793
E-Mail: leah@flinthillk9.com
Website: www.flinthillk9.com

Arizona

ELAINE ALLISON, CPDT-KA
Humane Society of Wickenburg
4000 Industrial Road
Wickenburg, AZ 85358
Phone: 928-684-8801
E-Mail: elainewhs@wickenburghumane.com
Website: www.wickenburghumane.com

JEFF BAME, CPDT-KA
Paws for Adventure
Paulden, AZ
E-Mail: paws4adventure@msn.com
Website: www.paws4adventure.
thedogtrainer.com

JOANN BLUTH, CDPT
A Canine Academy Int'l
Phoenix, AZ
Website: www.dogtrainerphoenix.com

CRYSTAL COLL
All Ways Pawsitive Pet Behavior & Training
Queen Creek, AZ 85243
Phone: 480-529-7947
E-Mail: info@allwayspawsitive.com
Website: www.allwayspawsitive.com

KRISTYN HAYES, CERTIFIED BEHAVIORAL THERAPIST AND TRAINER
Bark Busters Home Dog Training
Mesa, AZ
Phone: 877-500-BARK
E-Mail: mesa@barkbusters.com
Website: www.barkbusters.com

California

NAN ARTHUR, CDBC, CPDT-KA, KPACTP
Author of *Chill Out Fido!*
Whole Dog Training
Lakeside, CA
Phone: 619-561-2602
Website: www.wholedogtraining.com

AMY W. DE BENEDICTIS
The Puppylady
Menlo Park, CA
Phone: 650-255-5969
E-Mail: puppylady@pacbell.net

CATHY BONES, CPDT-KA
Pet Therapy Coordinator
Shriners Hospital for Children Northern California
CA
E-Mail: cbones@shrinenet.org

HOLLY BRAND, RVT, CDT
West Coast K-9 Training
Northern California, Contra Costa County
Brentwood, CA 94513
Phone: 925-516-1652
E-Mail: wck9t@sbcglobal.net

EMILY BURLINGAME
A Dog's Life
Sunnyvale, CA

SHANNON COYNER, RVT, CPDT-KA
Ventura, CA
Website: www.petwellnesscoach.com

MARY DISNEY
Dog Training/Walking/Sitting
Marina del Rey, CA
Phone: 310-339-9895
Website: www.marydisney.com

JANIS DOLPHIN
45851 Iversen Road
Gualala, CA 95445
E-Mail: dogwood@mcn.org

CYNTHIA EDGERLY
Bingo! Dog Training
854 San Miguel Canyon Rd
Watsonville, CA 95076
Email: bingodogtraining@yahoo.com
Website: www.bingodogtraining.com

JACQUELYN ENGLAND
A Dog's Life
1249 Birchwood Drive
Sunnyvale, CA 94089
Phone: 408-747-1111
Website: www.dogslife.biz

TERRI ERICKSON, CPDT-KA
Pawlite Pups, LLC
Glendora, CA
Website: www.pawlitepups.com

DIANA FOSTER
Assertive K-9 Training Kennels
Corona, CA
E-Mail: k9dogtrainer@sbcglobal.net

DONNASUE JACOBI
Just Like Home Pet Sitting and Training
Menlo Park, CA
Website: www.justlikehomepets.com

PENNY LOCKE
Dog Listener
All About Canines
1570 S. Novato Blvd.
Novato, CA 94947
Phone: 415-798-0223
E-Mail: penlocke@aol.com
Website: www.allabout-canines.com

TERRY LONG, CPDT-KA
DogPACT Training and Behavior Services
Long Beach, CA
Website: www.dogpact.com

JAMIE LURTZ
Solutions! Pet Services
Anaheim, CA
Phone: 714-404-9314
E-Mail: solutionspets@aol.com
Website: www.SolutionsPets.com

SHA NEWMAN
Training with Love for Canines
Valley Glen, CA
Website: www.trainingwithloveforcanines.com

LISA NEYER
Bark Busters
San Clemente, CA
Phone: 949-361-0077
E-Mail: beachcities@barkbusters.com
Website: www.barkbusters.com

DAVE PORT
The Way Of The Dog
Union City, CA
E-Mail: david@innu-no-michi.com

MARIAN POTT
Miramar Dog Training
Obedience, Herding, Behavior
Half Moon Bay, CA
Phone: 650-712-1192
E-Mail: miramark9@comcast.net
Website: www.MiramarDogTraining.vpweb.com

DONNA S. RINDSKOPF
Guide Dog Raiser
Doglovers Obedience of Ramona
Ramona, CA
E-Mail: DogloverDR@aol.com

ANDREA ROBINSON
Positive Pet Training and Supply
P.O. Box 613
Madera, CA 93639-0613
E-Mail: andreadogtrainer@yahoo.com
Website: www.positive-pet-training.com

VICKI RONCHETTE, CPDT-KA, CAP2
Braveheart Dog Training
San Leandro, CA
E-Mail: Braveheartdogs@sbcglobal.net
Website: www.braveheartdogtraining.com

LAUREL SCARIONI, CPDT-KA
Pawsitive Results Critter Academy
Santa Rosa, CA
Website: www.pawsitiveresults.net

WAYNE SHAFFER, ABCDT
Pawsitive Methods
P.O. Box 661
Kelseyville, CA 95451
Website: http://pawsitivemethods.com

SHAYNA STANIS, CPDT-KA
Berkely, CA
E-Mail: sstanisdt@comcast.net

M. CECILIA STERNZON, CPDT-KA
Canine Higher Learning
Serving the Silicon Valley, CA
Phone: 408-323-9987
E-Mail: dogtopia@earthlink.net,
Website: www.caninehigherlearning.com

REENA S. WALTON
Pups-R-Us Dog Training
Redwood City, CA
Phone: 650-366-2342
E-Mail: waltonmntn@aol.com

NICOLE WILDE, CPDT-KA
Author of *So You Wanna to Be a Dog Trainer*
(www.phantompub.com)
Gentle Guidance Dog Training
P.O. Box 2814
Santa Clarita, CA 91386
E-Mail: phantmwlf@aol.com
Website: www.gentleguidance4dogs.com

CARYL WOLFF, CPDT-KA, CDBC
Doggie Manners
12021 Wilshire Blvd., No. 298
Los Angeles, CA 90025
E-Mail: caryl@DoggieManners.com
Website: www.DoggieManners.com

Colorado

KARI BASTYR, MS, CDBC
Wag & Train
Denver, CO
Website: www.wagandtrain.com

PAT BLOCKER, CPDT-KA
Peaceful Paws Dog Training
Aurora, CO
E-Mail: pat@peacefulpaws.net
Website: www.peacefulpaws.net

SUE BROWN, CDBC, CPDT-KA
Love My Dog Training
Littleton, CO
Website: www.lovemydogtraining.com

RUTH BRUNETTE-MEANS, CPDT-KA
All Breed Rescue & Training
20 Mountview Lane, Suite C
Colorado Springs, CO 80907
E-Mail: info@csallbreed.org
Website: www.haveanicedog.org

ROBIN CARROLL
GAP dogs, Inc.
CO
E-Mail: dogmom702@msn.com

DENISE DAWSON
All Breed Rescue and Training
Colorado Springs, CO
Website: www.haveanicedog.org

CHRISTINE KELLY, CTC, CPDT-KA, TDI EVALUATOR, CGC EVALUATOR
K9to5
Colorado Springs, CO
E-Mail: ckelly@K9to5.us
Website: www.K9to5.us

LISA L. SICKLES, CPDT-KA, CDBC
WagWag Enterprises
Englewood, CO
Phone: 303-619-8013
E-Mail: lisa@wagwag.net
Website: www.wagwag.net

TERI THOMAS, CPDT-KA
Angels in the Making, LLC
Grand Junction, CO

Connecticut

MICHELLE DOUGLAS, CPDT-KA, CDBC
The Refined Canine, LLC
West Haven, CT
E-Mail: refinedk9@yahoo.com
Website: www.refinedcanine.com

Delaware

LYNNE YOUNG, CPDT-KA
PetsRx and Dog Training Club of
Chester Co.
Wilmington, DE
E-Mail: LynneYoung@aol.com

Florida

ANDREA CARLSON-CARTER
Courteous Canine, Inc.
3414 Melissa Country Way
Lutz, FL 33559

TERRY CUYLER, CPDT-KA, CGC, DELTA, THE GUNDOG CLUB
Pawsitive Results In Home
Dog Training
P.O. Box 953642
Lake Mary, FL 32795
Phone: 407-256-8906
Website: www.pawsprof.com

JANICE DEMADONA
Orlando, FL
Website: www.dogtrainingwithjanice.com

P.J. LACETTE
Best Paw Forward Inc.
1835 Oak Haven Plantation Road
Osteen, FL 32764-8872
E-Mail: bestpaw@iag.net
Website: www.bestpaw.com

SHEILA LIEBERMAN
Loving Obedience Dog Training
Miami, FL & Metro DC
Phone: 305-772-3647

PHYLLIS MAZZARISI
1128 24th Ave N.
St. Petersburg, FL 33704
E-Mail: nobonesaboutit2@aol.com
Website: www.nobonesaboutit.biz

LORENA B. PATTI, MS, CPDT-KA, ABCDT
Waggers Doggie Daycare & Training
Orlando, FL
E-Mail: info@waggersdogtraining.com
Website: www.waggersdogtraining.com

DEBBIE REVELL, RN, DIP. CABT, CDBC
Pets Behave LLC
297 County Line Road
Niceville, FL 32578
E-Mail: PetsBehave@earthlink.net
Website: www.PetsBehave.net

MAUREEN SCHOOLEY
Blue Paws, Inc.
New Port Richey, FL
E-Mail: maureen@CanineTalk.com
Website: www.CanineTalk.com

AMY WEEKS, CPDT-KA
Tampa, FL
E-Mail: drophammer@peoplepc.com

BARRY ZIONS
Alpha Dog Training
Spring Hill, FL

Georgia

DARLENE PINO
Clever Canines Dog Training
4820 Millbrooke Rd.
Albany, GA 31721
Phone: 229-878-0111

TRACEY SCHOWALTER
Puppy Adept, Inc.
Gainesville, GA
E-Mail: info@puppyadept.com
Website: www.puppyadept.com

TINA M. SPRING VAN WHY
Sit Happens Dog Training & Behavior
Athens, GA
E-Mail: tina@sithappens.us
Website: www.sithappens.us

Illinois

JAMIE DAMATO, CPDT-KA
Animalsense Canine Training and
Behavior, Inc.
Chicago, IL
Website: www.animalsense.com

WENDY DECARLO-YOUNG, CPDT-KA
Dog Obedience Group
1943 W. Estes Ave.
Chicago, IL 60626-2319
Phone: 773-973-2934
E-Mail: Wdecarlo@aol.com
Website: www.dogobediencegroup.com

LAURA DORFMAN, CPDT-KA
kona's touch, inc.
Glencoe, IL
Phone: 847-204-7100
E-Mail: konastouch@yahoo.com
Website: www.konastouch.com

TRISH MCMILLAN, MSc, CPDT-KA
ASPCA Animal Behavior Center
1717 South Philo Road, Ste. 36
Urbana, IL 61802
Website: www.aspca.org

ALICE PISZCZEK, CPDT-KA
BIG PAWS/little jaws
Naperville, IL
E-Mail: atpaws1@yahoo.com

MARY ANN RIECKE
Tail Waggers Dog Training Club
Chicago, IL
Website: www.tailwaggersdogtraining.com

PAIGE WILLIS, CPDT-KA
DeKalb, IL
E-Mail: paigewillis@gmail.com

Indiana

CHERIE A. BEATTIE, MS, CPDT-KA
The Pet Pro
Clarksville, IN
E-Mail: the-petpro@insightbb.com
Website: www.the-petpro.com

BONNIE KRUPA, CPDT-KA
Happy, Clean and Smart
5700 W Kilgore Ave.
Muncie, IN 47304
Phone: (765) 288-8186
Website: www.happycleanandsmart.com

AILIGH VANDERBUSH, CABT
Animalia, Inc.
5607 E. Washington St
Indianapolis, IN 46219
E-Mail: ailigh@animalia.us
Website: www.animalia.us

TONY VILLARREAL
Humane Society Calumet Area
Munster, IN
Website: www.hscalumet.org

SANDRA L. WIRE
K9 FunTime, LLC
6401 Westhaven Drive, Suite C
Indianapolis, IN 46254
Phone: 317-347-0035
E-Mail: Sandra@k9funtime.com
Website: www.k9funtime.com

Iowa

BETH HALEY, CPDT-KA
4RK9S
910 2nd Ave SW
Cedar Rapids, IA
Website: www.4RK9S.com

LUCINDA LUDWIG
Canine Connection LLC
Dubuque, IA
Phone: 563-451-9177
E-mail: getconnected@mchsi.com
Website: www.dubuquedogtraining.com

JILL SCHATZ, CPDT-KA
121 Dog Training
10815 78th Court NE
Bondurant, IA 50035
Phone: 515-967-7883 × 1
E-Mail: jill@121dogtraining.com

Kansas

PAT HENNESSY, CAP2, CPDT-KA
N2paws
12120 State Line #188
Leawood, KS
E-Mail: pat@n2paws.com
Website: www.n2paws.com

ROSIE STEEL
Rosie Steel Dog Training
P.O. Box 83
Mahaska, KS 66955
Phone: 785-245- 3348

Kentucky

LISA HOLLANDER, ABC CERTIFIED
1045 Georgetown Rd.
Lexington, KY 40510
E-Mail: lisadoggoneproud@aim.com
Website: www.doggoneproud.com

JASON MANN, ABCDT
Top Dog K9 Training Solutions
Lexington, KY
E-Mail: Jason@TopDogTrainingSolutions.com
Website: www.TopDogTrainingSolutions.com

SANDY OTTO
Puppy Preschool, Inc.
Bowling Green, KY
E-Mail: puppypreschool@insightbb.com

Louisiana
CAROLYN KERNER
Dog Gone Right
Amite, LA 70422
E-Mail: DogGoneRight@eatel.net

Maine
KAREN CAMPBELL
Karen Campbell's Pet Behavior Help Now!
Portland, ME
E-Mail: karenpethelp@gwi.net

ELIZABETH LANGHAM, MS, CPDT-KA
Tree Frog Farm Dog Training and Agility
North Yarmouth, ME
E-Mail: treefrogfarm@gmail.com
Website: www.treefrogfarmdogtraining.com

JENNIFER TUCK
Rip it Up! Dog Training
Skowhegan, ME
E-Mail: ripitupagility@yahoo.com
Website: www.ripitupagility.com

JENNY RUTH YASI
Head Trainer
Whole Dog Camp
Peaks Island, ME
E-Mail: info@wholedogcamp.com
Website: www.wholedogcamp.com

Maryland
CHRISTINE BEVILLARD, CPDT-KA
Great Canines (CR8K9S, LLC)
Mount Airy, MD
E-Mail: gr8k9s@gmail.com
Website: www.gr8k9s.com

KAREN COTTINGHAM
Primetime Pet Services
1109 Calebs Way
Salisbury, MD
E-Mail: primetimedogs@comcast.net

CRYSTAL FRANKLIN, CPDT-KA
Bethesda, MD
E-Mail: cfcare4pets@gmail.com

RACHEL B. LACHOW, CPDT-KA
Positively Obedient
Reisterstown, MD
Website: www.positivelyobedient.webs.com

LAURIE LUCK, CPDT-KA, KPACTP
Smart Dog University
P.O. Box 1111
Mount Airy, MD 21771
E-Mail: laurie@smartdoguniversity.com
Website: www.smartdoguniversity.com

CARI MESSICK, CPDT-KA
FitHound Puppy + Dog Training
Frederick, MD
E-Mail: cari@fithound.com
Website: www.fithound.com

JULES NYE, CPDT-KA
Sit Stay & Play
7863 Telegraph Rd #B
Severn, MD 21144
Phone: 443-791-3647
E-Mail: info@sitstayandplay.com
Website: www.sitstayandplay.com

CAROL ROSEN, MS
Positive Dog Training and Animal Actors,
LLC
Silver Spring, MD
Website: www.carolpositivedogtraining.com

JACKIE SHERIDAN-MOORE
1538 Deer Park Rd
Finksburg, MD 21048
E-Mail: jsheridanmoore@comcast.net

Massachusetts

ANN DUPUIS, CPDT-KA
Your Dream Dog
Randolph, MA
Phone: 877-K9Tcher
Website: www.yourdreamdog.com

MARNI EDELHART, CPDT-KA
Pioneer Pets LLC
Pioneer Valley, MA
E-Mail: pioneerpets@gmail.com
Website: www.pioneervalleypets.com

KATHY FARDY
Dog'sTime, It's Their Time!
P.O. Box 1133
Billerica, MA
Website: www.dogstime.com

PETER GOBEL
Training-U to train your pet
Randolph, MA
Phone: 781-249-5236
E-Mail: petergobel@usa.net

SUSAN M. MILLER, CVT, CPDT-KA, CDBC
The Canine Counselor
P.O. Box 117
Northampton, MA 01061
E-Mail: thek9counselor@yahoo.com

DONNA SAVOIE, CPDT-KA
Pack of Paws Dog Training
Charlton, MA
Website: www.packofpawsdogtraining.com

ANNE SPRINGER
Paws for Praise
119 Liberty St., 2nd Floor
Danvers, MA 01923
Phone: 978-356-7667
Website: www.pawsforpraise.com

JANE YOUNG
Foxfield Dog Training
Mansfield, MA
E-Mail: jyoung@wheatonma.edu
Website: www.foxfielddogtraining.com

Michigan

CJ BENTLEY, CPDT-KA
Michigan Humane Society
Detroit, MI
E-Mail: cjbentley@michiganhumane.org
Website: www.michiganhumane.org

DONNA FOURNIER
c/o Animal Talk
P.O. Box 1591
Royal Oak, MI 48068-1591
E-Mail: donna@animaltalkradio.com
Website: www.animaltalkradio.com

DEVENE GODAU, CPDT-KA
Trainers Academy, LLC
1016 Troy Court
Troy, MI 48083
Phone: 248-616-6500
Website: www.woofology.com

MONICA JOY
Happy Tails Pet Resort
Hubbard Lake, MI

LISA (LANEY) PATRONA, DIP. DTBC, CPDT-KA, PDT, CBC
Trainers Academy, LLC
1016 Troy Court
Troy, MI 48083
Phone: 248-616-6500
Website: www.woofology.com

Minnesota

JULIE HUMISTON, CPDT-KA
Puppy Love Dog Training
Minneapolis, MN
E-Mail: jehumiston@gmail.com

BECKY SCHULTZ, BA, CPDT-KA
Becky Schultz Dog Training and Behavior
Golden Valley, MN
E-Mail: beckyschultztraining@gmail.com

PAULA ZUKOFF
Coordinator of Behavior and Training
Animal Humane Society
Golden Valley, MN
Website: www.animalhumanesociety.org

Mississippi
LYNN RACHKISS
Behavior & Training Manager
Humane Society of South Mississippi
Gulfport, MS
E-Mail: lrachkiss@hssm.org
Website: www.sitstaygooddog.com

Missouri
CATHY HAWKINS, CPDT-KA
Cathy Hawkins Dog Training & Camp Jigsaw
1580 S. Wild Ridge Lane
Springfield, MO 65809
E-Mail: cathy@trackingdogcamp.com
Website: www.trackingdogcamp.com

BRAD JONES, ABCDT
Pettis County K9 Academy
P.O. Box 49
Sedalia, MO 65302
Phone: 660-827-5172
E-Mail: hotglass@iland.net
Website: www.pettiscountyk9.com

HEDDIE LEGER
The PawZone, LLC
Liberty, MO

MELINDA MURPHY
Goldog
Blue Springs, MO
E-Mail: murfhound@earthlink.net
Website: http://home.earthlink.
net/~murfhound

MARTY SWINDELL, BS, CPDT-KA
LickSkillet Dog Training
Lee's Summit, MO
Website: www.lickskilletdogtraining.com

Montana
JACKIE LOESER, CPDT-KA
Riverbend Agility Dogs
Stevensville, MT
E-Mail: jackie@blackdog.cc
Website: www.blackdog.cc

NANCY TANNER, CPDT-KA
Paws & People, LLC
Bozeman, MT
Phone: 406-522-1558
E-Mail: nancy@pawsandpeople.com
Website: www.pawsandpeople.com

Nebraska
**DAWN ANTONIAK-MITCHELL, ESQ.,
CPDT-KA**
BonaFide Dog Academy LLC
14840 Grover Street
Omaha, NE 68144
E-Mail: dawn@bonafidedogacademy.com
Website: www.bonafidedogacademy.com

SHANNAN BESSEY
The Well Trained Dog
Omaha, NE
Website: www.traineddogonline.com

STEPHANIE LARSON
1505 Independence
Lexington, NE 68850
E-Mail: gentlepaws.services@hotmail.com

Nevada
MONICA J. OESTERLING, CPDT-KA
Galaxy Dog Training
Reno, NV
E-Mail: galaxydogtraining@gmail.com
Website: www.galaxydog.net

New Hampshire

ANN. W. FIRESTONE
DogSense- In-Home Training and Behavior Service
South Acworth, NH
E-Mail: annimule@dishmail.net

JESSICA JANOWSKI
Puppy Please! Dog Training, LLC
Goffstown, NH
Phone: 603-261-9283
E-Mail: jessica@puppyplease.com
Website: www.puppyplease.com

LENORE SMITH, CPDT-KA
Downward Dog Companion Dog Training
NH
E-Mail: DownwardDogCDT@hotmail.com

New Jersey

NORA ANDERSON, ABC CERTIFIED
Anderson Canine Training LLC
Skillman, NJ
Phone: 609-240-7191
E-Mail: Andersoncanine@aol.com
Website: Andersoncanine.Tripod.com

VALERIE CASPERITE
WonderDogs
424D Kelly Drive
West Berlin, NJ 08091

KATE GORMAN, CPDT-KA
Gentle Spirit Pet Training
P.O. Box 201
Basking Ridge, NJ 07920
Phone: 908-626-0208
E-Mail: kategorman@aol.com

PHIL GUIDA
Canine Dimensions In-Home Dog Training
P.O. Box 1192
Marlton, NJ 08053
E-Mail: phil@caninedimensions.com

VYOLET MICHAELS, CTC, PDT, CPDT-KA
Urban Dawgs - Positive, Reward-Based Dog Training
Red Bank, NJ
Phone: 7320-758-8522
E-Mail: trainer@urbandawgs.com
Web: www.urbandawgs.com

ANGEL ROBINSON
Angels Tailwaggin Training LLC
Blairstown, NJ
E-Mail: ratdigger@angelstailwaggintraining.com
Website: www.angelstailwaggintraining.com

DAWN WATSON
Brother of the Wolf, LLC
700 Market Street
Gloucester City, NJ 08030
Phone: 856-210-6743
Website: www.brotherofthewolf.com

MARTHA WINDISCH, CPDT-KA
Personalized Dog Training, LLC
P.O. Box 312
Chatsworth, NJ 08019
E-Mail: mwindisch@att.net
Website: www.PersonalizedDogTraining.com

New Mexico

KATHERINE BRYCE, CPDT-KA
The Family Dog
Santa Fe, NM

HELENE KOBELNYK
My Lifelong Friend K-9 Academy
Capitan, NM

MARY LEATHERBERRY, CPDT-KA
Good Dog! Santa Fe
P.O. Box 2836
Santa Fe, NM 87504
Phone: 505-984-9831
E-Mail:mary@gooddogsantafe.com
Website: www.gooddogsantafe.com

New York

MARLA ABRAMS
Doggielove
412 West End Ave
New York, NY 10024
Website: www.doggielove.aol.com

DAINA BECKMAN
Happy Tails Dog Behavior & Training
Hornell, NY
Phone: 607-698-9122
E-Mail: daina@dogpsychologyhelp.com
Website: www.dogpsychologyhelp.com

STACY L. BRUSSEAU, CBC
Positive Pet Training
Rochester, NY
E-Mail: positivepet@frontiernet.net

SARAH CONNAUGHTON, CPDT-KA
Second Chance Pet Obedience
East Aurora, NY

JIM FIORINO
Jim's K-9 College
1 Omah Terrace
Albany, NY 12205
Website: www.jimsk9college.com

KRISTINA N. GAGE, CPDT-KA
SmartDog Dog Training
Saratoga Springs, NY
E-Mail: training@smartdogschool.com
Website: www.smartdogschool.com

HELEN HOLLANDER, CPDT-KA
The Educated Pup, LLC
Long Island, NY
E-Mail: HelenSue15@aol.com

PAULA KELMAN, CPDT-KA
291 Blackstone Blvd
Tonawanda, NY 14150
E-Mail: valiantannie@aol.com

ANN KING, CPDT-KA
Canine King
Westchester, NY
E-Mail: Canineking@aol.com

JOANN KOVACICH
Grateful Dog Pet Care, Inc.
Penfield, NY 14526
Phone: 585-288-4602
E-Mail: joann@gratefuldogpetcare.com
Website: www.gratefuldogpetcare.com

DARLENE KOZA
Scooter's School of Sit & Stay
P.O. Box 23272
Rochester, NY 14692
Phone: 585-755-7647
E-Mail: scootersschool@yahoo.com
Website: www.sitandstay.org

MIRA LEIBSTEIN, CBC, CPDT-KA
Click-n-Train
3074 Messick Ave
Oceanside, NY 11572
Phone: 516-993-0459
E-Mail: Mira@click-n-train.com
Website: www.Click-n-TrainYourDog.com

DAWN NARGI-FERREN
Metropolitan Pets
100 West 93rd Street
New York City, NY 10025
Phone: 917-687-3296
Website: www.metropolitanpets.com

NOELLE NASCA
Positive Puppy Southtown's
Dog Training Club
Hamburg, NY 14075
E-Mail: Luvapit2835671@aol.com
Website: www.southtownsdtc.com

DIANE PODOLSKY, CPDT-KA, CTC
The Cultured Canine, LLC
White Plains, NY
E-Mail: info@theculturedcanine.net
Website: www.theculturedcanine.com

LEIGH SANSONE, JD, CPDT-KA, PMCT
Ruff Customers Dog Training
314 W. 94th Street, Suite 1E
New York, NY 10025
E-Mail: RuffCustomers@gmail.com
Website: www.RuffCustomers.com

CHRISTINA SHUSTERICH, BA, CBC
NY Clever K9, Inc.
Queens, NY
Phone: 917-589-6296
E-Mail: info@nycleverk9.com
Website: www.nycleverk9.com

JULIE SONTAG, CPDT-KA
One Smart Puppy
New York, NY

SUE STERNBERG
Animals for Adoption and Great Dog
Productions
4628 Route 209
Accord, NY 12404
E-Mail: sue@suesternberg.com
Website: www.animalsforadoption.org;
www.greatdogproductions.com

ELIZABETH L. STROTER
TDI Evaluator, AKC CGC Evaluator
House Calls Dog Training
Highland, NY
Phone: 845-384-6546
E-Mail: elyonsstroter@earthlink.net

NANCY TUCKER
Tamarac Tollers
1420 Tamarac Rd.
Troy, NY 12180
Website: www.tamaractollers.com

North Carolina
ANN ISENHOUR
Bow Wow Boutique
103 Sherrill Road
Gastonia, NC 28056

BARBARA LONG, CPDT-KA
Paw in Hand Dog Training
Chapel Hill, NC
E-Mail: BarbaraLong815@msn.com
Website: www.pawinhanddogtraining.com

KAREN OWENS, M.ED., CPDT-KA
Clever Canine Dog Training
Concord, NC
Phone: 704-305-1008
Website: www.karensclevercanine.com

JENNIFER SHRYOCK, B.A., CDBC
Family Paws (Dogs & Storks programs)
Cary, NC
Phone: 919-961-1608
E-Mail: jen@familypaws.com
Website: www.familypaws.com; www.
dogsandstorks.com

Ohio
MEL BUSSEY-SILVERMAN, CPDT-KA, CDBC
Training Tracks Canine Learning Station
Oxford/Cincinnati, OH
E-Mail: trainingtracks@yahoo.com

AMY FLANIGAN
Civil Obedience Dog Training
Columbus, OH
E-Mail: CivilObedience1@aol.com
Website: www.civilobediencedogtraining.
com

MELANIE MCKEEHAN
Assistant Director of Operations
Red Dog Pet Resort and Spa
Cincinnati, OH

PAMELA SEMANIK, CPDT-KA
Walton Hills, OH
Phone: 440-232-5481

GLORIA J. WHITE, CPDT-KA
Pawsitive Waggers Training
Hannah House
3544 Behymer Rd.
Cincinnati, OH 45245
E-Mail: goldens2@roadrunner.com

Oklahoma
KRIS BUTLER
American Dog Obedience Center, LLC
Norman, OK
Website: www.DogPrograms.com

MERIT DAY
Top Dog Training
Broken Arrow, OK
E-Mail: merit@topdogschool.com
Website: www.topdogschool.com

PAM SHEEHAN
4 Paws Training, LLC
Broken Arrow, OK

Oregon
CYNTHIA BRUCKART
The Puppy Playhouse
Sherwood, OR
Website: www.thepuppyplayhouse.com

CARMEN BUITRAGO, MS, CAAB, CPDT-KA
Director of Behavior & Training
Cascade Pet Camp
3085 Lower Mill Dr.
Hood River, OR
E-Mail: Carmen@cascadepetcamp.com
Website: www.cascadepetcamp.com

CYNTHIA KURTZ
The Pet Geek
West Linn/Sandy, OR
Website: www.thepetgeek.com

DEENA MCIVER
K-9 Kind
Portland, OR
E-Mail: k9kind06@gmail.com

DEB WALKER
K9-Behavior Company
Lake Oswego, OR
Phone: 503-704-7481
E-Mail: www.k9-behavior.com

Pennsylvania
PATRICIA BENTZ, CPDT-KA, CDBC
K-9 Training & Behavioral Therapy
Philadelphia, PA
E-Mail: pabentz@earthlink.net
Website: www.k-9training.org

JANE BRYDON, M.S.ED., M.ED. CPDT-KA
Jane Brydon, Dog Training Coach, LLC
324 Prospect Avenue
Clifton Heights, PA 19018
Phone: 610-622-5183
E-Mail: jane@mydogtrainingcoach.com
Website: www.mydogtrainingcoach.com

DEBBY MCMULLEN, CDBC
Pawsitive Reactions, LLC
Pittsburgh, PA
E-Mail: Debby@Pawsitivereactions.com
Website: www.pawsitivereactions.com

TRICIA MOORE
Best Behavior
Newtown, PA
E-Mail: bestbehaviortpc@verizon.net

CAROL A. SIEGRIST, CPDT-KA
SIEGRIST LLC
Dog Training & Behavior Consultation
765 East Passyunk Avenue
Philadelphia, PA 19147
Phone: 215-514-0090

DAYNA VILLA, IACP
Taking the Lead Dog Training
PA
E-Mail: TakingTheLead@hotmail.com
Website: www.takingthelead.vpweb.com

ANN WITHUN
Dog Scouts of America Troop Leader,
Troop 161
Instructor, Fieldwood Dog Training Center
505 Barnstable Road
Carlisle, PA 17015
E-Mail: ann@withun.com
Website: www.dogscouts.org; www.
fieldwooddogtrainingcenter.org

VICKI WOOTERS, CPDT-KA
Wooters Dog Training
Malvern, PA
E-Mail: wooters2@comcast.net
Website: www.wootersdogtraining.com

Rhode Island

SUSAN M. PARKER
Dynamic Dog Training Services, LLC
President, The Little Rhodie Bully Breed
Club Inc.
50 Garnet Street
West Warwick, RI 02893
Phone: 401-823-8851
Website: www.DynamicDogtraining.net;
www.lrbbc.org

South Carolina

TEOTI ANDERSON, CPDT-KA
Pawsitive Results, LLC
Lexington, SC
Phone: 803-356-9170
E-Mail: PawsitiveResults@sc.rr.com
Website: www.getpawsitiveresults.com

Tennessee

ELAINE COUPÉ
For Pet's Sake & Memphis Agility
Oakland, TN
E-Mail: shadowspook@earthlink.net
Website: www.memphisagility.com

ELLEN MAHURIN, MA
Clever Critters
2810 Davenport Rd.
Knoxville, TN 37920
E-Mail: info@clever-critters.com
Website: www.clever-critters.com

KATHERINE ROLLINS, CPDT-KA
Kat's K9 Cadets
Greenville, TN
E-Mail: k9cadets@gmail.com

Texas

DANA COOPER, CPDT-KA
Woofers Canine Companion Training
@ Action Pack Dog Center
4 Lake Drive
Round Rock, TX 78665
Phone: 512-716-WOOF
E-Mail: training@wooferscaninetraining.com
Website: www.wooferscaninetraining.com

SANDRA ENGLAND
DogBoys Dog Ranch
2615 Crystal Bend Dr.
Pflugerville, TX 78660
E-Mail: Sandra@dogboys.com

REBECCA ENGLE, MA, CPDT-KA
First Steps and Beyond K-9 Obedience
Plano, TX
E-Mail: Rebecca@FirstStepsandBeyond.com

JOAN B. GUERTIN
Common Sense Dog Training & Behavior
Solutions
Mabank, TX
E-Mail: JBGuertin@aol.com

HEPZIBAH E. HOFFMAN-ROGERS, CPDT-KA
Thunderpaws Canine Solutions, LLC
206 S. Austin St.
Seguin, TX 78155
Phone: 830-379-7000
Website: www.thunderpawsdogs.com

VICTORIA HYNES
5016 Thompson Drive
The Colony, TX 75056
E-Mail: vhpublic@hotmail.com
Website: www.theeducatedcanine.com

MARGARET JOHNSON, CPDT-KA
The Humane Trainer, Inc.
Austin, TX
E-Mail: humanertrainer@austin.rr.com

NATALIA ROZAS DE O'LAUGHLIN, CPDT-KA
Houston Pet Help
TX
E-Mail: HoustonPetHelp@gmail.com
Website: www.houstonpethelp.frih.org

JERRY D. PATILLO, CPDT-KA
Happy Human, Happy Dog
P.O. Box 835655
Richardson, TX 75083
Phone: 214-789-8959
E-Mail: HappyHumanHappyDog@yahoo.com
Website: www.HappyHumanHappyDog.com

MAUREEN PATIN, CPDT-KA
What a Good Dog!
Prosper, TX
E-Mail: maureen@whatagooddogtx.com
Website: www.whatagooddogtx.com

AUDREY SCHWARTZ RIVERS, MS
PetShare: Pets and People for Positive
Change
Argos' Memories Blog
P.O. Box 590403
Houston, TX 77259-0403
E-Mail: asrivers@petshare.org;
argosmemories@gmail.com
Website: www.petshare.org; www.
argosmemories.com

HEATHER SCHAMERLOH
SmartDog Training
Dallas, TX

JOYCELYN SCHEDLER, CCTS
Tail Town Training
Bastrop, TX
E-Mail: TailTownTraining@gmail.com
Website: www.TailTownTraining.com

SUSAN SMITH, CPDT-KA, CDBC, CTC
Raising Canine, LLC, Animal Ed
TX
Phone: 512-916-40070
E-Mail: sue@raisingcanine.com
Website: www.raisingcanine.com; www.
animal-ed.com

KAREN VASS-DEEDS
Canine Connection
Ft. Worth, TX
E-Mail: canineconnection@charter.net

AGATHA WEISZ
The Not Naughty Dog
7200 Almeda Rd., Apt 528
Houston, TX 77054
E-Mail: agatha@thenotnaughtydog.com
Website: www.thenotnaughtydog.com

TONIA WHILDEN
Houston Dog Ranch
9602 Dalecrest Dr.
Houston, TX 77080
E-Mail: info@houstondogranch.com
Website: www.houstondogranch.com

Utah
ANN ALLUMS, CPDT-KA
Best Friends Animal Society
Kanab, UT
Phone: 435-644-2001 x4339
E-Mail: ann@bestfriends.org

NICOLE CORSON, CTC, CPDT-KA
Wag This Way™
Salt Lake City, UT
E-Mail: nicole@wagthisway.net
Website: www.wagthisway.net

Vermont
JILL HALSTEAD, BA, CTC
Follow the Leader Dog Training Services
Richmond, VT 05477
Phone: 802-578-9722
E-Mail: lookout@gmavt.net
Website: www.ftldogtraining.com

STEPHANIE JUHASZ
Smarter Than The Average Dog
P.O. Box 691
Bondville, VT 05340
E-Mail: vtsttad@yahoo.com

Virginia
WENDY ANASTASIOU, BA, CDBC, CPDT-KA
Life With Fido
Spotsylvania, VA
Website: www.lifewithfido.com

JIM BARRY, CDBC, CPDT-KA
Reston Dog Training
Reston, VA 20190
Website: www.restondogtraining.com

ROBERT JORDAN, CPDT-KA
Pavlov's Dogs Pet Dog Training
Mechanicsville, VA
E-Mail: pavlov1dog@aol.com

LORI MELHUISH
The Smiling Dog, LLC
Yorktown, VA
E-Mail: thesmilingdog@cox.net
Website: www.thesmilingdog-va.com

TERRY PRIDE
Missing Link Pet Services
Virginia Beach, VA
E-Mail: thistlepurple@yahoo.com

ERICA PYTLOVANY, CPDT-KA
WOOFS! Dog Training Center
4241-A N Pershing Dr
Arlington, VA 22203
Phone: 703-536-7877
Website: www.woofsdogtraining.com

VERONICA SANCHEZ, M.ED. CABC, CPDT-KA
Cooperative Paws LLC
Vienna, VA
E-Mail: veronica@cooperativepaws.com
Website: www.cooperativepaws.com

WENDY SCHMITZ, BA, CPDT-KA, CDBC
Life with Fido
Fredericksburg, VA
E-Mail: advice@lifewithfido.com
Website: www.lifewithfido.com

ELLEN TAYLOR, CPDT-KA
Community Initiatives Manager
ASPCA®
1604 Moore's Point Road
Suffolk, VA 23436
Phone: 757-745-7157
E-Mail: ellent@aspca.org
Website: www.aspca.org

LISA COLÓN TUDOR, CPDT-KA
KissAble Canine, LLC
Arlington, VA
E-Mail: trainer@kissablecanine.com

Washington
JEANNE HAMPL
Hampl's Dog Obedience
7898 Greyhawk Ave.
Gig Harbor, WA 98335
E-Mail: praise_luke@hotmail.com

JENNIFER SCHNEIDER, CPDT-KA
Pick of the Litter Dog Training
Seattle/Tacoma Area, WA
E-Mail: jennifer@pickofthelitterdogtraining.com
Website: www.pickofthelitterdogtraining.com

Wisconsin
SILVIA GOLZ, CPDT-KA
"Best Friend" – Companion Dog Training
Appleton, WI
Website: www.bestfriendcompaniondogtraining.com

ANGIE KOBER, BS
Canine Solutions
Neenah, WI
E-Mail: Akober@new.rr.com

JILL MILLER, CPDT-KA
Mad City Dog Training
813 Post Road
Madison, WI 53713
Website: www.madcitydog.com

HEATHER MOHAN-GIBBONS, MS, RVT, CPDT-KA, ACAAB
Collected Wisdom Animal Behavior, LLC
Milwaukee, WI
E-Mail: info@cwanimalbehavior.com
Website: http://cwAnimalBehavior.com

TIMOTHY REISINGER
Tomah, WI
E-Mail: reispinscher@yahoo.com

SHIRLEY RICHARDS, CPDT-KA
Coulee Region Humane Society
911 Critter Court
Onalaska, WI 54650
E-Mail: Shirley.richards@couleehumane.com

CINDY STEINKE, CPDT-KA, TDI, CGC, PETTECH
K-9 Elementary LLC
2190 Cty Rd X
Mosinee, WI 54455
Phone: 715-359-9587
E-Mail: k9elementary@charter.net
Website: www.k-9elementary.com

INTERNATIONAL

Belgium
DANY GROSEMANS, MAPBC
All Dog Training
Grootven 2, BE 3550
Heusden-Zolder
Belgium
E-Mail: Dany@Alldog.be
Website: www.Dierengedrag.be

Canada

DONNA HALL
Hot Diggity Dogs Services
3214 West 10th avenue
Vancouver, British Colombia
Canada
E-Mail: hotdiggity@shaw.ca
Website: www.hotdiggitydogs.ca

NICOLE JOHNSTON, CPDT-KA
Dogspaw LTD
Edmonton, Alberta
Canada
Phone: 780-471-BARK (2275)
E-Mail: nicole@dogspaw.ca
Website: www.dogspaw.ca

JANE NEVE
Canine Conduct Training Solutions
Black Creek, British Colombia
Canada
E-Mail: info@canineconduct.ca
Website: www.canineconduct.ca

WENDIE PATRICK-PRIDE
T.O.G.S. for Dogs
Wentzells Lake (serving all Nova Scotia)
Canada
E-Mail: changing_rooms@hotmail.com

MICHELLE SEVIGNY
DOGSAFE Canine First Aid
#2 - 151 Riverside Drive West,
North Vancouver, British Colombia V7H 1T6
Canada
E-Mail:info@dogsafe.ca
Website: www.dogsafe.ca

KIM WELLS, CPDT-KA
Kim Wells Companion Dog Training Services
Airdrie, Alberta
Canada
E-Mail: kmwells@telus.net

Greece

KATERINA HADZIYANNI
Athens, Greece
E-Mail: friendsforalife@yahoo.gr
Website: www.humane-training.gr

United Kingdom

NINA BONDARENKO, BA
Specialist Canine Services
Croydon, Surrey
United Kingdom
E-Mail: nina_dogs@hotmail.com
Website: www.ninabondarenko.co.uk

West Indies

LISA WHITE
FireStorm K9 Training
St George
Barbados, West Indies

INDEX

THE ASSOCIATION OF PET DOG TRAINERS (APDT)

THE ASSOCIATION OF PET DOG TRAINERS (APDT) is a professional organization committed to building better trainers through education, promoting dog-friendly methods and encouraging their use. Founded in 1993, the APDT has almost 6,000 members, including world-renowned speakers and authors, veterinarians, dog trainers, dog club members, humane society personnel, and service dog trainers, from 26 different countries worldwide. Through the APDT's conferences, membership directory, Journal, and seminars, the organization offers individual trainers a respected and concerted voice in the dog world.

PHOTO CREDITS

NATURAL with added VITAMINS

Nutri Dent ® MD

Promotes Optimal Dental Health!

MADE IN THE USA

Nylabone ®

Trusted For Over 40 Years

Our Mission with Nutri Dent® is to promote optimal dental health for dogs through a trusted, natural, delicious chew that provides effective cleaning action...GUARANTEED to make your dog go wild with anticipation and happiness!!!

Nylabone Products • P.O. Box 427, Neptune, NJ 07754-0427 • 1-800-631-2188 • Fax: 732-988-5466
www.nylabone.com • info@nylabone.com • For more information contact your sales representative or contact us at sales@tfh.com   TS446